DOCUMENTS OF MODERN HISTORY

General Editor:

A. G. Dickens

The Conflict of Nationality in Modern Ireland

A. C. Hepburn

EDWARD ARNOLD

Copyright A.C. Hepburn 1980
First published 1980 by
Edward Arnold (Publishers) Ltd
41 Bedford Square, London WC1B 3DQ

British Library Cataloguing in Publication Data

The conflict of nationality in modern Ireland. —
  (Documents of modern history).
  1. Ireland — Politics and government — Sources
  I. Hepburn A C   II. Series
  320.9'415'08   JN1411

  ISBN 0-7131-6261-9

Printed in Great Britain by The Camelot Press, Southampton

Contents

Acknowledgements

A number of friends and colleagues suggested documentary material for inclusion in this selection. In particular I am grateful to Dr M.R. Beames, Dr S.J. Connolly, Professor D.W. Harkness, Mr J.J. Leckey, Professor D.W. Miller, Mr G.J. Slater and Dr J.O. Springhall. My greatest debt is to Dr F.S.L. Lyons, who generously found time to read the entire manuscript and made many valuable suggestions and comments. A number of libraries and archives made material available, but I must express special thanks to Mr Brain Trainor and the staff of the Public Record Office of Northern Ireland. Gillian Coward of the New University of Ulster History Film and Sound Archive kindly helped with the preparation of the cover. The onerous task of typing was eased by Helen Agnew, and by the History secretarial staff at the University of Tennessee, Knoxville.

Every effort has been made to trace the owners of copyright material, and I must apologize for any unwitting infringement. My thanks, and those of the Publishers, are due to the following for permission to reproduce copyright material:

Her Majesty's Stationery Office for extracts from Parliamentary Papers, Government Reports, House of Commons Debates, Cabinet Papers and Public Record Office material; The Stationery Office, Dublin, for extracts from Dail Debates and Seanad Debates; The National Library of Ireland; The Bodleian Library; *The Times*, *The Observer*, *The Irish Times* and the *Belfast Telegraph*; Hamish Hamilton for extracts from *Diaries of a Cabinet Minister* by R.H.S. Crossman; Faber and Faber for lines from *Autumn Journal* by Louis MacNeice; Mr Mark Bonham Carter for the Asquith Papers; Mrs Christopher Sealy for the extracts from Douglas Hyde; Fr J. Anthony Gaughan for the extract from Jeremiah Mee; Rev. Professor F.X. Martin and Mrs Eibhlin Tierney for the extract from Eoin MacNeill's memoir; Anvil Books Ltd; John Murray Ltd; and the Merlin Press for the extract from *The Socialist Register*.

A.C. HEPBURN

Abbreviations

AOH	Ancient Order of Hibernians
EEC	European Economic Community
HC Deb	House of Commons Debates (UK Parliament)
INV	Irish National Volunteers
IRA	Irish Republican Army
IRB	Irish Republican Brotherhood
ITGWU	Irish Transport & General Workers' Union
LL	Land League
MP	Member of Parliament (UK or NI, according to context)
NI HC Deb	House of Commons Debates (NI Parliament)
NILP	Northern Ireland Labour Party
NLI	National Library of Ireland
PP	Parliamentary Papers
PR	Proportional Representation
PRONI	Public Record Office of Northern Ireland
RAMC	Royal Army Medical Corps
RIC	Royal Irish Constabulary
RUC	Royal Ulster Constabulary
SDLP	Social Democratic and Labour Party (of Northern Ireland)
UDA	Ulster Defence Association
USC	Ulster Special Constabulary (The 'B Specials')
UVF	Ulster Volunteer Force

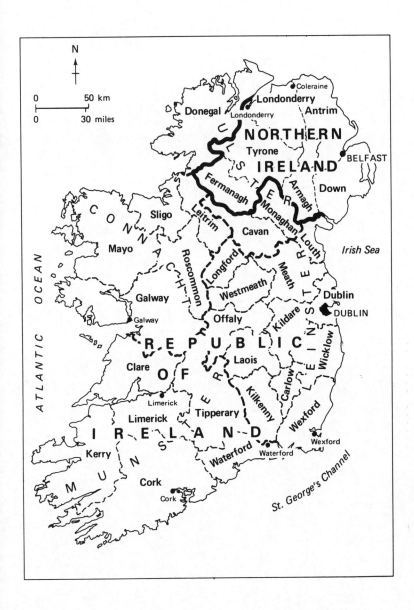

N

0   50 km
0   30 miles

Coleraine

Donegal

Londonderry

Londonderry

Antrim

NORTHERN

Tyrone

IRELAND

BELFAST

Fermanagh

Armagh

Down

Sligo

Leitrim

Monaghan

U L S T E R

Cavan

Louth

Irish Sea

Mayo

Roscommon

Longford

Westmeath

Meath

C O N N A C H T

Galway

Dublin

Galway

Offaly

Kildare

DUBLIN

R E P U B L I C

Clare

Laois

L E I N S T E R

Wicklow

O F

Carlow

Limerick

Kilkenny

M U N S T E R

Limerick

Tipperary

Wexford

I R E L A N D

Kerry

Waterford

Wexford

Waterford

Cork

Wexford

Cork

St. George's Channel

A T L A N T I C   O C E A N

Preface

I hate your grandiose airs,
    Your sob-stuff, your laugh and your swagger,
Your assumption that everyone cares
    Who is the king of your castle.
Castles are out of date,
    The tide flows round the children's sandy fancy;
Put up what flag you like, it is too late
    To save your soul with bunting.

Louis MacNeice *Autumn Journal* (London, 1939)

The Anglo-Norman expedition to Ireland in 1169, which began Ireland's formal association with England, followed barely a century after the successful Norman invasion of England. The date is largely symbolic, for in Ireland as in England the conqueror settled in relatively small numbers and within two or three centuries had effectively merged, on favourable terms, with the 'native' population. By the sixteenth century the 'Old English' were no longer reliable guardians of England's political interests in Ireland. While the forces of the Reformation swept England and Scotland, they retained the Catholic faith of their neighbours and tenants. England's developing great power status during this period caused her to undertake fresh measures to bring Ireland securely within her orbit, while financial weakness led her to meet the cost of her operations from expropriated Irish land. Concentration of interest in the northern province of Ulster, which had previously been the furthest removed from British control, combined with economic and population pressure in southern Scotland to bring about a major change in the demographic balance of that province. Immigrant Protestants from England and Scotland quickly became the largest group in much of the sparsely populated area, and the Catholics or 'native Irish' were driven to the hills or the far west. Elsewhere in Ireland most of the native tenantry stayed put, and a far narrower elite of landowning 'Anglo-Irish' families was thinly but firmly overlaid.

In the Cromwellian period, and again after an unsuccessful attempt by the deposed James II to use Ireland as a base for his French-backed efforts to regain the English throne in 1689-90, the government's grip on the country was tightened further. The penal laws cut sharply into the size of the Catholic and native landowning class once again. During the eighteenth century the city of Dublin grew into a large and elegant Georgian capital for Anglo-Irish society, built mainly from the profits of Anglo-Irish land. The Irish parliament reflected the wealth and power of this stratum of Irish society. A corrupt and previously powerless body, under the leadership of Henry Grattan in 1782 it won a small measure of independence from the British government, though of course it was a privilege restricted to the Anglo-Irish community of the Established Church. Such a concession had been extorted from London during the American revolutionary war. The following French revolutionary period, however, provoked a far more radical stream of protest, grounded in Catholic and Presbyterian discontent, which created modern Irish nationalism and gave it its first martyrs (1,2). The rest of the story may be followed in the commentary which accompanies these documents.

Introduction

National consciousness in history has proved a hardy creature, but not an immortal one. In some cases it can survive the flow of power and population across its territory, in other circumstances it may succumb or mutate. Perspective can be important — the mere passage of time is often a powerful force transforming invasion or occupation into assimilation. The most surprising feature in the history of Anglo-Irish relations is less why England would not 'take her paws out' of Ireland (134) than why Ireland so steadfastly declined to tread the path of assimilation into the United Kingdom previously taken by Scotland, Wales, Cornwall and the earlier Anglo-Saxon kingdoms. This Introduction will examine the components which sustained the national consciousness of Catholic Ireland through and beyond the period of the Union with Britain, 1801-1922, and at the same time consider the related problem of why Ulster Protestantism has equally vigorously resisted assimilation into the rest of Ireland.

Economic factors, in the form of the land question especially, played a central role in the growth of modern Irish nationalism. The great increase in population, from about three millions to over eight millions between 1750 and 1841, produced a pattern of population pressure, sub-division of farm holdings, and overdependence on the potato for food, that was not reversed until the disastrous rural breakdown of the Great Famine, 1845-7. Popular response to worsening conditions was at first seldom tinged by any degree of nationalism (2), and even during the Famine period itself Young Ireland writers who sought to make the connection between land and nationalism were by no means in complete agreement about the nature of the link or its efficacy as an organizational weapon (5, 6, 7). It was in Ulster, ironically, where Orange Protestants in areas like north Armagh came to see land-hungry Catholic peasants rather than rapacious landlords as the main cause of rent increases, that the land question was first perceived in nationalistic or ethnic terms (9). Elsewhere the connection was not made firmly until the period of the land war, that second decade of rural crisis which began in the late 1870s when American farm competition forced Irish landlords and tenants into a bitter and unequal struggle over declining profit margins (**21-27**). Once the links were established, however, constitutional nationalism took less than a decade to win Catholic Ireland completely to its cause, and less than a generation to persuade British governments to convert the tenantry into what was, self-consciously, 'a nation' of peasant proprietors (**30-32, 35**).

Tenants farmers were thus the great beneficiaries of Irish nationalism in the period 1880-1914. But tens of thousands of landless rural labourers, younger sons, and 'uneconomic' smallholders were less fortunate, and followed the Famine emigrants' trail in vast numbers to stoke the fires of expatriate nationalism in the cities of Britain and north America (**8, 21, 22, 44, 69**). Those who remained at home might in the circumstances have posed a serious challenge to the social cohesion of nationalism in the early twentieth century. As it was, such pressures were reduced to occasional outbursts of uncoordinated land agitation, initiated at the local level and often squashed by the national leadership (**73**).

In towns too, economic factors have helped to sustain both Irish nationalism and Ulster unionism. When they organized the unskilled workers of Dublin and the stagnant southern Irish towns James Connolly and James Larkin, in the words of one British cabinet minister, 'lifted the curtain upon depths below nationalism and the Home Rule movement'* (**40-42**). They and their successors failed either to build a majority political labour movement in Ireland or to divert the mainstream of the nationalist movement onto a socialist track. But they did deliver the toiling masses to nationalism for the crucial 1914-21 period in a way that the constitutional Home Rule movement had not been able to do. In a broader sense too, industrial urbanism stimulated ethnic consciousness to the advantage of both nationalism and unionism from the mid-nineteenth century onwards. This was true of the cities of Britain and America, where the occupational and residential solidarity of Irish migrants fashioned a storehouse of anti-English bitterness and later a nationalist financial reservoir which may only now be beginning to dry up (**124, 142**). It was also true of Belfast, Victorian Ireland's domestic centre for urban

---

*Augustine Birrell to H.H. Asquith, 26 Sept. 1913, in L.O Broin, *The Chief Secretary: Augustine Birrell in Ireland* (London, 1969), p. 75.

migration, where harsh working and living conditions, and tight competition for jobs, helped perpetuate and intensify old rural battles between Ulster Catholics and Protestants in an urban setting (Ch. **II**).

Since 1921 political movements associated to a greater or lesser degree with the IRA have attempted to find a basis of support for a 'workers' and small farmers' republic' which would bring down capitalism, clericalism and the border, but with very little electoral success north or south (**90**). Indeed a greater measure of success in binding together the dispossessed of town and country in a united movement has been achieved among Protestants in the north on the 'Bible' fundamentalist platform of men like the Rev. Ian Paisley (**118, 122, 128**). In the south there have been signs in recent years that some (though by no means all) politicians who once pursued radical social change through the medium of extreme nationalism are now couching their arguments instead in the language of cross-border conciliation (**136**).

But economic factors, important as they are, do not explain the full character and development of the conflict of nationality in modern Ireland. A whole range of cultural factors, though perhaps having their origin in economic circumstances, had by the nineteenth century gained a momentum of their own. To take religion first of all. Religious affiliation in early modern Europe was a test of political loyalty, and religious assimilation was part of the process of state-building — hence the brutal attempts in Ireland at forced assimilation, culminating in the penal laws. But by the end of the eighteenth century these measures were anachronistic, and their survival was limited and vestigial. Such an interpretation was implicit in the Catholic church's conciliatory and anti-nationalist posture during this period (**3**). The church's opposition to revolutionary and socially radical nationalism, established at this time, persisted into the twentieth century (**8, 29, 41**). But the career of Daniel O'Connell in the next generation created a new phenomenon of parliamentary or constitutional nationalism (**4**). Since then the mainstream of Catholic clerical opinion has usually, though not always, been firmly committed to the prevailing nationalist orthodoxy of the day, while remaining sensitive to popular criticisms of that orthodoxy (**50, 61**). In the political culture of nineteenth century Ireland, electoral choice was more a community than an individual activity — a united vote meant a united Catholic community (**17**). As the century progressed, moreover, the development of popular education made it increasingly

attractive for the Catholic church to have a strong voice in lay politics
(**33**, **103**).

The fact that religion had for centuries been the working test of
loyalties in Ireland led the Catholic church more rapidly down this
road. Once everyday use of the Irish language began to recede to the
western fringe of the country (as it had done by the early nineteenth
century), only differences in religious practice made it possible for
nationalists to characterize the predominantly Protestant landlord
class as 'Anglo-Irish' and 'foreign', and so perceive the land question in
national or ethnic rather than simply class terms (**6**). Irish nationality
came to be defined explicitly in the nineteenth and twentieth
centuries, as it had been implicitly in the seventeenth and eighteenth,
in religious terms (**38**). As Sir Lewis Namier wrote:

> . . . . there are permanent elements in the lives of communities
> which, refracted through the prism of ages, reappear in different
> colours. In the sixteenth century religion was the primary conscious
> bond of communities, in the nineteenth it was supplanted as such by
> nationality: the emphasis has changed and the terms in which
> certain things are expressed or disputed; much less the underlying
> reality—there always was a strong national element in religion, and
> there is a religious element in nationality. . . .*

The same was true on the Protestant side. Although Wolfe Tone had
argued for a Presbyterian-Catholic alliance against the Episcopalian
church (which was not disestablished in Ireland until 1869), the nineteenth century witnessed steady development in the other direction,
towards 'Protestant unity' (**1b**). William Johnston of Ballykilbeg
regarded political Protestantism and the Orange Order as a response
to Catholic nationalism (**16**). Others have explained the polarization
of Ulster in terms of sectarian initiatives on the Protestant side (**18-20**).
But in fact there is little point in attempting to attribute the
introduction of 'sectarian' or ethnic politics to one side or the other.

Both nationalism ('political Catholicism') and unionism ('political
Protestantism') developed in nineteenth century Ireland from the
same root—the democratization of electoral politics. As the British
parliamentary franchise was extended in 1832 and—more important
for Ireland—in 1867 and 1884, the locus of communication between
candidate and constituency shifted from the corporation chamber
and dinner-table to the hustings. In England the existing parlia-

*L.B. Namier, *Avenues of History* (London, 1952), p.3

mentary parties were able to convert themselves, with slight changes in rhetoric, into mass parties. But in Ireland ethnicity offered a far more powerful and compelling tool for organizing the newly enfranchised masses — creating the constitutional nationalist Home Rule party on the Catholic side, and transforming the Conservative party, through the medium of the Orange Order, into the Unionist party on the other (17). If democracy was not the father of modern Irish nationalism and unionism, it certainly proved a benevolent uncle to both during their formative years.

The movement for the revival of the Irish language, literature, and sports, known overall as the 'Irish-Ireland' movement, is another facet of nationalism which will be considered in the documents that follow. Much of this writing has worn badly, reflecting the prevalence, even in Ireland, of the obsessional race-thinking which was characteristic of the age of imperialism (36, 37, 52). The language-revival movement, though it has not been without academic and literary distinction, has been disappointing as a popular movement, confirming the fears of its early critics (39, 95). In particular the hope of some early language enthusiasts that Irish would form a viable basis for an all-Ireland nationalism, where religion had so obviously failed, was especially ill-founded. The way in which Catholic schools took up the Irish language and Protestant schools did not has effectively made possession of the language simply another guide to religious affiliation — and in the Irish civil service, until very recently, an unintended but effective *de facto* mechanism for excluding Protestants. At the popular level the Irish language has simply reinforced religion as a badge of nationality. Its importance in the history of nationalism lies rather in the fact that it provided the main ideological stimulus for the new elite which swept aside the constitutional Home Rulers and carried out the revolution of 1916-21. Notwithstanding the frenzied religious imagery of Patrick Pearse's writing, it was the Gaelic League and the Gaelic Athletic Association which supplied the manpower and the motivation for him and his fellow-insurgents (52). On the Unionist side there has been no real equivalent of this. Like the Conservative party in Britain the Unionist elite has proved remarkably adaptable, swallowing the radical Orangeman Johnston of Ballykilbeg in the 1870s and stifling, outflanking, or occasionally embracing similar challengers in the twentieth century (105-107, 114). What it will do with Ian Paisley, its most formidable challenger to date, remains to be seen.

By the beginning of the twentieth century Irish nationalism, and

Ulster unionist resistance to it, were both firmly established as political traditions and machines. This momentum was sufficient to carry the Home Rule party through the long period of 'killing home rule with kindness' when the land purchase and congested districts' policies of successive British governments threatened to eliminate the basis of agrarian tenant discontent on which the nationalist movement appeared to rest (35). Similarly in Belfast and industrial Ulster, the momentum of tradition helped unionism to survive unscathed the challenges of an organized labour movement which sought to straddle the religious divide (97).

The political developments of 1909-14, especially the out-of-office frustration of the Conservatives and the fortuitous outcome of the 1910 general elections in Great Britain, gave the Home Rule party a firm grip on the parliamentary balance of power, generating a degree of polarization and excitement in Ireland from which both nationalism and unionism could draw new energy (44-49). Once the north had begun the threat of armed resistance the failure of the Home Rulers to follow suit convincingly gave the more extreme nationalists their first opportunity (52, 53, 58). With an issue and a military force at their disposal, the progress of these ideologues towards rebellion and blood-sacrifice was rapid and steady (64, 65). A variety of factors enabled them to carry the support of the great mass of ordinary humanity with them down such a path, the most important of which was probably opposition to wartime military conscription (55-57, 59-62, 67, 68, 70, 73, 74, 77). The early development of the new southern Irish state thus took place in an intensely nationalist context, and nationalism provided much of the framework for subsequent political debate (81-83, 87, 88, 91). Remarkably, the emphasis during the immediate post-revolution years was less on the question of national unity than on sovereignty for that part of Ireland which had secured independence — 'three-quarters of a nation once again'. At this stage few expressed concern over the future of Catholics in the north under partition (84, 85, 89, 98). Inter-related with national sentiment was an anti-English and anti-Protestant cultural puritanism which extended on occasion almost to general xenophobia (92, 95, 96). A stable and humane state was established and maintained in the south, but it avoided serious conflict with a resurgent Catholic episcopate only by permitting a large measure of clerical influence and control in areas which most modern states have regarded as their own preserve (93, 94, 96).

In Northern Ireland the British government's decision, embodied in the 1920 Government of Ireland Act, to delegate direction of the province's affairs to a local parliament ensured that Unionist and Orange ideology would remain at the centre of the political stage. The application of the principles of majoritarian democracy in such a context meant that the Unionist political leadership was in practice expected to maintain control of the area by whatever means it could (**99, 100, 101, 138**). The security of the state implied the maintenance of the exclusive Orange political tradition (**106, 114**), and for two generations British policy continued to acknowledge the implications of earlier decisions by according the Northern Ireland government a degree of independence akin to dominion status in internal affairs (**99, 110, 111**). Only the massive political upheaval of the 1960s and the inability of that government to contain it brought any change in this policy (**116, 133**).

The main stems of nationalism and unionism in Ireland share some common historical roots. They also have much in common so far as social philosophy is concerned, notwithstanding the frequent proclamation of perceived differences (**117, 126, 134**). Aside from a few specific questions like divorce, abortion and contraception, they share strongly conservative attitudes on many social issues: opposition to secularism and support for clerical influence in education; resistance to the growth of a strong political labour movement; and general support for the political and social values of rural and small town society over those of the city (**33, 34, 40, 41, 94, 103**). But in both societies these values are defined to a great extent in denominational terms, and hence in terms of opposition to the other. Separation and polarization in a sense help to preserve the *status quo* in both parts of Ireland. Whether those who would change this should seek to do so in an all-Ireland or in a greater United Kingdom context is open to debate (**90, 133**).

What is clear is that the experience of the 1970s offers no hope of a general political settlement by agreement among Irishmen in the foreseeable future (**130, 132, 137, 138, 139, 141**). This view is implicit in the recent trend of British policy towards separating the military and political aspects of the Northern Ireland problem almost entirely (**140**). A military solution to the IRA problem is effectively what is being sought, while the political settlement may well turn out to be an indefinite continuation of 'direct rule'. Ironically, it is the IRA which now hopes, through its military policy of terrorism, to compel a political settlement (**144**).

Whether the 1973 entry of both the Irish Republic and the United Kingdom into the European Economic Community will make any fundamental impact on the nationality conflict in Ireland is hard to predict — as, of course, is the political future of the EEC itself. EEC oversight should certainly do something to restrain the governments concerned from intemperate actions, as well as encourage liberal-progressive policies (it is said that fear of rejection by the EEC stimulated the expansion and reform of the Irish schools' system in the 1960s). Should the Common Market bring about increased economic prosperity and expansion, especially in the skilled and white collar sectors, the alleviation of occupational inequalities in the north would be facilitated (**129**), and perhaps the hopeless and desperate sectarianism of the urban working class would begin to erode. But the present beneficiaries of EEC membership appear to be the farming class, whose influence north and south is likely to remain a conservative one. More widespread economic benefits, if they come, are likely to be delayed in their social effects. Inter-governmental co-operation, even in Ireland, could well proceed at administrative and governmental level without making any deep impact on local community relations. Worse still may be the danger of the elected European parliament being used by Irish politicians simply as a wider stage for the enactment of traditional political theatre (**143**). The grass-roots political culture of Ireland will have to change in some way before the problem can be 'solved', and in that context Sir Lewis Namier's dictum does not encourage hopes of an early solution: 'maladjustment in human affairs is a concomitant of change. Forms, procedure and ideas outlive the conditions which gave them rise: disbodied they continue an independent existence. . . . nations fight ghosts. . . .'*

---

*L.B. Namier, *Avenues of History* (London, 1952), p.2

I The formation of modern Irish nationalism

1 Wolfe Tone: An oppressed, insulted and plundered nation

Wolfe Tone (1763-98) was an Anglican by birth, and a graduate of Trinity College, Dublin. After an early career as a law student and would-be colonial adventurer in London, he returned to Dublin in 1788 to practice as a barrister. He soon became active as a political pamphleteer however, and a central figure in the Society of United Irishmen, a body committed to ending British rule in Ireland by whatever means possible. In 1796 he arrived in France, via America, to work for French involvement in an Irish uprising. He was arrested by the British authorities after a short sea battle with a small French invading force off Donegal, and committed suicide while awaiting execution. Meanwhile a series of uncoordinated uprisings, determined but brutally anti-Protestant in Co. Wexford, puny but theoretically nonsectarian in Counties Antrim and Down, had in the absence of French support been crushed with little difficulty and less mercy. These extracts from Tone's posthumously published autobiography reveal the importance to his nationalism of the ideals of the French revolution, his hopes for a revolutionary alliance between the Catholics and the Protestant Dissenters against the Established church, and at the same time his deep distrust of the Catholic clergy.

(a) . . .Animated by their unconquerable hatred of France, which no change of circumstances could alter, the whole English nation, it may be said, retracted from their first decision in favour of the glorious and successful efforts of the French people; they sickened at the prospect of the approaching liberty and happiness of that mighty nation: they calculated, as merchants, the probable effects which the energy of regenerated France might have on their commerce. . . .

But matters were very different in Ireland, an oppressed, insulted, and plundered nation. As we well knew, experimentally, what it was to be enslaved, we sympathized most sincerely with the French people, and watched their progress to freedom with the utmost anxiety; we had not, like England, a prejudice rooted in our very nature against France. As the Revolution advanced, and as events expanded themselves, the public spirit of Ireland rose with a rapid acceleration. The fears and animosities of the aristocracy rose in the same, or a still higher proportion. In a little time the French Revolution became the test of every man's political creed, and the nation was fairly divided into two great parties, the Aristocrats and the Democrats (epithets borrowed from France), who have ever since been measuring each other's strength, and carrying on a kind of smothered war, which the course of events, it is highly probable, may soon call into energy and action.

It is needless, I believe, to say that I was a Democrat from the very commencement, and, as all the retainers of Government, including the sages and judges of the law, were, of course, on the other side, this gave the *coup de grâce* to any expectations, if any such I had, of my succeeding at the bar, for I soon became pretty notorious; but, in fact, I had for some time renounced all hope, and, I may say, all desire, of succeeding in a profession which I always disliked, and which the political prostitution of its members (though otherwise men of high honour and of great personal worth) had taught me sincerely to despise.

(b) The dominion of England in Ireland had been begun and continued in the disunion of the great sects which divided the latter country. In effectuating this disunion, the Protestant [Episcopalian] party were the willing instruments, as they saw clearly that if ever the Dissenters and Catholics were to discover their true interests and, forgetting their former ruinous dissensions, were to unite cordially and make common cause, the downfall of English supremacy, and, of course, of their own unjust monopoly, would be the necessary and immediate consequence. They therefore laboured continually, and, for a long time, successfully, to keep the other two sects asunder, and the English Government had even the address to persuade the Catholics that the non-execution of the penal laws, which were, in fact, too atrocious to be enforced in their full rigour, was owing to their clemency; that the Protestants and Dissenters, but especially the latter, were the enemies, and themselves, in effect, the protectors of the Catholic people. Under this arrangement the machine of government moved forward on carpet ground, but the time was, at length, come when this system of iniquity was to tumble in the dust, and the day of truth and reason to commence.

(c) . . .Clarke then, after some civilities in reply, asked me what I
thought of some of the Irish priests yet remaining in France. I
answered, that he knew my opinion as to priests of all kinds; that
in Ireland they had acted, all along, execrably; that they hated
the very name of the French Revolution, and that I feared, and
indeed was sure, that if one was sent from France, he would immediately, from the *esprit de corps,* get in touch with his brethren in
Ireland, who would misrepresent everything to him. . . .

> R. Barry O'Brien (ed.), *The Autobiography
> of Theobald Wolfe Tone* (Dublin 1893), I,
> 38-9, 43, 300

2 'If the rich would alleviate the sufferings of the poor. . .'

The gulf between Tone's cosmopolitan world of revolutionary enlightenment
and the social conditions of rural Ireland was enormous. Rapid population
growth, subdivision of holdings, and an exploitative system of sub-letting,
produced recurrent waves of protest in the traditional form of intimidation
and secret society activity. Most movements in the south of Ireland, like the
Whiteboys and the Rightboys (followers of 'Captain Right, who comes by
night'), were simply agrarian. In Ulster, as we shall see, sectarian factors
caused a nationalistic pattern to be imposed on this background. The
Defenders movement, originating in Ulster, is credited with having been the
Catholic-nationalist rival to the alliance of Protestant forces which became the
Orange Order. Indeed, known Defender oaths contain garbled republican
references—'The French Defenders will protect our cause, and the Irish
Defenders put down the British laws'. But while the Defenders' style caught the
imagination of the rural poor and spread throughout Ireland, the following
extract suggests that outside the areas of mixed religion in Ulster, agrarian
questions were not readily perceived in nationalistic terms, at least in the early
stages of the movement. Lawrence O'Connor, a rural schoolteacher in Co.
Kildare, was executed in 1795 for administering a Defender's oath. His speech
from the dock following sentence was reported in the contemporary press.

. . .he proceeded in stating substantially that the paper produced in
evidence against him and which had been called an oath, was symbo-
lical. Three words were observable in it, Love, Liberty and Loyalty,
the meaning of which though well known to his fraternity was not
known to their lordships, and he would explain them. By *Love* was to
be understood that affection which the rich ought to show to the poor
in their distress and need, but which they withheld from them; and
here he animadverted with severity upon this subject. *Liberty* meant

that liberty which every poor man had a right to use when oppressed by the rich, in laying before them and expostulating with them on their sufferings — but the poor man in this country had no such liberty. Here he stated several grievances the poor laboured under, as landholders refusing them land to their cottages, rack-rents and particularly obliging them to take potato ground at six guineas an acre — a rent, considering the price of labour, that swallowed all their earnings and left them in debt and poverty, etc., etc. *Loyalty* he defined as meaning that union which subsisted among the poor — he would die in that loyalty — it meant that the poor who formed the fraternity to which he belonged would stand by each other. He expatiated at large upon this subject, insinuating that he died in a cause which he and many others thought a good one, and held out the admonition that the rich should immediately take such measures as would alleviate the distresses of the poor; that prosecutions were not the means of bringing about peace in the country; but if the rich would alleviate the sufferings of the poor, they would hear no more of risings or Defenders and the country would rest in peace and happiness. He denied any intention of dividing the lands — and as a last request of a dying man, he called upon the judges not to afflict him with a sudden execution, but to allow him some time to appear before his God in a state of repentance for such sins as he had committed.

Hibernian Magazine, November 1795 pp. 431-3.

Reprinted in: M.R. Beames, 'Peasant Movements, 1785-95', in *Jnl. of Peasant Studies*, II, 4(1975), 505.

3   Archbishop Troy: Loyalty and its rewards

The Catholic church in late eighteenth-century Ireland was concerned primarily with rebuilding an ecclesiastical structure which the Williamite period and the penal laws had destroyed. Secret societies, however their oaths might be framed, were denounced firmly by the church, as they were to be in most subsequent phases of Irish history. But senior clerics of the period, especially John Thomas Troy (1739-1823) Catholic archbishop of Dublin, were also strongly opposed to more open expressions of republican sentiment, and even to any kind of nationalist tendency at all — thus providing some justification for Tone's opinion of them. Troy's Pastoral Address of 1798 contained the usual denunciations of Whiteboyism, Defenderism, and oath-taking in general, a long account of the treatment of the continental Catholic church and the papacy by the forces of revolutionary France, and in this passage, a vision of the re-establishment of Irish Catholicism in terms entirely independent of any form of nationalism.

At present, when these kingdoms are seriously menaced with invasion by a formidable and implacable enemy, when too many may have been seduced into a persuasion, that French Republicans are our friends and allies, desirous to fraternize with us, for the sole purpose of delivering us from pretended bondage, and securing our religion and liberty, I cannot be silent, nor withhold my pastoral endeavours to warn the unreflecting, or recall to a sense of duty such as may unhappily, have become the proselytes of that dangerous delusion.

. . .in publishing different pastoral instructions, I have been influenced by no other motive than a conscientious sense of duty, and a most sincere friendship for my beloved flock; not only without pension or other temporal emolument, but without even the expectation or desire of any; neither have I ever published or preached any doctrine at the instance or insinuation of Government. . . .

Compare your present situation with the past. Twenty years ago the exercise of your religion was prohibited by law; the ministers of it were proscribed; it was penal to educate Catholic youth at home or abroad; your property was insecure, at the mercy of an informer; your industry was restrained by incapacity to realize the fruits of it. At present you are emancipated from these and other penalties and disabilities, under which your forefathers, and some amongst yourselves, had laboured. You are now at liberty to profess your religion openly, and to practise the duties of it; the ministers of your religion exercise their sacred functions under the sanction of law, which authorizes Catholic teachers; a College for the education of your Clergy has been erected at the recommendation of his Majesty; it is supported and endowed by parliamentary munificence; the restraints on your industry are removed, together with the incapacity to realize the fruits of it for the benefit of your posterity. What, let me ask you, has effected this favourable change — this great difference between your past and your present situation? I answer: Your loyalty, your submission to the constituted authorities, your peaceable demeanour, your patience under long sufferings. . . .

You will perhaps reply, that some legal disabilities still exclude the most loyal and peaceable Roman Catholics from a seat or vote in Parliament, from the privy council, from the higher and confidential civil and military departments of the State. I grant it. But, is it by rebellion, insurrection, tumult, or seditious clamour on your part, that these incapacities are to be removed? Most certainly not. . . .

Reprinted in: P.F. Moran (ed.), *Spicilegium Ossoriense* (Dublin, 1884), iii, 553-9

4   Daniel O'Connell: Towards a friendly connection

The uprisings of 1798, together with Robert Emmet's tailpiece in 1803, became the basis for an enduring republican tradition. But a more immediate outcome was the Act of Union of 1801 binding Ireland to Britain in legislative union. The granting of full civil rights to Roman Catholics, promised as an accompanying measure, did not materialize. For twenty years there was little interaction between the essentially middle-class world of political protest and the crude, direct responses to material distress offered by the agrarian secret societies. Not until 1823 did a Catholic barrister, Daniel O'Connell (1775-1847), member of a gentry family from Kerry, bring together these forces in a formidable new body, the Catholic Association. Cooperating closely with the priests at local level and drawing financial strength from the 'Catholic rent', a penny a month contributed by almost a million peasants, the Association soon had the Catholic electorate sufficiently well organized to return O'Connell to Westminster by an overwhelming majority at the Clare by-election in 1828. Within a year Parliament had given way, and O'Connell was admitted as the first avowedly Catholic MP since the seventeenth century. The political energy and organization generated by the drive for emancipation was carried on in O'Connell's new movement for repeal of the Act of Union, and so constitutional nationalism was born.

I would not. . . fling British connection to the winds. I desire to retain it. I am sure that separation will not happen in my time; but I am equally sure that the connection cannot continue if you maintain the Union on its present basis. What, then, do I propose? That there should be that friendly connection between the two countries which existed before the Union. I propose it not as a resolution; but what I look for is that friendly connection by which both countries would be able to protect each other. As Ireland exported corn to England, so could England export her manufactures to Ireland — both countries would afford mutual advantage to the other. I propose that you should restore to Ireland her Parliament. We have our viceroy and our Irish peers; we only want a House of Commons, which you could place upon the same basis as your Reformed Parliament. This is the claim of Ireland upon you; this is what I ask from you. I have shown you that Ireland is entitled to an independent Legislature. I have shown you the

effects of that independence. I have shown you the incompetency of
the Irish Parliament to vote itself away. I have shown you that the
Union was accomplished by crimes the most unparalleled. I have
shown you that the terms of the Union were unjust to Ireland. I have
shown you that the Union has been ruinous to us, and that some of its
consequences have reverted to yourselves. I have shown you that the
legislative terms of the Union were unjust. I have shown you that the
Union has deprived my country of the protection of the law and the
benefits of the Constitution, and that it has despoiled the people of the
means of existence. I have shown you that the English labourers and
artisans have suffered equally from the poverty of Ireland. I have
shown you the probable consequences of continuing the Union. I have
shown, or rather I have suggested, with what facility the connection
could be placed on the basis of right and justice. You are unable to
govern Ireland, even to your own satisfaction; for two-thirds of the
time you have presided over her destinies you have ruled her, not by
the powers of the law, but by undisguised despotism. You have not
made Ireland prosperous, and her misery has been of no advantage to
you. In the name, then, of Ireland, I call upon you to do my country
justice. I call upon you to restore her national independence.

> Speech to the House of Commons, 22 April
> 1834, in M.F. Cusack (ed.), *The Speeches
> and Public Letters of the Liberator* (Dublin,
> 1875), i, 433-4.

5 John Mitchel: The vast brute mass of England

The repeal movement ultimately foundered on its failure to achieve the same
kind of rapid results which had been won in the case of emancipation. Its
decline, and O'Connell's own death, coincided with an event which was to
affect the lives of Irish people in a more powerful way than any political
movement had ever done. Between 1845 and 1847 rural Ireland was so
devastated by potato famine as to reduce the total population by one-quarter
within the space of five years, and reverse the general trend of early marriage
and subdivision of holdings so sharply that emigration reduced the population
from eight millions to four millions by the end of the century. The Young
Ireland group of nationalists, which partly grew out of the repeal movement
and was partly a reaction against O'Connellite organization, attempted to
address itself to this crisis, even though its intellectual middle-class leadership
had little direct experience of the problem. The movement's most militant
writer, John Mitchel (1815-75), a solicitor and the son of a Presbyterian

minister from Ulster, laid the blame for the famine unequivocally at England's door.

The Conquest was now consummated—England, great, populous, and wealthy, with all the resources and vast patronage of an existing government in her hands—with a magnificent army and navy—with the established course and current of commerce steadily flowing in the precise direction that suited her interests—with a powerful party on her side in Ireland itself, bound to her by lineage and by interest—and, above all, with her vast brute mass lying between us and the rest of Europe, enabling her to intercept the natural sympathies of other struggling nations, to interpret betwen us and the rest of mankind, and represent the troublesome sister island, exactly in the light that she wished us to be regarded—England prosperous, potent, and at peace with all the earth besides—had succeeded (to her immortal honour and glory) in anticipating and crushing out of sight the last agonies of resistance in a small, poor and divided island, which she had herself made poor and divided, carefully disarmed, almost totally defranchised, and totally deprived of the benefits of that very British 'law' against which we revolted with such loathing and horror. England had done this; and whatsoever credit and prestige, whatsoever profit and power could be gained by such a feat, she has them all.

John Mitchel, *The Last Conquest of Ireland (Perhaps)* (Dublin, n.d.), p. 210

6 Fintan Lalor: A people and a class

A latecomer to the Young Ireland movement was James Fintan Lalor (1807-49), member of a prosperous Protestant farming family in the Irish midlands. Though politically associated with Mitchel, Lalor differed from him in identifying not 'England' but his own Anglo-Irish landlord class as the cause of the famine and of Ireland's national degradation. In a prophetic letter to the editor of a new national journal, *The Irish Felon*, on 24 June 1848, Lalor sought to find in the land question a new and more enduring basis for the national movement.

. . .It is a mere question between a people and a class—between a people of eight millions and a class of eight thousand. They or we must quit this island. It is a people to be saved or lost—it is the island to be kept or surrendered. They have served us with a general writ of ejectment. Wherefore, I say, let them get a notice to quit at once, or we shall oust possession under the law of nature. . . . They do not now, and never did belong to this island. Tyrants and traitors have they ever been to us and ours since first they set foot on our soil. Their crime it is and not England's that Ireland stands where she does to-day—or rather it is our own that have borne them so long. Were they a class of the Irish people the Union could be repealed without a life lost. Had they been a class of the Irish people that Union would have never been. But for them we would now be free, prosperous and happy. . . .

I hold and maintain that the entire soil of a country belongs of right to the people of that country, and is the rightful property not of any one class, but of the nation at large, in full effective possession, to let to whom they will on whatever tenures, terms, rents, services, and conditions they will; one condition, however, being unavoidable, and essential, the condition that the tenant shall bear full, true, and undivided fealty, and allegiance to the nation, and the laws of the nation whose lands he holds, and own no allegiance whatsoever to any other prince, power, or people, or any obligation of obedience or respect to their will, orders, or laws. . . .

. . .A people whose lands and lives are. . . in the keeping and custody of others, instead of in their own, are not in a position of common safety. The Irish famine of '46 is example and proof. The corn crops were sufficient to feed the island. But the landlords would have their rents in spite of famine, and in defiance of fever. They took the whole harvest and left hunger to those who raised it. Had the people of Ireland been the landlords of Ireland, not a single human creature would have died of hunger, nor the failure of the potato been considered a matter of any consequence.

Between the relative merits and importance of the two rights, the people's right to the land, and their right to legislation, I do not mean or wish to institute any comparison. I am far indeed from desirous to put the two rights in competition, or contrast, for I consider each alike as the natural complement of the other, necessary to its theoretical completeness, and practical efficacy. But, considering them for a moment as distinct, I do mean to assert this—that the land question contains, and the legislative question does not contain, the materials from which victory is manufactured; and that, therefore, if we be truly in earnest and determined on success, it is on the former question, and not on the latter that we must take our stand, fling out our banner, and hurl down to England our gage of battle.

Reprinted in: L. Fogarty (ed.), *James Finton Lalor* (Dublin 1918), pp. 59-65

7   Charles Gavan Duffy: Creatures of the imagination

The Young Ireland rising of 1848 was stimulated less by any awareness of a widespread insurrectionary feeling in the country than by the excitement of the Young Irelanders themselves at the example of revolution in continental Europe. A series of lame and uncoordinated escapades, it scarcely justified the name of rebellion at all. Many of the leaders were transported, and some later appeared on opposing sides in the American civil war. Charles Gavan Duffy (1816-1903), a Catholic from Ulster, who edited the leading Young Ireland publication, *The Nation,* was in prison facing charges of sedition at the time of the 1848 risings. He later became an MP for the short-lived Tenant Right League, before emigrating to Australia in 1855, ending a chequered career as prime minister of the state of Victoria. His later reflections on this period in Irish politics are frequently to the point, although the assessment of his own role in affairs owes much to the benefit of hindsight.

My opposition to Lalor's policy was based not on moral but strictly on political grounds. I believed it had not the slightest chance of success. His angry peasants straining to break their chains were creatures of the imagination. The actual peasants had endured the pangs of famine with scarcely a spurt of resistance. They had been taught by O'Connell that armed resistance to authority was justifiable under no circumstances; while they were perishing in every county in the island they were still taught that submission was their duty, and they submitted and died. Pauper alms carried to their homes, pauper works, which even to their eyes where worthless, further demoralized them, till the spirit of manhood was almost extinct. Mitchel had never been in Munster or seen the peasants on whom we were bid to rely, and his sincere patriotism and courage were not fortified by practical capacity or the inestimable faculty of knowing what can be accomplished. . . .

> C. Gavan Duffy, *My Life in Two Hemispheres*
> (London, 1903), i, 242-3

8   Fenianism: The importance of revolutionary mythmaking

The famine did generate mass political bitterness, but its growth was slow. Its fruit was the Fenian (or Irish Revolutionary) Brotherhood, an oath-bound secret society founded in 1858 along lines which owed something to the organization of continental movements like the Italian *Carbonari.* Fenianism was the first in a long line of Irish nationalist movements to draw strength, especially financial strength, from the feelings of exiled Irishmen in Britain (where it was said to have penetrated the army on a large scale) and particularly in the

United States. The American civil war was an added stimulus, bringing military experience to large numbers of Irish-Americans. It was hoped in a vague way that such forces might find their way to Ireland. They did in fact stage an 'invasion' of Canada in 1867.

In Ireland, the leaders of the movement were a group of journalists associated with *The Irish People* newspaper between 1863 and 1865, and dominated by James Stephens (1824-1901), an indefatigable travelling organizer who built a large network of nominal Fenians throughout Ireland. But the moment for a rising, if it ever existed, was missed, and the movement fizzled out with a series of bombings in England and more escapades on the Canadian border. The long-term importance of Fenianism lies in its creation of the tradition of an Irish Republic 'now virtually established', maintained by a revolutionary elite which had a broader class base than the men of 1848 and which, unlike the men of 1798, survived to hand on that tradition. In America the tradition continued to supply money and advice to Ireland, and also enjoyed reciprocal benefits with aspiring Irish-American politicians. The Catholic church in Ireland denounced Fenianism more thoroughly than it had done any other nationalist monifestation since the peasant movements of the pre-union period—ostensibly because it was an oath-bound movement. The church's success in maintaining this resolute position is perhaps a measure of the movement's limited popular support. This extract is believed to have been written by the novelist Charles Kickham (1828-82), later Head Centre of the reorganized IRB during its quiescent years.

Nothing would please us better than to keep clear of the vexed question of 'priests in politics' if we could do so without injury to the cause which we are endeavouring to serve. But the question was forced upon us. We saw clearly that the people should be taught to distinguish between the priest as a minister of religion and the priest as a politician before they could be got to advance one step on the road to independence. The people for whom God created it must get this island into their own hands. If they do not the fruitful land will become a grazing farm for the foreigner's cattle, and the remnant of our race wanderers and outcasts all over the world if English rule in Ireland be not struck down. Our only hope is in revolution. But most of the bishops and many of the clergy are opposed to revolution. Is it not then the duty of the Irish patriot be he priest or layman to teach the people that they have a right to judge for themselves in temporal matters? That is what we have done. We have over and over declared it was our wish that the people should respect and be guided by their clergy in spiritual matters. But when priests turn the altars into a platform; when it is pronounced a 'mortal sin' to read *The Irish People,* a 'mortal sin' even to wish that Ireland should be free; when priests actually call upon the people to turn informers, and openly threaten to set the police upon the track of men who are labouring in the cause for which our Fathers so often bled; when true men are reviled and slandered; when the uprooting of the people is called a 'merciful dispensation of Providence' — when, in a word, bishops and priests are doing the work of the enemy, we believe it is our duty to tell the people that bishops and priests may be bad politicians and worse Irishmen. . . .

The Irish People, 16 September 1865

II The development of Ulster Unionism

9 The emergence of the Orange Order

The unprecedented rate of population growth in late eighteenth-century Ireland put an intolerable strain on the resources of the country. In the northern parts of Co. Armagh, where many small farming families had the skill and opportunity to eke out their income by the domestic spinning and weaving of linen, the rate of growth and density of habitation was higher than elsewhere. Competition for land among the Protestant descendants of seventeenth-century English and Scots planters was acute, aggravated by a growing Catholic demand for land as the enforcement of the penal laws became less strict. Just as in England and the rest of Ireland during this period, agrarian secret societies proved to be the only effective form of political organization available to the peasantry. In north Armagh and some other parts of Ulster, bodies like the Protestant Oakboys and Peep o'Day Boys, and the Catholic Defenders, saw their situation more in ethnic-sectarian than in class terms. In Co. Antrim in the 1770s the Steelboys embraced both attitudes in their bitter complaint that 'some of us refusing to pay the extravagant rent demanded by our landlords have been turned out, and our lands given to Papists, who will promise any rent'. Feelings similar to this were the background to the fiercely-fought 'Battle of the Diamond', near Loughgall, Co. Armagh, in 1795, where the struggle for what was essentially local economic-territorial ascendancy seemed to merge into the wider question of national allegiance. From the victorious Protestant side at this encounter, reinforced by Protestants of a higher social class, sprang a new and far more durable body, the Orange Order. The following narrative by Joseph Atkinson, a local justice of the peace sympathetic to the Protestant side, was recorded in a contemporary account of the battle.

For several days prior to the 21st of September, 1795, this neighbourhood was disturbed by mobs of Defenders. On the 18th they took possession of the gravel pit of Annaghmore, their number amounting to at least 500 men, and they hoisted a white flag, upon which all the good and loyal Protestants of the neighbourhood became much alarmed, and assembled on the hill of Cranagill, opposite

Annaghmore. On the morning of that day a skirmish took place in the townland of Teaguy, in which there was a man killed of the name of McCann, a Defender. Some time during the day Mr Archdall Cope and his brother Robert Camden Cope, Mr Hardy, Councillor Archdall, Priests Taggart, McParland, and Traynor, came to my house, and we all went to where the Protestants were stationed on Cranagill Hill. Mr Archdall Cope and Taggart proposed to me to make the Protestants lay down their arms; in reply to which I declared they should not do so, until the others had laid down theirs first, as I considered the Protestants were entitled to carry arms, which the others were not. Upon which Taggart said, 'that they should fight it out', to which I replied, 'With all my heart'. We then rode over to where the priests' party were assembled, when a woman called out, 'There's Atkinson, the traitor'. Immediately one of the party presented his gun at me, when a woman, a tenant on my property, caught hold of the gun, and said, 'her landlord should not be shot'. . . .

On Monday morning, the 21st, I got up at 5 o'clock, and soon after the firing commenced at the Protestant houses at the Diamond . . . We did not expect this after what had occurred at my house. A number of Protestants came to me, finding they were attacked. I gave them all the ammunition I had, and set out with my family for the Fort of Charlemont, being well aware their object was to destroy my house, and all who were in it. On the road I heard the Protestants were likely to be successful, and I sent my family home and went on to Charlemont. I got Captain Killeney, and sixty invalids who were stationed there, to accompany me. When we arrived at the Diamond the battle was over.

> Reprinted in: M.W. Dewar, J. Brown, S.E. Long, *Orangeism: A New Historical Appreciation* (Belfast, 1967), pp. 93-4

10   Thomas Drew: Looking for good in the church of a brother

The early Orange Order had been predominantly Episcopalian. Irish dissenters, mainly Presbyterians, were slower than members of the Established Church to achieve that amalgamation of views on religion, nationality, and politics which has characterized Ulster since the mid-nineteenth century. But by the late 1820s the struggle between the conservative Presbyterian Henry Cooke (1788-1868) and the liberalism of his rival Henry Montgomery (1788-1865) was beginning to swing in favour of the former. In mid-century, furthermore, all the major denominations in Britain, Ireland, and elsewhere began to make serious efforts to proselytize the new urban masses. In Ulster this development coalesced with the national question in such a way as to complete the polarization between Protestant and Catholic. This extract is from a sermon delivered by Thomas Drew (1808-70), rector of Christchurch, Belfast, to a congregation of Orangemen on 12 July 1857.

. . .The Sermon on the Mount is an everlasting rebuke to all intolerance, and all legislative and ecclesiastical cruelty. Of old time, lords of high degree with their own hands, strained, on the rack, the delicate limbs of Protestant women; prelates dabbled in the gore of helpless victims; and the cells of the Pope's prisons were paved with calcined bones of men and cemented with gore and human hair. Would that such atrocities were no longer formidable! What has been done may be repeated, and, at this hour, the world had its record of existing wrong. Austria crushes the throbbing hearts of Italy. France basely upholds the Pontiff's detested throne; and America has not yet regarded the cry of millions she calls 'chattels' and not men.

This sad anomaly cannot forever last. . . . The Word of God makes all plain; puts to eternal shame the practice of persecutors; and stigmatizes, with enduring reprobation, the arrogant pretences of popes, and the outrageous dogmata of their bloodstained religion.

. . .He who lives, labours, plans and gives for the prosperity of his own church alone is a narrow-minded Christian. He may be a believer; he may be, to some extent, a good Christian—a pious and generous member of some particular denomination. Let him, however, not dream of taking to himself the honoured name of Protestant. That glorious and eloquent name is reserved for those only who can rise above congregational littleness; who can unite on broad and evangelical principles against the common foe, and who look for what is good in the church of a brother, and care not to know what is uncongenial. . . . It is a miserable triumph to propagate rancour. . . . Such troubles in the camp of God's hosts will find no countenance from true Protestants. To the honour of Orangemen, they have always discouraged these internecine clamours which gladden the hearts of Rome's children and subserve the aggression of the ever-watchful Papacy.

. . .At no period were the resources of Rome more available. All that literature and the fine arts; all that painting, sculpture and music can do, are employed in her service. The strangest result of all this fascination is, that men of intelligence and learning, who have drunk of her cup, are men so intoxicated by its poison, as to endorse and uphold the most fantastic and incredible inventions, lies and practices of the Romish sect. . . . It is painful to see how false views of the real state of Ireland are still maintained by wily statesmen, and by persons from whom better things might reasonably be expected. By reason of a falsified census, the numbers of the Protestants were set down vastly below their amount. In many instances, treacherous census takers actually returned no Protestants, and counted those who are really Protestants as Romanists! Famine, pestilence and emigration have diminished the Romish population by several millions. Thousands have left the errors of Rome for the truth of God's word; and the greater portion of those who remain are of a class so priest-ridden, impulsive, uncertain and disloyal, as to make it wonderful that statesmen should prescribe for Ireland as if it were a Popish, and not, as its real strength, worth, industry and loyalty constitute it, a great Protestant country.

. . .The faint-hearted clergy of the past century have to answer, to some extent, for the race of semi-infidel legislators and pro-Popery legislators which abound. It is not to be credited, if preachers had really been scriptural (and to be really Scriptural they must be really Protestant) preachers, that their flocks, especially the young, would have grown up in such deplorable deficiency of Protestant feeling and conduct. . . . Our princes want prelates like Latimer and Ridley to stand at their sides. Italy wants another Savonarola; Scotland another Knox; and England another Wicliff!

Transcription from: PP 1857-8 XXIV (*Report on Riots in Belfast*, 1857), Evidence, pp. 248-52.

11   Industrial Belfast: The creation of a battleground

The most significant development in nineteenth-century Ulster was the growth of Belfast from a small port, no larger than two or three others on the Ulster coast, into the only large industrial city in Ireland. Its strength, based initially on world leadership in the production of linen, was buttressed subsequently by the development of a major shipyard in the 1850s, in turn generating the development of engineering and ropeworks. A town of some 19,000 people in 1800 had 121,000 inhabitants by 1851, and at the end of the century had grown into a city of more than 400,000 people. In this extract the medical officer of health describes the other face of Victorian prosperity — the state of the poorer parts of the town — at mid-century. Although similar conditions abounded in British industrial cities, only Belfast had to house two large and indigenous, but self-consciously distinct, communities with an established predisposition to violent hostility.

Our main streets, for width and regularity of outline, are proverbially a model; but we cannot say so for the myriad approaches to the poorer residences. Upwards of 1,800 houses, in courts, etc., are accessible only by a covered archway. Of these the majority have only one outlet, and, under these circumstances, it is impossible that any current could ventilate such localities. Indeed, as regards the tenements of the poor, the tendency to crowd them into the smallest space is so great, that it would seem to be an understood law of nature that the indigent do not actually require as much fresh air as the wealthy. . . .

. . . The great majority of the poorer class of houses in this town consist of four rooms in two storeys. These are generally occupied by two families. Each room varies from seven to ten feet square, and from six to eight feet high in the lower storey — the same dimensions with a lower storey in the upper. Each room, though not always, contains one window, the upper sash of which is almost invariably, in the older houses, made immoveable. . . . Such a house is manifestly insufficient to be the domicile of ten individuals; but we have known, and not unfrequently, so many as eighteen or even twenty persons sleeping within such limited apartments. . . .

. . . There are in this town 48 flax and cotton spinning and weaving factories, 53 bakeries, and 33 confectioneries, 14 large clothing-establishments, and 14 foundries, besides several large sewed muslin work-rooms. All of these establishments are characterized by having numbers (in many instances amounting to many hundreds) of young persons congregated for many hours daily in a limited space. In some, it is a great object to keep the rooms at a certain, and that a high temperature. It is plain that, unless the utmost precautions are taken to prevent the accumulation of respired, and therefore vitiated air, the greatest danger to health may be expected. . . .

Fever may be said to be endemic in this town. The memory of the oldest inhabitant fails to refer to a time when it was represented merely by an isolated case. During the last thirty years it has attacked above 62,000 inhabitants, of whom nearly 6,000 perished. Next to Dublin, no town in Ireland, or the sister kingdoms, of similar character or dimensions, has been so severely visited. Thus, while the proportion of fever deaths in all Ireland of the total deaths is only 6 per cent, it is here

16.2 per cent; and while the proportion of deaths from zymotic diseases is 38 per cent for all Ireland, here it is 47.1 per cent.

. . .When we consider that, little more than twenty years ago, we could boast of but a single flax-spinning factory, and that now upwards of forty tall chimneys spring from similar establishments, it is little wonder that we should find disease, and especially epidemic disease, on the increase. To give accommodation to the thousand operatives which the giant demand of an unusually properous manufacture created, strings of houses on the simplest plan were hurried up, generally without sufficient carefulness as to drainage, ventilation, house wants, or situation, and the more ancient and cheaper districts, though already sufficiently crowded, were resorted to by the unthinking artisan, in his desire to have a dwelling sufficiently near his employment.

> A.G. Malcolm, 'The Sanitary State of Belfast'
> (1852), reprinted in *Problems of a Growing
> City: Belfast, 1780-1870* (PRONI 1973) pp.
> 156-61

12   The battle-lines drawn

The early development of segregated Catholic and Protestant working-class districts in Belfast was greatly intensified by the waves of sectarian rioting which became a regular feature of the city from mid-century onwards. This extract describes the distribution of forces at the time of the most severe outbreak in 1886.

Belfast is a great manufacturing town, which in progress and wealth enjoys a foremost place among the centres of population of the United Kingdom. Its population in 1881, according to the Census returns, was 208,122, and since that time has probably increased to about 230,000. It has an area of 6,805 acres, and a valuation of £604,537.

The town is, in its present proportions, of very recent growth; and the result is that the poorer classes, instead of, as in other cities, occupying tenements in large houses, reside mainly in separate quarters, each of which is almost entirely given up to persons of one particular faith, and the boundaries of which are sharply defined. In the district of West Belfast, the great thoroughfare of Shankhill-road, with the network of streets running into it, and the side streets connecting those lateral branches, is an almost purely Protestant district; and the parties referred to in the evidence as 'the Shankhill mob', are a Protestant mob. The great Catholic quarter is due south of the Shankhill district, and consists of the thoroughfare known as the Falls-road, and the streets running south of it; and the parties referred to in the testimony before us as the 'Falls-road-mob', are therefore a Catholic mob. Due south of the Falls district is Grosvenor-street; almost entirely inhabited by Protestants, so that the Catholic quarter lies between two Protestant districts. The Shankhill-road and Falls-road are both largely inhabited by shopkeepers who supply the wants of the population, and whose houses are sometimes large and comfortable. The streets running off these thoroughfares consist of long rows of cottages of artisans and labourers. The great points of danger to the peace of the town are open spaces in the border land between the two quarters; and two of these spaces — the Brickfields and Springfield — will be found to have been the theatres of some of the worst scenes of the riots.

The great number of working people who dwell in the districts we have described are, at ordinary times, a most peaceable and industrious community. But unfortunately a spirit has grown up amongst these people, which has resulted in that, on three previous occasions within the last thirty years, in 1857, 1864, and 1872, the town was the scene of disturbances and long-continued riots.

> PP 1887 XVIII *(Report of the Belfast Riot Commissioners)*, Report, p. 4.

13   Triumph of the Romish mobs, 1857

The Irish census took no account of religion until 1861. But we may be fairly certain that Belfast in 1800 was a predominantly Protestant town, numbering only about 2,000 Catholics (10 per cent) in its population. But the large-scale urban migration which followed was for half a century disproportionately Catholic, for Catholics occupied the least secure position in Ulster's rural economy. The famine, we may be certain, accentuated this trend, so that by 1861 the Catholic proportion of the population reached its registered peak at 34 per cent (41,000). The proportion in the early 1850s may have been even higher. But with the onset of an era of major riots in 1857, Ulster Catholic migrants tended increasingly to choose Britain or America as their destination in preference to the Orange citadel of Belfast. The immediate cause of the 1857 disturbances was an outbreak of evangelical and aggressively Protestant street-preaching in the town, and attempts by Catholics to disrupt it. In origin, at least, the movement was part of a revival movement which extended far beyond Ireland. But to many people in Belfast the issue came to be seen as a struggle for mastery in the city, as the Protestant daily newspaper discerned clearly when the magistrates intervened to cancel a meeting.

The Romish mobs have triumped in our town. They have succeeded in accomplishing what no Protestant in Belfast ever supposed he should live to see realized. The preaching of the Gospel in our streets to the destitute, ragged poor is put down. Belfast ranks now with Kilkenny, or Cork, or Limerick. In these Romish cities, where priests are regnant, and their mobs omnipotent, and the authorities bow to their behests, no Protestant minister dare lift his voice in the streets or highways, to proclaim the peaceful message of the Cross — he would be stoned or murdered. We write what everybody knows to be fact. It is one of the dark features of the Romish South that there is no religious liberty tolerated there by the priesthood; and the mobs, under their complete influence and domination, obey their fiats, and resist with the violence of fiends, every public effort to make known to the benighted masses the blessed tidings of salvation.

But no one ever supposed that it should be thus in Protestant Belfast. Hitherto fullest liberty has been given to our ministers to carry out their benignant purposes of doing good. They have preached in the streets — in all parts of the town — without let or hindrance. The Romanists interfered not. Hitherto they had a deep policy to carry out. They were without influence in this town — they were poor — they feigned great gratitude for the foolishly bestowed, and ill-requited benefactions of so-called liberal Protestants. We remember their solitary chapel near the precincts of Smithfield. When Donegall-street chapel was built, lasting gratitude was expressed to the generous Protestants who had aided Dr Crolly [parish priest] in the erection of that edifice. Dr Crolly was one of our most eloquent lip-advocates of toleration, forbearance, good-will among Christian brethren. And many of our townsmen were deceived. They began to think Romanism a changed, mild, humble, harmless system.

Look at the daring, intolerant, and triumphant attitude and operations of the system now? We do not think lightly of the Papal mob-law domination. We have the worst fears because of it. Is our town henceforward to be degraded by the reproach that a Protestant minister shall not dare to preach in its streets? Are our magistrates to rebuke ministers of God for obeying their divine Master's command, 'to go into the streets and highways', to discharge the functions of their office?

. . .a mighty Romish movement is now in operation in this town to assimilate it to the degraded Popish towns of the South and West of Ireland. . . .

. . .Our object is not to inflame Protestant against Papist. We advocate the right of the poor and of the outcasts to have the Gospel preached to them on the streets.

Belfast Newsletter, 5 September 1857

14   The hateful system of street-preaching

To Catholics on the other hand, street-preaching seemed less the exercise of a religious right than an abuse of free speech.

Every unprejudiced person — every man of common sense — knows that street-preaching is not got up for the purpose of enlightening Protestants 'who sit in darkness'. That is not the object of the raving system. Its real object and aim is to insult the feelings of Catholics and deride their faith; to show that here, in the midst of a population of 50,000 Catholics, there is a tyrannical, rampant, and 'dominant' faction, struggling for mastery over those who do not agree with them either religiously or politically. That faction must be at their old work of division, disunion, and religious hate. . . .

The exercise of a public or private right when it becomes obnoxious to the community and results in violence, has no longer the character of right; it then becomes a wrong; and it is the duty of those intrusted with the administration of the law to act with determination and vigour, and put down this hateful system, which in defiance of judicial remonstrance, promises us a reign of confusion, terror, and, possibly, bloodshed. We warn the authorities in time, and thus have done our duty.

Belfast Morning News, 5 September 1857

15   Roaring Hanna

Faced with the disapproval of the magistracy and the incontrovertible fact that street-preaching was in practice likely to be followed by serious rioting, the Church of Ireland Mission called a halt to its 1857 programme. But a young Presbyterian clergyman, Hugh 'Roaring' Hanna (1824-92), though opposed by his own Belfast Presbytery, came forward to take up the challenge. He would, he said in his 'First Letter to the Protestants of Belfast', uphold the right to preach in the open. Hanna later became a prominent public figure in Belfast, as a commissioner for national education and a leading opponent of home rule. The 1857 troubles were something of a stepping-stone in his career. His decision to proceed with his service on 6 September, leading as it did to the inevitable rioting, made him an important witness before the subsequent riots commission. His evidence under cross-examination by a Catholic counsel gives some impression of his brash and irrepressible style.

(a) MEN AND BRETHREN, — Your blood-bought and cherished 'RIGHTS' have been imperilled by the audacious and savage outrages of a Romish mob. The well-meant but foolish leniency of an easy-natured magistracy, vainly hoping to disarm resentment by conciliation, has hastened and aggravated the present crisis. . . .

Your ministers have a legal right to preach in the open air. No man can honestly deny that. You have also a right to listen to them. Let them choose *convenient* places for their services. When you assemble around, leave so much of the thoroughfare unoccupied that such as do not choose to listen may pass by. Call that clearance the 'Pope's pad'. No man has any right to interrupt the services. . . .

(b) Mr O'Rorke— *You have the character of being a controversialist?* — I do not know that I have that character, but some people are kind enough to say that I was rather a smart hand at it.

Well, certainly you do not want for a trumpeter — you can blow your own trumpet? — To be sure.

You have preached very often on controversial subjects? — Yes.

And you have advertised these sermons? — Some of them.

What were the subjects of these sermons? — The various subjects that are litigated between the two churches; and I think I have logically overturned, among other things, the Pope's supremacy; and if you wish for something more specific, I will go on and tell you what further damage I have done your church.

What further damage have you done my church? — I intended it.

Do you think you have moved one stone out of it? — I think I have.

You have not removed the roof off it yet? — The covering is very scanty.

You do not like coverings at all? You like open air better? — Yes.

At the risk of a shindy? — Let the people who precipitate the shindies take the consequences.

You are just in the Presbyterian Church what Mr McIlwaine is in his church? — I just wish to be a faithful minister, a useful man, and a loyal citizen.

Do you not wish to be simply what Mr McIlwaine is? — I have no particular anxiety to be what Mr McIlwaine is. Mr McIlwaine is only an incumbent. I would never be satisfied till I realized the top of my ambition. I would not be satisfied with his ecclesiastically humble position. If I were in the Episcopalian Church, I would not be satisfied till I was Archbishop of Canterbury.

About how far are you off the head of your own church? — Oh! I am a considerable distance off; but I am climbing as fast as I can.

And you want to climb by notoriety? — I want to climb by honest endeavour.

Honest endeavour, on Sundays, to create riots? — No; that is not part of my policy or principle either.

You take the Regium Donum? * — I do. I am only sorry that it is not more than twice as much.

> PP 1857-58 XXVI *(Report on Riots in Belfast, 1857),* Evidence pp. 169, 252-3

16   William Johnston of Ballykilbeg

Although it was religious affiliation that delineated the two communities in Ulster, and although outbursts of religious enthusiasm on either side might serve to bring the communities into sporadic conflict, Christian rhetoric alone could not easily sustain a regular political movement, particularly on the Protestant side where church attendance was lower and the diversity of denominations posed an organizational problem. The Orange Order had been officially dissolved by its Grand Lodge in 1836, but the grass-roots refused to die and indeed flourished as strongly in the new working-class districts of Belfast as they had done in rural Armagh. One of the Order's most active spokesmen from about 1860 onwards was William Johnston (1829-1902), a small landowner from Ballykilbeg, Co.Down. He won attention, imprisonment, and a political career at Westminster, in that order, following an Orange march which he led from Newtownards to Bangor in 1868 in defiance of the Party Processions Act, a measure through which British governments sought unsuccessfully to stifle political excitement in Ireland between 1850 and 1872. Following the wide extension of the franchise implemented by the second reform act, Johnston stood as an independent in the Belfast parliamentary election of 1868, entering Westminster at the expense of an official Conservative. His victory, and his endorsement as Conservative candidate at

---

*The *Regium Donum* (Royal Bounty) was a grant made from public funds to Presbyterian ministers in Ireland. Initiated by William III in 1690 in return for Irish Presbyterian support against James II, it was discontinued in 1869 when the Church of Ireland was disestablished.

future elections, mark the establishment of a formal link between the Ulster Conservatives and the popular Protestantism of the Orange Order. In this extract, from an early speech to the Grand Orange Lodge of Belfast, Johnston expounds the basic political justification for Orangeism.

Such a demonstration as this is a glorious thing. Would to God there were more of them all over the length and breadth of Ireland. (Hear, hear). We should not then be told that Orangeism was a thing of the past, that the Orange Institution was not in existence, that the thing had passed away, and that only a man here and man there was engaged in maintaining Orangeism. We should then be able to point to our glorious demonstrations, and say—Are these the men that are not in existence? Such a glorious demonstration as we can show here tonight is a proof that, under God, Orangeism shall never be extinguished in Ireland. (Loud cheers). There are some who dread demonstrations. There are some who tell us we should confine ourselves to our monthly meetings in our lodge-rooms. We are forbidden by the law of the land to go forth in procession on the 12th July. . . . Are we not then, to show our force in any way? Are we to hide ourselves in holes and corners for fear of giving offence to our fastidious fellow-countrymen? God forbid it. If they believed that we were extinguished, if that belief could be entertained by those who hate us, we would see re-enacted in this country those deeds of blood which stained the hills and alleys in byegone days. . . .

. . .The Orange Institution is a religio-political institution. . . . But Popery is something more than a religious system; it is a political system also. It is a religio-political system for the enslavement of the body and soul of man, and it cannot be met by any mere religious system, or by any mere political system. It must be opposed by such a combination as the Orange Society, based upon religion, and carrying our religion into the politics of the day. We must carry our religion into the politics of the day. We must tell our representatives in Parliament that they must support Protestantism in their politics as well as go down on their knees before God on the Sabbath Day. (Cheers). . . .

Belfast Newsletter, 15 May 1861

17 A sectarian voting pattern

In mid-Victorian England the Protestant nonconformist churches provided much of the grass-roots support for the growing Liberal party. Earlier, Presbyterians in some parts of Ulster had been associated with the United Irishmen against what they regarded as an Anglican-dominated ascendancy. But even in 1798 the Orange Order had been a force working in the other direction, emphasizing the common bonds of the Protestant churches. In party politics the same trend developed, although vestigial Presbyterian support for the Liberal party lingered on, handicapped still further by Gladstone's adoption of home rule in 1886. Until the secret ballot was established in 1872, an individual's voting behaviour was public knowledge, and often *published* knowledge if it suited the dictates of party propaganda or commercial interests. Pollbooks are therefore an important, if neglected, source for historians. The first two extracts are from a full list of the poll for the parliamentary borough of Newry, Co. Down, in 1868. Kirk was the successful Liberal, and Lord Newry the Conservative candidate. Notice that the Liberals polled 97 per cent of the Catholic votes cast, 15 per cent of Presbyterian votes, and less than 5 per cent of Episcopalian votes. Analysis of the full list of voters also reveals that the average rateable value of Catholic electors was £14-11-2, of Presbyterians £21-8-0 and of Episcopalians £16-5-0. The third extract illustrates the response of one Ulster Liberal to the changing circumstances. Col. E.J. Saunderson (1837-1906), who had been critical of Orangeism in the 1860s, later became leader of the Ulster Unionist group at Westminster.

(a) Summary of Voting

There voted in all 765, Of this number Mr. Kirk polled—

Roman Catholics	341
Episcopalians	9
Presbyterians	30
Methodists	1
Independents	1
Quakers	4
Total	380

Lord Newry polled—

Episcopalians	174
Presbyterians	171
Roman Catholics	11
Methodists	16
Independents	7
Quakers	0
Total	379

(b)   Extract from list of voters for the borough of Newry

Name of Voter.	Name or Description of Premises Rated.		Rated Value.			Newry	Kirk	Religion
			£	s.	d.			
Burns, Walter	17 Hill street	house	20	0	0	1	..	P
Burns, James	2 Kildare street	same	23	0	0	..	1	P
Burnside, Wm. J.	81 Canal street —	same	22	0	0	1	..	E
Byrne, Michael	11, 12 Lower Water street	same	00	0	0	..	1	R C
Byrne, James	13 Monaghan street	same	17	0	0	a	a	R C
Byrne, James	76 Hill street	same	42	0	0	..	1	R C
Byrne, Edward	40 Mill street	same	18	0	0	..	1	R C
Byrne, Michael	Hide Market	same	5	0	0	..	1	R C
Byron, Archibald	114 Chapel street	same	7	0	0	1	..	E
Cahill, Peter	35 Kilmorey street	same	5	10	0	..	1	R C
Callan, Owen	1 Courtenay hill	same	10	0	0	..	1	R C
Callaghan, James	117 Canal street —	same	11	0	0	..	1	R C
Callaghan, Owen	11 Caulfield place	same	8	0	0	..	1	R C
Campbell, Patrick	32 Ballinacraig —		8	10	0	..	1	R C
Campbell, Bernard	82 Commons	house and land	6	0	0	1	..	R C
Campbell, Michael	13 Lower Water street	house	5	10	0	..	1	R C
Campbell, Patrick	34, 35 Boat street	same	32	10	0	..	1	R C
Campbell, Francis,	127 High street	same	8	10	0	1	..	E
Campbell, Francis	14 Basin walk	same	10	0	0	1	..	E
Campbell, Hugh	81 Ballinacraig —	house, land, & c	150	0	0	a	a	P
Campbell A.F., jun	81 Ballinacraig —	same	150	0	0	1	..	P
Campbell, Robert	39, 40 Upper Water street	house	24	10	0	1	..	P
Caldwell, John	10 Maginnis street	house and yard	6	0	0	..	1	R C
Cardwell, Thomas	45 Lower Water street	same	4	15	0	..	1	E
Cardwell, Thomas	17, 18 Edward street	same	50	0	0	..	1	R C
Carey, Thomas	7 Marcus square	same	36	0	0	..	1	R C

(c)   Col. E.J. Saunderson to William Johnston   16 August 1874

. . .I believe we are now in a transition state, and that the old lines of political demarcation have lost to an extent their political signi-ficance. If you wish to ask me to define by a name my political sentiments I should answer that I am a Protestant. If you were to ask what party I should support I should say the Protestant party. I could define my political principles in no other way. . . .

PRONI, Johnston Papers

18   The end of a sectarian police force

Law and order were maintained in mid-nineteenth-century Belfast by the Town Police, a force raised by the local corporation. The Royal Irish Consta-bulary, a centrally-controlled and semi-military body, which since 1836 had been responsible for the rest of Ireland outside Dublin, kept only a small force in the town. The Catholic section of the population had little confidence in the local body, which it customarily distinguished from the RIC by the title 'the Protestant police'. The commission of inquiry into the 1857 riots confirmed widespread allegations that the Town Police had not always acted impartially between rioters. The charges were renewed following the next major bout of rioting in 1864, and the town force was abolished. The riot commissioners on that occasion laid more emphasis on the force's lack of resources and professional skills than on its partisan conduct, but they also set down a useful analysis of the operation of discriminatory selection procedures in one particular area of employment.

. . .It certainly is somewhat remarkable that in this body of 160 men, only five Roman Catholics are to be found; the proportion of Roman Catholics to Protestants (of all sects) in Belfast being a third, and in the class in life whence the police is recruited, considerably higher. . . . It must then be regarded as strange that in these circumstances Roman Catholics are to be found in the Belfast police force in the proportion of only one to thirty-one, compared with Protestants; the facilities of admission being equally afforded to both, and the temptations to seek it being certainly as great in the case of the former as of the latter. . . .

. . .Various reasons were suggested by witnesses, such as the superior physical condition of the Protestant population in the rank of life whence the police force is recruited; the existence amongst them of more education, intelligence, and the like. We incline to the opinion that other causes operate far more powerfully. The Council which nominates and controls the force consists, with the exception of a couple of its members, of Protestants. The chief of the force has always been of that religion; and, in 1857, the person holding that post was a member, and had been master of an Orange lodge. The officers have been Protestants in like manner. All this naturally tends to produce an impression amongst Roman Catholics, whether justly or not — certainly very naturally — that their chances of admission into the force would be small, and that promotion in it would be hopeless. The mode of filling vacancies also encourages this idea, and greatly tends to keep the police Protestant, it having once become so. No proper advertisement is published inviting candidates to apply, a mere written notice, posted on the walls of the police-office, being the sole intimation to them. The members of the force, it may be presumed, circulate amongst their relatives and friends (who are most likely to be of their own creed) the intelligence thus withheld from the general public; so that, without any direct exclusion of Roman Catholics as such, they are virtually shut out, almost as completely as if there was a positive rule against their admission. . . .

While we are far from adopting the idea that in ordinary circumstances it is necessary or desirable to preserve any kind of proportion between the members of different religious communities in a police force and the members of the same communities in the population amongst whom they are placed, we yet recognize the expediency of such a course in cases where religious animosities run high, and where the non-observance of some such system would lead to a want of confidence detrimental to the efficiency of the force. We trust sincerely that the day may not be distant when even in Belfast it may be safe and wise in the case of the police, and indeed in all cases, to nominate men without regard to aught than their personal fitness for the duties assigned to them. But beyond a doubt this cannot be done now. Here again the Royal Irish Constabulary offers the way to obviate any difficulty. Its numerical strength is so considerable that, composed as it is of members of the different religious denominations in the country, in the selection of men for Belfast there need be no difficulty in preserving amongst them the proportion which the members of different congregations there bear to each other, and in preserving it till a wiser and happier time renders it unnecessary to take such a circumstance into consideration. . . .

In closing this part of our report to your Excellency, we must add that, when opening our inquiry, we fully believed there had been exaggeration in the accounts that had been made public of the riots. It is with pain we must now avow our conviction, based on the testimony of witnesses of every class, that the reality was far worse than any description we had met with. . . .

> PP 1865 XXVIII *(Belfast Riots Inquiry Commission),* Report, pp. 2-17.

19   Ulster fights. . . 1886

The provision of a more fully professional police force seemed to make little impact on the situation in Belfast. There were further serious riots in 1872, and in 1886 came the worst outbreak to date, lasting intermittently from May until September, with 32 killed and 371 injured. The occasion was the introduction and prompt defeat of the Liberal government's Home Rule Bill. The response of the Protestant mob to the RIC, described below by the riots commissioners, makes an interesting comparison with the previous extract, and indicates the powerful impact of rumour in a tense situation.

Unquestionably, however, a main cause of the prolonged continuance of the disturbances was the wild and unreasoning hostility exhibited by a large section of the Protestants of Belfast against the police. . . .

It was an expression of the extraordinary belief which so largely prevailed amongst Belfast Protestants — a belief that the late Government of the Queen was packing the town of Belfast with Catholic policemen, carefully selected from certain southern counties, and charged with the duty of shooting down the Protestants. There can be no doubt that this belief was honestly held by large sections of the humbler Protestants in Belfast, and was the secret of the bitter hostility shown against the Royal Irish Constabulary. . . .

We are sorry to add that certain persons having great influence in Belfast, thought proper, at various periods during the riots, to indulge in language, written and spoken, well calculated to maintain excitement at a time when all men of influence should have tried to assuage it. . . . We feel it our duty to draw special attention to a letter of the 4th day of August, 1886, written by Mr De Cobain, Member of Parliament for one of the divisions of the town — a letter the publication of which the Mayor of Belfast most properly brought under the notice of the Government. Another cause of the continuance of the riots was the unhappy sympathy with which, at certain stages, the well-to-do classes of Protestants regarded the proceedings of the rioters. At one stage of the riots it seemed as if the greater part of the population of the Shankhill district united against the police. This is the more to be regretted as it was on all sides admitted that no more valuable aid could have been given to the police than that afforded by respectable and influential people of the localities in which the troubles arose. . . .

Some few witnesses appeared to think that it was desirable to organize a kind of vigilance committee consisting of respectable men acting solely in their own localities and among their own co-religionists. Such proposals are more specious than feasible, and the efforts of many of the peace-makers in Belfast during the riots did more harm than good. At the same time we direct attention to the evidence of Mr Combe (of the firm of Combe, Barber, and Combe), which shows plainly that in large works it is perfectly possible to make such arrangements as will tend to keep order among the workmen, and to prevent religious difficulties interfering with the earning of a livelihood. We regretted to find that in some other large works no effort was made to check cruelty and intolerance, and that in one, the workmen freely carried away large numbers of iron bolts and nuts, which they and others afterwards used in the riots; nor was any effort made to check such misconduct. . . .

PP 1887 XVIII *(Report of the Belfast Riots Commissioners)*, Report pp. 16-19.

20   Derry follows suit

The city of Derry (renamed Londonderry by the seventeenth-century planters) never developed successful industries in the way that Belfast had done. Its population growth—from about 12,000 to 40,000 during the course of the century—was due as much to unbearable circumstances on the land in Co. Donegal and mid-Ulster as to real demand for labour in the city. Its remote situation and poor hinterland proved insurmountable obstacles to sustained economic growth, so that only shirtmaking, based on the plentiful supply of cheap female labour, developed as a flourishing industry. The city's origins as a frontier fortress for the seventeenth-century plantation, and its legendary siege against the Catholic forces of James II in 1689, when a group of apprentices closed the gates in defiance of the faltering governor, gave it emotional significance for Protestants. But urban migration from the late eighteenth century onwards ensured that it would become a predominantly Catholic city. Sectarian rioting, though easier to contain than in Belfast, broke out in 1870 and 1883. The following extract reveals many of the same features that were apparent in the case of Belfast. Behind all the immediate causes lies a struggle for domination of territory between two irreconcilable groups, but in this case the territory was the historic walled city centre, and the local Protestant forces required at least ritual reinforcement from outside the city, especially the Orangemen on 12 July and the Apprentice Boys of Derry, virtually identical in membership, on 12 August.

When the city was very limited in extent and population, when its inhabitants were almost exclusively Protestant, and when such Catholics as had gathered under its walls were poor and few in number, it is easy to imagine that anniversaries, celebrated by those who virtually were the citizens, passed off without opposition. But, as Londonderry increased in extent and prosperity, it, almost of necessity, underwent other changes. Trade and commerce attracted population, much of it from the largely Roman Catholic county of Donegal. Of the immigrants of this class, some had wealth, perhaps; others acquired it, in the pursuits of industry. Legislative enactments concurrently altered the relations of the Catholic and the Protestant; and, gradually, from being an almost exclusively Protestant community, with a few Catholics amongst the humblest class, a large majority of the population is of the latter creed, some of them affluent in means and of good social station, several in comfortable circumstances, and nearly all acquainted, more or less, with the history of events that cause them to look on the local anniversaries as offensive to themselves. Here then we find one reason for the existence of increased discontent with the celebrations.

Another reason we glanced at, in the commencement of our Report. The city of Londonderry, geographically cut off from the strictly Protestant districts of Ulster, has been for some time past brought into rapid communication with those portions of them in which the Orange organization is most general, by the railways to which we have already referred. As a matter of private speculation, the railway companies, of late years, have taken to running excursion trains to Derry, on the two historic anniversaries; and this, by causing a large influx of strangers to take part in the proceedings, naturally leads to a more angry feeling amongst the great body of the Catholics of that city, than would exist had they been, as of old, exclusively conducted by their fellow-townsmen. The character of the demonstrations has certainly undergone a change, and amongst the Catholic lower classes, at least, they are now regarded with the most hostile feelings. . . .

Amongst the reasons assigned for desiring changes in respect to these arrangements one, which we regretted to find put forward, was the existence of distrust in the impartial administration of justice, by the members of the local bench. . . .

In point of fact, there was no real foundation for the charges made, though, of course, anything that could reasonably be done to remove the suspicion of partiality, however unfounded, is desirable. If it were possible to add some Roman Catholic gentlemen to the Bench of local magistrates, now very exclusively Protestant in its constitution, we are sure doing so would produce good effect. . . .

From what we have previously said, we need hardly observe that the police arrangements of the borough need complete alteration. The existing body is, on all sides, condemned, as wholly inadequate to the local necessities. The opinion, in Londonderry, seems unanimous that the proper substitute for it would be a sufficient number of the Royal Irish Constabulary, specially empowered, as in Belfast, to discharge the regular duties of a watch and ward. . .

PP 1870 XXXII *(Londonderry Riots Inquiry Commission),* Report, pp. 17-20.

III   The drive for Home Rule, 1879-1906

21   Michael Davitt—a Fenian retrains

Just as the Famine dispersed a wave of Irish emigrants throughout the English-speaking world, so the Fenian movement and its collapse sent forth another group, infinitely smaller in number, but retaining a degree of sustained commitment to Irish nationalism which had eluded earlier Irish revolutionaries. For some the commitment was inseparable from fruitful careers in Irish-American politics; for others it led only to long prison sentences and a subsequent life of bitterness and dependence on the charity of old colleagues. The background of Michael Davitt (1846-1906), which he describes below, was fairly typical of the revolutionaries of the Fenian generation. He lost an arm in a Lancashire mill accident at the age of sixteen, and from 1870 to 1877 was imprisoned in Dartmoor following conviction for his part in a Fenian assassination plot. But his subsequent role in Irish politics was to prove very different from that of his early associates. Although recent historical analysis has demonstrated that Davitt's autobiography exaggerates his role in affairs generally and in particular credits him with a prescience he did not possess so far as the linking of the land and national questions was concerned, there is no doubt that he played an important linking role in 1878-9 between Irish-American nationalists of the Fenian generation and new developments taking place in Ireland.

. . .almost my first-remembered experience of my own life and of the existence of landlordism was our eviction in 1852, when I was about five years of age. That eviction and the privations of the preceding famine years, the story of the starving peasantry of Mayo, of the deaths from hunger and the coffinless graves on the roadside — everywhere a hole could be dug for the slaves who died because of 'God's providence' — all this was the political food seasoned with a mother's tears over unmerited sorrows and sufferings which had fed my mind in another land, a teaching which lost none of its force or directness by being imparted in the Gaelic tongue, which was almost always spoken in our Lancashire home. My first knowledge and impressions of landlordism were got in that school, with an assistant monitor of a father who had been the head of some agrarian secret society in Mayo in 1837, and who had to fly to England in that year to escape a threatened prosecution for Ribbonism.

> Michael Davitt, *The Fall of Feudalism in Ireland* (London, 1904), p. 222

22   The new departure

At the same time as Michael Davitt was readjusting to the world outside Dartmoor, a man of very different background was developing another nationalist weapon. Charles Stewart Parnell (1846-91), a Protestant Irish landlord and a member of parliament for the moderate home rule party, was the central figure in a small group of MPs who were evolving techniques for impeding the business of the House of Commons in order to publicize the nationalist cause. Parnell's arrogant, forceful style won attention not only at Westminster and in Ireland, but also amongst ex-Fenians in Irish-America who had grown up with nothing but contempt for constitutional nationalism. His strategy, in so far as one can be identified in so pragmatic a figure, was to pull together under his control as many strands of the nationalist movement as possible—the moderate home rule party (preferably with more militant personnel) and the respectable forces, clerical and lay, which underpinned it at local level; the re-emerging forces of agrarian radicalism; and the sensitive guardians of the revolutionary tradition and purse-strings in America. Although Parnell was never able to obtain formal support from the old Fenian leadership of the IRB itself, he was able to do for some years what no other constitutional leader was ever able to do—win over the mainstream of revolutionary sentiment in America, in the form of the ex-Fenian John Devoy (1842-1928) and his Clan na Gael organization. It now seems that Devoy's original telegram to Parnell of 25 October 1878, which initiated the 'new departure in Irish politics' was based on a mistaken assumption that Parnell had broken with his moderate parliamentary associates. It is certainly clear that at a subsequent meeting in Dublin Parnell did not in fact promise what Devoy thought he had promised. But the new link held out more real hope of achievement for Irish nationalism than any previous movement had done.

Nationalists here will support you on the following conditions:-
First. Abandonment of the Federal demand and substitution of a general declaration in favour of self-government.
Second. Vigorous agitation of the Land Question on the basis of a peasant proprietary, while accepting concessions tending to abolish arbitrary evictions.
Third. Exclusion of all sectarian issues from the platform.
Fourth. Irish members to vote together on all Imperial and Home

Rule questions, adopt an aggressive policy and energetically resist coercive legislation.

Fifth. Advocacy of all struggling nationalities in the British Empire and elsewhere.

New York Herald, 26 October 1878

23   The priest as landlord: Irishtown, 1879

During the 1870s, developments in refrigeration and shipping exposed European farmers to serious transatlantic competiton for the first time. In Ireland the general slump in agricultural prices was compounded by a series of bad harvests, so that by the end of the decade there were more grounds for concern about the situation on the land than at any time since the famine. The land war that developed was essentially a struggle between a poverty-stricken tenantry and a mortgaged landlord class over a disappearing profit margin, the penalties being destitution or emigration on the one side, bankruptcy or a reduced standard of living on the other. The landlord class, even after the restructuring of the post-famine years, was still largely Anglo-Irish. Thus when Davitt founded the Land League in 1879, to resist evictions and reduce rents, and Parnell took up the question at parliamentary level, it was not difficult to associate the land and national questions in a way that Lalor had dreamed of thirty years before. It was an irony more apparent to historians than contemporaries that the meeting at Irishtown, Co. Mayo, on 20 April 1879, which inspired the birth of the Land League, was directed against the rent levels, not of an Anglo-Irish aristocrat, but of a Catholic priest.

The Dublin press did not report the demonstration, nor even allude to it in any way. It was not held under official home-rule auspices, while the fact that one of its objects was to denounce rack-renting on an estate owned by a Catholic clergyman would necessarily, at that early stage of a popular movement, frighten the timid editors of Dublin from offering it any recognition. But the local prestige won by the meeting was enormous. The speeches were fully given in the *Connaught Telegraph*. The meeting had within a few days knocked five shillings in the pound off the rentals of the estate which was singled out for attack. This news flew round the county, and requests for meetings reached the organizers from various districts. It was generally known that the active spirits in the organizing of the meeting were members of the Fenian body, and on this account, but chiefly owing to the 'attack' made upon Canon Burke, many of the altars in Mayo rang with warnings and denunciations against gatherings called by 'irresponsible people' and which showed 'disrespect' towards the priests.

Michael Davitt, *The Fall of Feudalism in Ireland* (London, 1904), p. 151

24   Charles Stewart Parnell: The leper of old

For Parnell, agrarian radicalism appeared at the ideal moment. It provided a burning material issue to stimulate grass-roots organization, and cut the ground from beneath the feet of his moderate opponents in the home rule party. At the same time it provided a rationale and method of agitation in the countryside which captured the imagination of the revolutionary elements at home and abroad. When the National Land League came into being on 21 October 1879, Parnell was its president. His speeches during the following five years transferred the determination and intransigence which had charac-terized the campaign of disruption in the House of Commons onto the larger canvas of rural Ireland. In a speech at Ennis, Co. Clare in 1880, typical of a number he delivered in Ireland during this phase of his career, he gave support to the techniques of boycotting which had been developed against obnoxious landlords and 'blackleg' tenants.

. . .Depend upon it that the measure of the Land Bill of next session will be the measure of your activity and energy this winter. It will be the measure of your determination not to pay unjust rents; it will be the measure of your determination to keep a firm grip of your home-steads; it will be the measure of your determination not to bid for farms from which others have been evicted, and to use the strong force of public opinion to deter any unjust men amongst yourselves and there are many such, from bidding for such farms. If you refuse to pay unjust rents; if you refuse to take farms from which others have been evicted, the land question must be settled, and settled in a way that will be satisfying to you. It depends therefore, upon yourselves, and not upon any Commission or any Government. When you have made this question ripe for settlement, then and not till then will it be settled. . . . Now, what are you to do to a tenant who bids for a farm from which another tenant has been evicted? I think I heard somebody say shoot him. I wish to point out to you a very much better way, a more Christian and charitable way, which will give the lost sinner an opportunity of repenting. When a man takes a farm from which another has been evicted, you must shun him on the roadside when you meet him, you must shun him in the streets of the town, you must shun him in the shop, you must shun him on the fair-green and in the market place, and even in the place of worship, by leaving him alone, by putting him into a moral Coventry, by isolating him from the rest of his country, as if he were the leper of old, you must show him your detestation of the crime he has committed. . . .

> Transcription from: *The Times,* 20 September 1880

25   The rule of the Land League

The Land League alarmed government and landlords because it possessed the strength, unity and techniques of a militant trade union, supported by a nightly campaign of terror which was no doubt carried out from within its membership, but was not under its official aegis. Its organization could be suppressed, but the spirit of united resistance which it engendered could only be deflated by substantive concessions. During 1880 it became clear that W.E. Gladstone's newly-elected Liberal government would tackle the Irish land question on the basis of what was called dual ownership, or the 'three Fs' — fair rent for the tenant as set by a land court, free sale by the departing tenant of improvements he had made to his property, and fixity of tenure. This was likely to satisfy the more moderate elements and so split the united front, without either restructuring Irish land tenure in the way that agrarian radicals wanted, or carrying the national question any further forward. Davitt's report to Devoy, though clearly angled so as to retain the support of a secret revolutionary for an open, semi-constitutional movement, conveys a fair impression of the Land League at its height. Note that 'Nationalist' here is used not in the usual sense but as a code name for the IRB.

Michael Davitt to John Devoy   16 December 1880

. . .It would take me a week to give you anything like an account of immense growth and power of the L.L. It now virtually rules the country. . . . The income of the League is now about £100 a day. *Nearly all of which comes in from Irish branches.* Our expenditure is enormous as we are sparing no money in the work of organization, boycotting, relief to evicted people, legal fights with landlords, etc. Land League Courts are being established everywhere in which the affairs of the district are adjudicated! The London Press declares that all the League has got to do now, in order to have the complete government of the country in its hands, is to issue a League currency. . . . You would be astonished to find the class of men who are now joining us inside a movement with which *I* am connected. There is a danger, however, of this class and the Priests coalescing by and by, and ousting the advanced men or gaining control of the whole thing and turning it

against us. I am taking every precaution, however, against this Whig
dodge. . . .

. . .The landlords are scaring old Forster [Chief Secretary for
Ireland] with stories of an intended Rising, importation of arms, etc.,
in order to have the League squelched. I am necessitated, therefore, to
take a conservative stand in order to stave off coercion, for if the H.C.
[Habeas Corpus] is suspended the whole movement would be crushed
in a month and universal confusion would reign. These damned petty
little outrages are magnified by the Tory organs, copied into the
English Press and play the devil with us on outside public opinion. The
Government Land Bill is certain to be on the line of the three Fs. This,
of course, will not be enough, but it will satisfy a great number inside
the League, and be accepted by the Bishops and the Priests almost to a
man. I anticipate a serious split in the League when the Government
measure comes out. . . . If we could carry on this Movement for
another year without being interfered with we could do almost
anything we pleased in the country. The courage of the people is
magnificent. *All classes are purchasing Arms openly.* . . . The
Government does not know what to do in the presence of such a state of
affairs as we have created, and all our former enemies — Nationalist
[IRB] *Leaders* excepted — are silenced and subdued before the
enormous power at our back. . . .

This is something like an outline of the situation at the present
moment. All we want is to be left alone for a few months longer by the
Government *and the Nationalists* [IRB], and we will have Ireland in
such a state of organization as she never was in before. . . .

Reprinted in: W. O'Brien and D. Ryan
(eds.), *Devoy's Post Bag* (1948), ii, 22-4

26 'No Rent': The passive resistance of an entire population

The Land Act of 1881, as expected, embodied the principle of dual ownership.
It was accompanied by a Coerion Act to suppress further agitation. Parnell
and the League were in a quandary, for there was no doubt that the Land Act,
whatever its deficiencies as a radical measure, was likely to bring ·about
substantial rent reductions for many thousands of League supporters. But
accepting the act implied a collapse of the Parnellite alliance. The policy was
thus devised of 'testing the act', of holding back the mass of tenants while the
Land League put forward a small number of selected cases in order to discern
the land court's likely attitude. It was a procrastinating policy, likely to collapse
with the passage of time if it did not give way earlier in the face of militant

ex-Fenians and agrarian radicals on the one side, and tenants anxious to submit their own cases to the court, regardless of politics, on the other. Parnell's tone became more militant during the course of the year, and he was almost certainly relieved by the cabinet's decision to imprison him under the Coercion Act in October 1881. But the 'No Rent Manifesto', which his followers immediately brought forward, was endorsed by him without conviction, and proved more important as a rallying call to a disintegrating nationalist coalition than as a mechanism for disrupting the Land Act.

Fellow-countrymen! — The hour to try your souls and to redeem your pledges has arrived. The executive of the National Land League, forced to abandon the policy of testing the land act, feels bound to advise the tenant-farmers of Ireland from this day forth to pay no rents under any circumstances to their landlords until the government relinquishes the existing system of terrorism and restores the constitutional rights of the people. Do not be daunted by the removal of your leaders. Your fathers abolished tithes by the same method without any leaders at all, and with scarcely a shadow of the magnificent organization that covers every portion of Ireland today. Do not suffer yourselves to be intimidated by threats of military violence. It is as lawful to refuse to pay rents as it is to receive them. Against the passive resistance of an entire population military power has no weapons. Do not be wheedled into compromise of any sort by the dread of eviction. If you only act together in the spirit to which, within the last two years, you have countless times solemnly pledged your vows, they can no more evict a whole nation than they can imprison them. The funds of the National Land League will be poured out unstintedly for the support of all who may endure eviction in the course of the struggle.

Our exiled brothers in America may be relied upon to contribute, if necessary, as many millions of money as they have contributed thousands to starve out landlordism and bring English tyranny to its knees. You have only to show that you are not unworthy of their boundless sacrifices in your cause. No power on earth except faint-heartedness on your own part can defeat you. Landlordism is already staggering under the blows which you have dealt it amid the applause of the world. One more crowning struggle for your land, your homes, your lives — a struggle in which you have all the memories of your race, all the hopes of your children, all the sacrifices of your imprisoned brothers, all your cravings for rent-enfranchised land, for happy homes and national freedom to inspire you — one more heroic effort to destroy landlordism at the very source and fount of its existence, and the system which was and is the curse of your race and of your existence

will have disappeared forever. The world is watching to see whether all
your splendid hopes and noble courage will crumble away at the first
threat of a cowardly tyranny. You have to choose between throwing
yourselves upon the mercy of England and taking your stand by the
organization which has once before proved too strong for English
despotism; you have to choose between all powerful unity and
impotent dis-organization; between the land for the landlords and the
land for the people. We cannot doubt your choice. Every tenant-
farmer of Ireland is today the standard-bearer of the flag unfurled at
Irishtown, and can bear it to a glorious victory. Stand together in the
face of the brutal and cowardly enemies of your race. Pay no rents
under any pretext. Stand passively, firmly, fearlessly by while the
armies of England may be engaged in their hopeless struggle against a
spirit which their weapons cannot touch. Act for yourselves if you are
deprived of the counsels of those who have shown you how to act. No
power of legalized violence can extort one penny from your purses
against your will. If you are evicted, you shall not suffer; the landlord
who evicts will be a ruined pauper, and the government which
supports him with its bayonets will learn in a single winter how powerless is armed force against the will of a united, determined, and self-
reliant nation.

> Signed CHARLES S. PARNELL, President, Kilmainham Jail;
> MICHAEL DAVITT, Hon. Sec., Portland Prison; THOMAS BRENNAN,
> Hon. Sec., Kilmainham Jail; JOHN DILLON, Head Organizer,
> Kilmainham Jail; THOMAS SEXTON, Head Organizer, Kilmainham
> Jail; PATRICK EGAN, Treasurer, Paris.

> Reprinted in: Michael Davitt, *The Fall of
> Feudalism in Ireland* (London, 1904) pp.
> 335-7

27 Parnell and the march of a nation

When Parnell emerged from prison in the spring of 1882 it was under the terms
of a 'Kilmainham Treaty' with the government whereby he undertook to cease
resistance to the Land Act (which the government in turn agreed to amend in
the interests of tenants with long arrears of rent and those with leases) and to
cooperate with the Liberals in a broad programme of reform in Ireland.
Henceforward his policy was increasingly one of open constitutionalism. If the
three-sided alliance of revolutionaries, parliamentarians and agrarians had
effectively broken up, it was nonetheless clear that a good proportion of the

grass-roots attracted initially by the alliance remained adhering to the parliamentarian centre after the final breach. Parnell had got from militant agrarianism the stature to take advantage of the next great development, the parliamentary Reform Act of 1884. This enfranchised the bulk of the Irish peasantry who, in 1886, swept Parnell at the head of a united, militant home rule party to the centre of the parliamentary stage with 85 out of 103 Irish MPs and one from Liverpool. The election victory of the '86 of '86' had destroyed the Irish Liberal party, the moderate home rulers, and the entire power of Irish Unionism outside Ulster. At Westminster they now constitued a large and cohesive group, with reasonable hopes of winning the balance of power often enough to command the attention of the English parties. An Irish republic might not emerge from an English parliament, but as Parnell explained at Cork on 21 January 1885, the possibility of a half-way house emerging by constitutional means was no longer the remote dream it had been in O'Connell's time.

I go back from the consideration of these questions to the consideration of the great question of National self-government for Ireland. I do not know how this great question will be eventually settled. I do not know whether England will be wise in time and concede to constitutional arguments and methods the restitution of that which was stolen from us towards the close of the last century. It is given to none of us to forecast the future, and just as it is impossible for us to say in what way or by what means the National question may be settled, in what way full justice may be done in Ireland, so it is impossible for us to say to what extent that justice should be done. We cannot ask for less than restitution of Grattan's Parliament, with its important privileges and wide and far-reaching constitution. We cannot under the British Constitution ask for more than the restitution of Grattan's Parliament, but no man has the right to fix the boundary to the march of a nation. No man has a right to say to his country 'Thus far shalt thou go and no further', and we have never attempted to fix the *ne plus ultra* to the progress of Ireland's nationhood, and we never shall.

Transcription from: *The Times*, 22 January 1885.

28 Gladstone: An Irish motor muscle and imperial patriotism

By the end of 1885 Gladstone had announced his conversion to the home rule cause. The return of Parnell to Westminster with the balance of power in his hands confirmed the Liberal leader's decision to press forward with the new policy. A bill was introduced by Gladstone on 8 April 1886 in a speech which is summarized below. But he had already lost the support of the Whig group within his party, and when the full scope of the bill became clear he also lost the backing of Joseph Chamberlain's radical group. The Home Rule Bill was defeated on its second reading in the House of Commons by 341 votes to 311, and Gladstone's government resigned. The weakened Liberal party remained in opposition for seventeen of the following twenty years. Gladstone introduced a second Home Rule Bill in 1893, which passed the Commons but was roundly defeated in the Lords by 419 votes to 41. Home rule was no nearer, but the Liberal party's commitment to it after 1886 forged a 'union of hearts' with Parnell and his successors which survived until the first world war. The prolonged association between the two parties produced a modified style of nationalism and a new view of Irish nationality, foreshadowed by Gladstone himself in his speech introducing the 1886 bill.

We are not called upon to constitute another Co-ordinate Legislature. While I think it is right to modify the Union in some particulars, we are not about to prepare its repeal. . . . A supreme statutory authority of the Imperial Parliament over Great Britain, Scotland, and Ireland, as one United Kingdom, was established by the Act of Union. That supreme statutory authority it is not asked, as far as I am aware, and certainly it is not intended, in the slightest degree to impair.

. . . There are those who say, 'Let us abolish the Castle'; and I think that gentlemen of very high authority, who are strongly opposed to giving Ireland a domestic Legislature, have said nevertheless that they think that there might be a general reconstruction of the administrative Government in Ireland. Well, sir, I have considered that question much, and what I want to know is this—how, without a change in the Legislature, without giving to Ireland a domestic Legislature, there is to be, or there ever can possibly be, a reconstruction of the Administration. . . . The fault of the administrative system of Ireland, if it has a fault, is simply this—that its spring and source of action, or, if I can use an anatomical illustration without a blunder, what is called the motor muscle is English and not Irish. Without providing a domestic Legislature for Ireland, without having an Irish Parliament, I want to know how you will bring about this wonderful, superhuman, and I believe, in this condition impossible result that your administrative system shall be Irish and not English. . . . Well, sir, what we seek is the settlement of that question; and we think that we find that settlement in the establishment by the authority of Parliament, of a legislative body sitting in Dublin for the conduct of both legislation and administration under the conditions which may be prescribed by the Act defining Irish, as distinct from Imperial affairs. There is the head and front of our offending. . . . I cannot conceal the conviction that the voice of Ireland, as a whole, is at this moment clearly and constitutionally spoken. I cannot say it is otherwise when five-sixths of its lawfully chosen representatives are of one mind in this matter. There is a counter voice; and I wish to know what is the claim of those by whom that counter voice is spoken, and how much is the scope and allowance we can give them. Certainly, sir I cannot allow it to be said that a Protestant minority in Ulster, or elsewhere is to rule the question at large for Ireland. I am aware of no constitutional doctrine tolerable on which such a conclusion could be adopted or justified. But I think that the Protestant minority should have its wishes considered to the utmost practicable extent in any form which they may assume. . . .

We stand face to face with what is termed Irish nationality. Irish nationality vents itself in the demand for local autonomy or separate and complete self-government in Irish, not in Imperial affairs. Is that an evil in itself? Is it a thing that we should view with horror or apprehension? Is it a thing which we ought to reject or accept only with a wry face, or ought we to wait until some painful and sad necessity is incumbent upon the country, like the necessity of 1780 or of 1793? Sir, I hold that it is not,. . . . I do not believe that local patriotism is an evil. I believe it is stronger in Ireland even than in Scotland. Englishmen are eminently English, Scotchmen are profoundly Scotch, and if I read Irish history aright, misfortune and calamity have wedded her sons to her soil. The Irishman is profoundly Irish, but it does not follow that because his local patriotism is keen he is incapable of Imperial patriotism. There are two modes of presenting the subject. The one is to present what we now recommend as Good, and the other to recommend it as a choice of Evils. Well, sir, I have argued the matter as if it were a choice of evils; I have recognized as facts entitled to attention the jealousies which I do not share or feel. . . . But in my heart I cherish the hope that this is not merely the choice of the lesser evil, but may prove to be rather a good in itself. . . .

> HC Deb. 3rd series, vol. 304, cols. 1049-83 (8 April 1886).

29 Saxon wolves, Irish bishops, and the fall of Parnell

After 1886 Parnell's leadership of the Irish party became more spasmodic. He gave no encouragement at all to the new agrarian 'Plan of Campaign' which his lieutenants developed to force down rents, preferring to press the home rule case entirely through parliamentary links with the Liberal opposition. A sustained attempt by *The Times* newspaper, with discreet help from the Conservative government, to discredit him through evidence of past association with terrorist movements collapsed in 1889 when the crucial documents in the case were admitted to be forgeries. But this vindication was offset within the space of a few months when the husband of Katharine O'Shea (with whom Parnell had been living for several years) filed for divorce, naming Parnell. Parnell had no defence, and did not offer one. He and Mrs O'Shea were later married. But the lodging of O'Shea's suit, after years of apparent complaisance, was inspired by a complex mixture of political and pecuniary motives (Mrs O'Shea had at last inherited a long-awaited and substantial fortune in 1889).

The immediate political outcome was a denunciation by Gladstone, in December 1890, of the continued leadership of the Irish party by a convicted adulterer, and Parnell's subsequent refusal to bow to the majority view of his colleagues and step down. Debate revolved initially around the question of whether an English political leader should be permitted to impinge upon the 'independent opposition' of the Irish party or whether, on the other hand, the cause of home rule should be jeopardized for the sake of one man's career. But when the struggle was carried from Westminster to a bitter series of by-elections in Ireland, the main appeal of the anti-Parnellites was to the Catholic clergy, who endorsed them wholeheartedly. Parnell, meanwhile, appeared to reverse his political direction entirely, turning back once more to the revolutionary tradition for support. How he would resolved his position was never put to the test, for he died, aged only forty-five, in October 1891.

These two extracts are from manifestos issued during the North Kilkenny by-election of December 1890 although the first, issued by independent supporters of Parnell, was repudiated by him.

(a) Men of the Hillsides, Gather in your thousands to support the leader of your race, Charles Stewart Parnell MP. What Englishman shall dare to tell you who shall be your chief or what shall be the method of your warfare? We have fought for liberty in defiance of England. We have advanced along the path of freedom in spite of England's fraud and force. In the past we have succeeded because we have trusted ourselves alone. In the future we shall succeed by fighting along the same lines, by defying the English dictation, by acting with the spirit and the resolution of the self-respecting nation. Shall the radicals of England choose your leader? Men of the hillsides, will you, the countrymen of Grattan and the volunteers of O'Connell, Davis and Wolfe Tone, of gallant Father Murphy, priest and patriot, who fought and bled for the independence of our country; will you, men of the hillsides, inspired by the glorious memories of the past, will you abandon your chief? Will you give him up to the Saxon wolves who howl for his destruction or will you rally round him as your fathers rallied round the men of '98, and shout with a thousand united voices, 'No Surrender'. Hurrah for Charles Stewart Parnell, the leader of an independent Irish party, and down with the faction which would make Irish people the servants of a foreign power. . . .

Reprinted in: *The Times,* 18 December 1890

(b) . . .Mr Parnell speaks as if he were an injured man, but the facts cannot be forgotten. Mr Parnell is responsible, and he alone, for the present deplorable situation. He pledged himself, again and again, to repel the charge against him. His pledges were accepted in good faith. When the time for speaking came, he remained silent. The pledges were broken. The charge was not repelled. Upon these facts a strong opinion was formed by multitudes of Englishmen, true friends of the liberty of Ireland. Mr Parnell does not hesitate to denounce them as 'English wolves'. But the fact remains that the 'English wolves' and the Irish bishops express the same opinion about him, and he cannot mend the matter by calling nicknames. . . .

Reprinted in: *The Times* 11 December 1890

30 Agrarianism again: The United Irish League

The Parnellite split continued throughout the 1890s. In face of continued Unionist government in Britain and a clear loss of Liberal enthusiasm for the home rule issue after Gladstone's retirement in 1894, constitutional nationalism seemed to be a declining force. But although the bad rural conditions of the 1880s had been eased considerably by controlled rents and continued emigration, there remained large areas of the country where the problem was more complicated. In the far west the barren coastline was quite unable to support its relatively dense population in acceptable conditions, and a government board had been set up in 1891 to stimulate farming, fishing, and other occupations in these 'congested districts'. In the eastern area of Connaught and parts of Munster the problem differed again in that many landlords, faced with the application of the new land laws to permanent tenancies, let most of their best land on 'eleven months' leases to large graziers, whose 'ranches' were typically surrounded by small and relatively very poor tenanted holdings. It was against this background that a disillusioned Anti-Parnellite MP, William

O'Brien (1852-1928) founded the United Irish League in 1898. In later years the League was to become a rather sleepy constituency organization for the parliamentary party, but from 1898 to 1902, and more sporadically from 1907 to 1909, it was a formidable force on the land. It also provided a platform for the reunification in 1900 of the Irish parliamentary party, under the chairmanship of John Redmond (1856-1918). George Wyndham (1863-1913), who served as Chief Secretary for Ireland in the Unionist cabinet of 1900 to 1905, described the situation to a colleague soon after taking office.

George Wyndham to A.J. Balfour   26 November 1900

The *United Irish League* started two and more years ago by O'Brien in Mayo, has spread over the country. Redmond discouraged it; Healy stabbed it, the Priests fought it at the election. It won 'hands down'. Redmond acquiesces. The Bishop of Raphoe, Father O'Hara, and a few more of the abler Priests, are sailing with it in the hope of getting a hand on the tiller. The so-called 'National Convention' to meet whilst our December Parliament is sitting will be composed of delegates from the League and will — see Dillon's speech at Tullamore of yesterday — construct a Parliamentary Party to the exclusion of Healy and his remnant. . . .

Agrarian Agitation. The League began by an attack upon 'graziers'. Thanks to T.W. Russell [Ulster Liberal unionist MP, later Liberal home ruler] they are now doubling this policy with 'Compulsory Land Purchase'. All the 103 Irish members with the exception of Col. Saunderson 'sans phrase' and McCartney [both Irish Unionists], with a minimum of hedging, have committed themselves to that policy. The only material difference between the Unionists and Nationalists is that the former wish to give a fair, the latter an unfair, price to the Landlord.

All, friends and foes, are strangely cut off from British sentiment. They believe that in spite of War taxation and Imperial Politics, Ireland is going to bathe once more in the limelight. The Nationalist party, armed with a mandate from the Convention and assisted by Russell, mean, if they can, to imitate Parnell's Parliamentary tactics. . . .

Reprinted in: J.W. Mackail and Guy Wyndham, *The Life and Letters of George Wyndham* (1925), ii, 409-11

31   Attacking home rule with kindness

After 1886 it was clear that the Unionist party in Great Britain had lost all flexibility on the question of Irish self-government. Confronted nonetheless with the responsibility of governing Ireland for most of the following twenty years, it evolved a policy known as 'killing home rule with kindness', of part-conciliating, part undercutting the Irish party by pressing forward with reform measures in a number of areas — land tenure, agricultural self-help, rural labourers' housing, university education and local government — while holding coercive measures in reserve for meeting agitation. Democratic local councils were created in 1898, and plans for subsidized public housing for labourers were implemented by the incoming Liberal government in 1906. The fortunes of some other aspects of the policy are considered below. George Wyndham, the paternalistic idealist entrusted by the Unionists with developing what proved to be the last phase of that policy, came to grief in 1904-5 when his attempts to ease Protestants, landlords and 'moderates' back into Irish politics by means of a negotiated scheme for very limited devolution were stifled by opposition from the Unionist side. Earlier the 'Wyndham Land Act' of 1903, making the credit facilities of the state, plus an attractive bonus, available to facilitate the sale of entire estates to the tenants on the basis of voluntary sale, had ensured his reputation as the instigator of nationwide peasant proprietorship in Ireland. Even this measure came under attack from the mainstream of the Irish party however, on the overt grounds that it would saddle tenants with repayment obligations which they would regret, would perpetuate the problem of the grass ranches, and did nothing to strengthen the power of the Congested Districts Board or assist the evicted tenants, 'the wounded soldiers of the land war'. Another reason for giving the measure a guarded reception was that it was a product of the party of 'conference and conciliation', and as such calculated to undercut the position of the nationalist movement.

George Wyndham to Moreton Frewen   14 November 1903

. . .I am disappointed and chagrined by recent events. Nor can I take the sanguine view that the Land Act will fulfil the objects of the Land Conference if it is to be assailed daily by the *Freeman*, Davitt and Dillon. My power of usefulness to Ireland is already diminished and may be destroyed.

I have convinced my colleagues, a majority of our supporters in the House, and a still larger majority in the large towns of England, that it was right in itself to foster Union among Irishmen, and to obliterate the vestiges of ancient feuds without troubling ourselves about the ultimate effect of social reconciliation on Ireland's attitude towards the 'Home Rule' versus 'Union' controversy.

And if this is set back, you cannot deal with the 'University Question' or the 'Labourers' question if so large and beneficient a measure as the Land Act is to be used only to divide classes more sharply. . . .

Unless those who care for Ireland can show that the Conference and the Land Act have produced social reconciliation, I cannot get a hearing for using *Imperial* credit and *Irish* savings in accordance with the views of a United Ireland. . . .

If, however, I had a united Irish Party, with leaders not subject to repudiation, prepared to cooperate, to a certain extent with Irish landlords, scholars and business men, I could get Irish savings for Irish purposes and equivalent grants whenever England helps herself too freely out of the common Exchequer.

My point is that I get beaten in detail if I am rebuffed by jeering allusions to Irish reconciliation. I am nearly tired out. . . .

> Reprinted in: J.W. Mackail and Guy Wyndham, *The Life and Letters of George Wyndham* (1925) pp. 472-3

32   Butter on nationalist principles

It was widely held by 'non-political' observers and by many Unionists at the end of the nineteenth century that the root of the continuing 'Irish problem' lay in inefficient agriculture. One such agricultural reformer was Sir Horace Plunkett (1854-1932), younger son of an Anglo-Irish nobleman, who emerged in Irish public life during the 1890s with a movement for agricultural cooperation. Plunkett at first sought the backing of Nationalist politicians for his 'non-political movement', but rather queered his pitch in that quarter when he fought and won the South County Dublin constituency as an independent Unionist (1892-1900). But the Unionist government took up his ideas, and in 1900 he became Vice-President and working head of the new Department of Agriculture and Technical Instruction. Although immediately losing his parliamentary seat he continued to hold what Nationalists argued was a political appointment until 1907, when the Liberal government responded to Irish party pressure to dismiss him. He remained a middle-of-the-road conciliationist, no matter where the road wandered, and in 1917 reappeared at the centre of the stage as an advocate of dominion home rule. In this extract he quotes a story originally told by his deputy in the Irish Agricultural Organization Society.

It was hard and thankless work. There was the apathy of the people and the active opposition of the Press and the politicians. It would be hard to say now whether the abuse of the Conservative *Cork Constitution* or that of the Nationalist *Eagle,* of Skibbereen, was the louder. . . . Once when I thought I had planted a Creamery within the precincts of the town of Rathkeale [Co. Limerick], my cooperative apple-cart was upset by a local solicitor who, having elicited the fact that our movement recognized neither political nor religious differences—that the Unionist-Protestant cow was as dear to us as her Nationalist-Catholic sister—gravely informed me that our programme would not suit Rathkeale. 'Rathkeale', said he, pompously, 'is a Nationalist town—Nationalist to the backbone—and every pound of butter made in this Creamery must be made on Nationalist principles, or it shan't be made at all'. This sentiment was applauded loudly, and the proceedings terminated.

> Horace Plunkett, *Ireland in the New Century*
> (John Murray, London, 1904) pp. 190-1

33   Catholic higher education: a Catholic view

Trinity College, the sole constituent college of the ancient University of Dublin, had long been resented by majority nationalist opinion as an Anglo-Irish episcopalian institution which monopolized higher education in Ireland. In 1879 an examining body, 'The Royal University' was created, awarding degrees and endowing fellowships at five small colleges (including a Jesuit foundation in Dublin). But most of the Royal's graduates were in fact private students, unattached to any of the five colleges, and by the end of the century such a concept of university education was very much at variance with prevailing trends in Britain and elsewhere. Successive British governments as well as Nationalist politicians were anxious to come to terms with the problem, but repeatedly found themselves at an *impasse*—the Catholic church in Ireland, without whose support any move would have been pointless, wanted an institution where a prevailing Catholic atmosphere could be ensured and maintained, whereas the weight of backbench parliamentary opinion in Britain was against any such endowment. Efforts by successive Unionist governments to tackle the problem, in 1898 and 1904, petered out. The following extract is a fairly extreme statement of the Catholic position made in the 1870s.

. . .Now, it is a plain fact that by giving Catholic youth a higher education you open a new and large avenue, by which the godless spirit of the times may gain admittance. And unless they be furnished with fully sufficient moral and intellectual protection, you expose them to imminent danger, not merely of holding the Faith with less simplicity and heartiness (though this would be bad enough), but of wilfully admitting a fully deliberate doubt as to its truth—or, in other words, of actual apostasy. It is this which makes the whole subject so anxious, and which makes one a little impatient with commonplaces about marching with the times, and aiming at progress, and growing in largeness of thought. We are very far from meaning that ignorance is the Catholic youth's best preservative against intellectual danger, but it is a very powerful one, nevertheless, and those who deny this are but inventing a theory in the very teeth of manifest facts. A Catholic destitute of intellectual tastes, whether in a higher or a lower rank, may, probably enough, be tempted to idleness, frivolity, gambling, sensuality; but in none but the very rarest cases will he be tempted to that which (in the Catholic view) is an immeasurably greater calamity than any of these, or all put together, viz. deliberate doubt on the truth of his religion. It is simply undeniable, we say, that the absence of higher education is a powerful preservative against apostasy, and those who watch over souls will reasonably refuse to bear part in withdrawing that preservative, until they are satisfied that some other very sufficient substitute is provided. It is the work of higher education, as such, to cultivate and enlarge the mind; but it is the work of Catholic higher education as such, so to cultivate and enlarge the mind as to guard against the danger that such cultivation do immeasurably more harm than good. Now, the Church's interest is not in higher education, as such, but in Catholic higher education. . . .

Dublin Review, vol. xxii new series (January-April 1874), p. 192.

34 Catholic higher education: a Protestant view

On the issue of higher education for Catholics, nonconformist church pressure tended to influence the Liberal party in the same inflexible direction as the Ulster contingent led the British Unionists. It was therefore with some foreboding that the new Liberal government in 1906 set out to find a mutually acceptable solution. The Irish party, which began by suspecting incorrectly that the government intended only a foredoomed attempt to 'make Trinity College acceptable to Catholics', was prepared to consider a number of other options, notably the creation of a separate but equal college in the University of Dublin, or alternatively an entirely new federal university, embracing existing colleges at Cork and Galway, and centred on a major new college in Dublin. Irish government and much of educated Catholic lay opinion tended to favour the former solution, involving more prestige and the hope of less segregation, but the Irish party bowed to majority clerical opinion and in 1908 the National University of Ireland and its constituent University College, Dublin, came into

being. The more progressive elements in Trinity College had hoped for an
expansion of their own institution, but Nationalist politicians regarded these
aspirations as those of 'monopolists in a corner', and were probably more at
ease in countering the frankly reactionary position expounded by Vice-Provost
Barlow of Trinity before the Royal Commission's enquiry in 1906.

. . .I am very far from agreeing with some who hold that inasmuch as
the ratio in Ireland of Catholics to Protestants is at least three to one,
we should have three times as many Catholics as Protestants at Trinity
College. These persons quite ignore the fact that the great Catholic
majority consists of poor and ignorant peasants, and I think that to
facilitate the education of a poor and perhaps stupid youth by paying
his college fees. . . is but a cruel kindness. I would gladly see a clever
boy helped through his course. . . but a stupid or even mediocre
youth, turned by charitable assistance into a profession would very
likely starve, and if he did not emigrate might become a discontented
and possibly dangerous member of society, instead of remaining a
useful agriculturalist as, but for misplaced charity, he might have
been. This plan of turning universities into gigantic charity schools, as
has been done by Mr Carnegie, may be successful in Scotland, but
would certainly not suit the atmosphere of Ireland. . . .

> PP 1907 XLI *(Royal Commission on Trinity
> College, Dublin and the University of Dublin)*
> Final Report, Appendix, p. 38.

35   James Bryce: When they have the land. . . .

Gladstone had made the cause of Irish home rule something of a crusade for a
generation of rank-and-file Liberals. But many others, especially the younger
ones who had grown up in a party twice wrecked on the issue, were less enthusiastic. Liberal sentiment in the post-Gladstone era was less anti-home rule as
such than based on a feeling that the Irish question ought no longer to be the
burning question of the hour, that it stood between the new Liberalism and a
major programme of social reform in Britain, and that any attempt to reintro-
duce it implied a head-on collision with the Unionist-dominated House of
Lords. Apart from a radical minority who saw it as an issue inextricably linked
with the overblown power of the upper house, many Liberals were coming
implicitly to share the Unionist analysis — that political nationalism might
wither away when exposed to a modicum of prosperity and widespread reform
on all material fronts. This was certainly the view of James Bryce (1838-1921),
who became Liberal Chief Secretary in December 1905. His correspondent
Dicey was a fellow constitutionalist and a Unionist propagandist, so that Bryce
may have taken a certain academic delight in emphasizing and exaggerating

any covert home rule tendency in the recent Unionist administrations.

James Bryce M.P. to A.V. Dicey   3 February 1905

You are right in thinking that a policy tending towards wider self-government must be pursued by a Liberal government. But then it will be pursued, to judge from the past, by a Tory government also. The last ten years have under the Tories done more than a Liberal government with a bare majority could have done in that direction. No Liberal government could, perhaps would, have given the land to the tenants; probably could not have given the local government scheme. Both measures bring home rule nearer in two ways—they give more power to the masses and they lessen the dangers feared in 1886 and 1893. The forces of nature seem to me to be working for Home Rule; and it will come about under one English party just as much as another *if,* an important *if,* the Irish continue to press as strongly for it. That is perhaps not so certain. When they have the land, much of the steam will be out of the boiler.

[Joseph] Chamberlain would of course give them anything they asked in return for support for him. He has tacitly made offers, but they don't trust him. . . a succession of Chamberlains would be far more dangerous to England than the Irish are.

That Home Rule will come in our time seems unlikely. But under our democratic government a resolute section is pretty sure to get sooner or later whatever does not conflict with the direct interests or direct passions of the English masses. So I expect it to come, if the Irish go on pressing as they have done since O'Connell.

NLI, Bryce Papers, Ms. 11011

IV The search for more differences: Irish-Ireland and a Socialist Republic

36 Douglas Hyde: The hideousness of an artistic race

The Irish parliamentary party never felt the need to look any further than the land question and the loyalty of the Catholic clergy to provide steam for its boiler and illustration that Irish administration would make Ireland a prosperous and loyal state within the Empire where English administration has so patently failed. The party leadership remained very much in the hands of men who had learnt their nationalism as Parnell's lieutenants in the Land League, and who showed little interest in alternative bases for Irish national consciousness. In particular the party failed to associate itself in the public mind with either the Gaelic Athletic Association, founded in 1884 to foster an interest in Gaelic football and other 'national' games (and which excluded from participation all members of the armed forces and RIC), or the Gaelic League, founded by Eoin MacNeill, Dr Douglas Hyde, and others in 1893 to stimulate a revival of the Irish language. Hyde (1860-1949) was a Protestant, the son of a Church of Ireland rector in Connaught, who later became President of Ireland, 1938-45. He always maintained that his movement was non-political, and staved off a radical nationalist revision of its constitution until 1915. But although his personal commitment to Irish culture was strongly positive, there was a negative element in the movement, especially at the popular level, inasmuch as it defined Irish nationality and Irish problems in contradistinction to the values and influence attributed to England. This feature is clearly apparent in Hyde's own seminal lecture, 'The necessity for de-anglicizing Ireland'.

If we take a bird's-eye view of our island to-day, and compare it with what it used to be, we must be struck by the extraordinary fact that the nation which was once, as every one admits, one of the most classically learned and cultured nations in Europe, is now one of the least so; how one of the most reading and literary peoples has become one of the least studious and most un-literary, and how the present art products of one of the quickest, most sensitive, and most artistic races on earth are now only distinguished for their hideousness.

I shall endeavour to show that this failure of the Irish people in recent times has been largely brought about by the race diverging during this century from the right path, and ceasing to be Irish without becoming English. . . .

It is a fact, and we must face it as a fact, that although they adopt English habits and copy England in every way, the great bulk of Irishmen and Irishwomen over the whole world are known to be filled with a dull, ever-abiding animosity against her, and — right or wrong — to grieve when she prospers, and joy when she is hurt. . . I believe it is our Gaelic past which, though the Irish race does not recognize it just at present, is really at the bottom of the Irish heart, and prevents us becoming citizens of the empire, as, I think, can be easily proved. . . .

Let us suppose for a moment — which is impossible — that there were to arise a series of Cromwells in England for the space of one hundred years, able administrators of the empire, careful rulers of Ireland, developing to the utmost our national resources, whilst they unremittingly stamped out every spark of national feeling, making Ireland a land of wealth and factories, whilst they extinguished every thought and every idea that was Irish, and left us, at last, after a hundred years of good government, fat, wealthy, and populous, but with all our characteristics gone, with every external that at present differentiates us from the English lost or dropped.

How many Irishmen are there who would purchase material prosperity at such a price? It is exactly such a question as this and the answer to it that shows the difference between the English and Irish race. Nine Englishmen out of ten would jump to make the exchange, and I as firmly believe that nine Irishmen out of ten would indignantly refuse it.

And yet this awful idea of complete anglicization, which I have put here before you in all its crudity is, and has been, making silent inroads upon us for nearly a century. . . .

What we must endeavour to never forget is this, that the Ireland of today is the descendant of the Ireland of the seventh century; then the school of Europe and the torch of learning. It is true that Northmen made some minor settlements in it in the ninth and tenth centuries, it is true that the Normans made extensive settlements during the succeding centuries, but none of these broke the continuity of the social life of the island. Dane and Norman drawn to the kindly Irish breast issued forth in a generation or two fully Irishized, and more Hibernian than the Hibernians themselves and even after the Cromwellian plantation the children of numbers of the English

soldiers who settled in the south and midlands, were after forty years'
residence, and after marrying Irish wives, turned into good Irishmen,
and unable to speak a word of English, while several Gaelic poets of the
last century have, like Father English, the most unmistakably English
names. In two points only was the continuity of the Irishism of Ireland
damaged. First, in the north east of Ulster, where the Gaelic race was
expelled and the land planted with aliens, whom our dear mother
Erin, assimilative as she is, has hitherto found it difficult to absorb,
and in the ownership of the land, eight-ninths of which belongs to
people many of whom have always lived, or live, abroad, and not half
of whom Ireland can be said to have assimilated.

> D. Hyde, *The Revival of Irish Literature and
> Other Addresses* (T. Fisher Unwin, London,
> 1894), pp. 126-7.

37   D.P. Moran: We are all Palemen now

D.P. Moran (1871-1936) was probably the most gifted Irish journalist of his
generation. Always an independent figure, he nonetheless voiced more clearly
than anyone else the developing 'Irish-Ireland' ethos which the Irish party
failed to capture. His thinking, though clearly influenced by Hyde, was more
overtly nationalist, and sometimes crudely so, as in the first extract below, but
probably none the less influential for that. In the second extract he argues that
every nationalist movement in modern Irish history had failed in its task of
resisting English encroachment. The basis of nationality in a generalized
hostility to English influence is very clear.

(a)   . . .It takes an Englishman to get the most out of English
literature, as it takes a Frenchman to get the most out of French
literature. A literature steeped in the history, traditions, and
genius of one nation, is at the best only an imperfect tutor to the
people of another nation; in fact, the common, half-educated
people of another nation will have none of it. The Irish nation has,
this century, been brought up on English literature. Of course it
never really kindled their minds or imaginations; they were driven
to look at literature as a thing not understandable and above
them — a position, I need scarcely say, not making for the development of self-respect or intellectual self-dependence. In most cases
when they left school they ceased to read anything but the
newspapers. Of course there are many exceptions to this generali-
zation. If an Irishman received a higher English education and
lost touch with Irish aspirations, he practically became an

Englishman, and many people with less advantages, by force of exceptional ability, got their heads above the entanglements around them and breathed something like free air. But I am talking of the common run of men who make up a nation, and not of the few exceptions. Tell me of any ordinary man in Dublin, Cork or elsewhere, who professes an appreciation for the best products of English literature, and I will have no hesitation in informing you that he is an intellectual snob, mostly composed of affectation.

> D.P. Moran, 'The Battle of Two Civilizations', Originally published in *The New Ireland Review,* Reprinted in *The Philosophy of Irish Ireland* (James Duffy & Co. Ltd., Dublin 1905), p. 101

(b) No one wants to fall out with [Thomas] Davis's comprehensive idea of the Irish people as a composite race drawn from various sources, and professing any creed they like, nor would an attempt to rake up racial prejudices be tolerated by anyone. We are proud of Grattan, Flood, Tone, Emmet, and all the rest who dreamt and worked for an independent country, even though they had no conception of an Irish nation; but it is necessary that they should be put in their place, and that place is not on the top as the only beacon lights to succeeding generations. The foundation of Ireland is the Gael, and the Gael must be the element that absorbs. On no other basis can an Irish nation be reared that would not topple over by force of the very ridicule that it would beget. However, since the glories of 1782 the process has been reversed, and we are all Palemen now. . . .

The movement of 1782 placed the Pale at the head of Ireland for the first time in history, and ever since the Pale has retained that place. The '98 and '48 movements, the Fenians and the Parnellite agitation, were Pale movements in their essence, even when they were most fiercely rebellious. In many respects they were tinkering movements, for, while they were making a loud noise the great canker was left unheeded. The passions and excitements of those days distracted all men's attention from one long monotonous series of fateful sounds. No one heeded the dull incessant sap, sap, of English ideas, ideals and manners—mostly of the worst English kind too—that were all the time rotting the only possible foundation for the Ireland that the people were vaguely, incoherently seeking after. . . .

The great present result of our conquest by the Pale, and of the failure of subsequent partly national movements — whose success would probably have long since put Pale influence into its proper subordinate place — is that Irishmen are now in competition with Englishmen in every sphere of social and intellectual activity, in a competition where England has fixed the marks, the subjects, and has had the sole making of the rules of the game.

> D.P. Moran, 'The Pale and the Gael', *The New Ireland Review*, reprinted in *The Philosophy of Irish Ireland* (James Duffy & Co. Ltd., Dublin 1905) pp. 37-47.

38   *The Leader:* Nationalism in a Catholic atmosphere

Moran's most powerful weapon was *The Leader*, a weekly newspaper which he founded in 1900 and edited for a generation. In essence the paper took up the thinking of the Gaelic League and Irish-Ireland movement generally, simplified the issues and disseminated them far more widely. In later years, as a subsequent group of extracts shows, *The Leader* took an active part in the destruction of the Irish parliamentary party. But during this early period its role was rather in helping to create an atmosphere in which a different style of nationalism might thrive. In particular Moran's journalism played a key part in linking the 'Catholic' and 'Gaelic' concepts of Irish nationality, and in winning widespread support amongst the younger clergy for 'Irish-Ireland'.

(a) It has been hinted to us that it is our opinion that no one but a Catholic can be an Irishman. We never said so, nor do we think so. . . . We are prepared to be perfectly frank with our sympathizers who think we are 'too Catholic'. We have great admiration and respect for Thomas Davis, but his 'Tolerance' scheme did not work. . . . When we look out on Ireland we see that those who believe, or may be immediately induced to believe, in Ireland a nation are, as a matter of fact, Catholics. When we look back on history we find also, as a matter of fact, that those who stood during the last three hundred years for Ireland as an Irish entity were mainly Catholics, and that those who sought to corrupt them and trample on them were mainly non-Catholics. . . .

Such being the facts, the only thinkable solution of the Irish national problem is that one side gets on top and absorbs the other until we have one nation, or that each develops independently. As we are for Ireland, we are in the existing circumstances on the side of Catholic development; and we see plainly that any genuine non-Catholic Irish nationalist must become reconciled to Catholic development or throw in his lot with the other side. . . . If a non-Catholic nationalist Irishman does not wish to live in a Catholic atmosphere let him turn Orangeman. . . .

The Leader, 27 July 1901

(b) Douglas Hyde to Lady Gregory   7 January 1901
    . . . The fact is that we cannot turn our back on the Davis ideal of every person in Ireland being an Irishman, no matter what their blood and politics, for the moment we cease to profess that, we land ourselves in an intolerable position. It is equally true, thought, that the Gaelic League and the Leader aim at stimulating the old peasant, Papist aboriginal population, and we care very little about the others, though I would not let this be seen as Moran has done. . . .

> Gregory Ms, Berg Collection (New York Public Library), cited in L.P. Curtis Jnr., *Anglo-Saxons and Celts*, p. 147 (Conference on British Studies, University of Bridgeport, Conn. — New York University Press).

39   The National University: A question of educational method

Although much of the early work of the Gaelic League was in the study and revival of Irish literature, its most vigorous and politically significant activity was in the field of language agitation. Much of this consisted of contests and 'test cases' with petty bureaucracy, but the League's most distinguished operation was its successful campaign to establish Irish as a compulsory matriculation requirement for entry into the new National University. The deputy leader of the Home Rule party, John Dillon (1851-1927) very much a Victorian liberal on issues of this nature, delivered a strong attack on compulsion to the National Convention in February 1909, but the University senate bowed to the League's pressure. Although intolerance and dictation of policy by zealots had been a hallmark of agrarian movements since the days of the Land League, if not the eighteenth-century Whiteboys, such an approach was new to the more genteel world of higher education.

. . . After all, it is our own university. The constitution is such that the will of the people must in the long run prevail in its government. If it fails, the shame and discredit of its failure will not rest on the British government, but on the Irish people (applause). 'Blow the university to fragments if Irish is not immediately made compulsory', says one controversialist. 'Burn it down' says another.

A delegate — Right (hear, hear).

Mr Dillon — Right, says my friend here. . . . We must at least wait for the university before we can blow it up or burn it down. And I would ask you again why didn't you blow up or burn down the Royal University?

A delegate — It was not national.

Mr Dillion — And is it to be contended by my friend that we are to tolerate every institution except a national institution (applause) which is your own, and which in the long run you can do what you like with? It is the first time since the Union. . . that the British government has to meet us fairly on the question of higher education; and is it wise, does it not tend to discredit our country, that now when for the first time a British government has met us fairly and given us an institution which we can control ourselves, that we should select that opportunity to fall upon each other with fury for a detail? ('Not a detail'). Not a detail? You may think there is a great deal involved in the detail, but it is a detail. ('No, no') I do not attach importance to the point, but I ask does it not tend to discredit our country that after all these hundred years during which primary education and university education in our country has been enslaved, and our language and the literature of our country has been trampled underfoot, that when the British government for the first time gives us the opportunity of modelling our own university we should select this opportunity of failing upon each other with fury over this question. . . .

. . .It has been said and repeated that this is a fight between the friends and foes of the Gaelic revival ('Right' and 'No, no'). . . To my own knowledge many of those most strongly opposed to making Irish compulsory for matriculation in the new university are just as keen friends of the language and of the Gaelic movement as the most violent of the advocates of compulsory Irish. The question truly stated is not an issue between friends and foes of the Gaelic revival. It is a question of educational method. . . .

Transcription from: *Weekly Freeman*, 20 February 1909

40   Jim Larkin's nationalist plot, 1907

What appeared to be an entirely different line of attack on the English connection developed in the Irish labour movement during the years leading up to the first world war. The most flamboyant figure in this movement was the Liverpool-born 'strike organizer' Jim Larkin (1876-1947). The Irish labour movement at the turn of the century was a small affair based on craft unions. Its main strength lay among Belfast Protestants, and for that reason it took little interest in nationalist politics. But when Larkin arrived in Belfast in 1907 to organize unskilled workers on behalf of the English-based National Union of Dock Labourers, he found that much of his potential support inevitably lay in the Catholic section of the city. The strike and agitation which he organized cut across, for a brief period, the usual sectarian lines of conflict. The private response of Fred Crawford, a small businessman who later achieved public fame as the leading gun-runner for the Ulster Volunteer Force, 1911-14, is a good illustration of Belfast sectarian thinking.

F.H. Crawford to Major R.W. Doyne   20 August 1907

I am thankful to say our strike troubles are over for the present. It was simply a political move on the part of a section of the Nationalists to discredit Belfast. . . .

What a blessing all the rioting took place in the Catholic quarter of the city. This branded the whole thing as a Nationalist movement. Larkin the leader is the grandson of Larkin the Manchester martyr.*

The whole strike was a big political plot to ruin Belfast trade. The Nationalists are sick of people pointing out to them the Prosperity of Belfast and Protestant Ulster, they want to ruin us and this is one move in that direction. The serious part of the business is that they have duped a lot of protestants, who call themselves Independent Orangemen, and a few demagogues who love to hear their own voice. . . .

> PRONI   Crawford   Letter-book,   D.
> 1700/10/1/1, pp. 148-9

41   Jim Larkin's English invasion, 1913

Larkin's career as Irish organizer for the NUDL ended suddenly in 1908 with the withdrawal of support by an executive alarmed at the outflow of English funds to Ireland. By then he had moved his base to Dublin, and his prompt response was to convert the branches he had initiated into the basis for a new Irish Transport and General Worker's Union. Although the emphasis

---

*Larkin's grandfather was in fact still alive in Liverpool ten years after three Fenians named Allen, Larkin and O'Brien were executed for the murder of a policeman in Manchester in 1867.

remained on the organization and recognition of trade unionism among the
dockers, carters and other labourers of Dublin, Cork and the smaller Irish
ports, it was inevitable, especially after the 1910 general elections brought
home rule back to the forefront of politics, that the ITGWU should come to
terms with nationalism. The focus of concern was that Labour's potential
strength in urban areas would be given good political representation in the
arrangements for distribution of seats in the Home Rule parliament, and that
partition should not be allowed to separate industrial Belfast from the rest of
Ireland.

But more important to Larkin's career was the great strike and lockout
which dominated Dublin throughout the winter of 1913-14. The living conditions and wage rates in the city were deplorable by the standard of other United
Kingdom cities of the time, but Larkin's ambitious policy of confrontation and
general strike was based on too slender a financial base, and failed to win
steady support from English unions. The strike, which had set nationalist
workers against nationalist employers, ended in lockout and defeat for the
men. Larkin's policy aroused the opposition of all strands of nationalism
except for the radical wing of the revived IRB, and was openly denounced by
the Catholic church. The *Irish Catholic* weekly, endorsed by the Cardinal
Archbishop of Armagh as 'a clever exponent of Catholic views and a fearless
vindicator of Catholic interests', published a series of editorials on Larkinism,
one under the heading 'Satanism and Socialism'.

. . .We earnestly trust that our workers will display a more keen capacity in the future than they appear to have done in the past for
discerning where and to what extent their confidence should be
bestowed. A palpable attempt has been made within the last few days
to win them over to the ranks of the Labour-Socialist party of England,
wherein they would soon be taught to forget their Nationality and to
rank Home Rule on the same level as the Eight Hour Day. Everyone
knows there is a design afoot to wrest the parliamentary representation
of one of the Dublin divisions from the Irish party and bestow it on the
secretary of the Transport Union, as if there were no decent native
representative of industry available who would worthily defend the
interests of his class as well as of his nation. We know what Labour-
Socialism has done in France — how it has poisoned patriotism in the
minds of those who have yielded to its seductions, how it has striven to
make the profession of arms hateful in the eyes of a gallant people,
how it has scoffed at the valorous legends of the most glorious army in
the world and sought to teach the conscript that he should forsake the
sabre for the Socialists' gutter-broom, how it laughs at the ties of
frontier and of race, and would make the Frank the bondsman of the
Teuton if thereby could be purchased a craven and ignoble peace. We

refuse to believe that our brethren among the workers of Ireland will ever allow English Labour-Socialists to degrade them to such a level as this, but it is highly time they were on their guard against sophistry, and realized that the most sacred Right of all at stake today is the Right of Ireland to the support of all her children in the defence and vindication of her national and industrial independence. Our motherland has had enough, and more than enough, of English garrisons!

The Irish Catholic, 13 September 1913

42 James Connolly: Plebeian conquerors and conquered

Larkin was not closely associated with any particular branch of the nationalist movement, and his absence in the United States from 1914 until 1923 meant that he was not called upon to spell out his position fully. His colleague in the ITGWU, James Connolly (1868-1916), was a more systematic thinker, and developed what remains the most cogent exposition of Irish republican socialism. Though occupying a respected place in the canon of international Marxist thought, and arguing for a united Catholic and Protestant working class, Connolly's work is not always entirely free from the nostalgia and race-thinking of the Gaelic movement.

(a) The seventeenth, eighteenth and nineteenth centuries were, indeed, the Via Dolorosa of the Irish race. In them the Irish Gael sank out of sight, and in his place the middle-class politicians, capitalists and ecclesiastics laboured to produce a hybrid Irishman, assimilating a foreign social system, a foreign speech, and a foreign character. In the effort to assimilate the first two the Irish were unhappily too successful, so successful that today the majority of the Irish do not know that their fathers ever knew another system of ownership, and the Irish Irelanders are painfully grappling with their mother tongue with the hesitating accent of a foreigner. Fortunately the Irish character has proven too difficult to press into respectable foreign moulds, and the recoil of that character from the deadly embrace of capitalist English conventionalism, as it has already led to a revaluation of the speech of the Gael, will in all probability also lead to a re-study and appreciation of the social system under which the Gael reached the highest point of civilization and culture in Europe. . . .

James Connolly, *Labour in Irish History* (1910), pp. 5-6

(b) The underlying idea of this work is that the Labour Movement of Ireland must set itself the Re-Conquest of Ireland as its final aim, that the re-conquest involves taking possession of the entire country, all its power of wealth-production and all its natural resources, and organizing these on a cooperative basis for the good of all. To demonstrate that this and this alone would be a re-conquest, the attempt is made to explain what the Conquest of Ireland was, how it affected the Catholic natives and the Protestant settlers, how the former were subjected and despoiled by open force, and how the latter were despoiled by fraud, and when they protested were also subjected by force, and how out of this common spoliation and subjection there arises to-day the necessity of common action to reverse the Conquest, in order that the present population, descendants alike of the plebeian Conquerors and the Conquered plebeians, may enjoy in common fraternity and good-will that economic security and liberty for which their ancestors fought, or thought they fought.

James Connolly, *The Re-Conquest of Ireland*
(1915), p. 1

43 Patrick Pearse: The people who wept in Gethsemane

Social radicalism, other than on the question of land tenure, was not a central feature of Irish nationalism in the early twentieth century. Only among the militant republicans of the IRB, which had maintained a nominal continuity from the Fenian period, was there support for the Dublin strikers and a general interest in organizing the urban working class. Patrick Pearse (1879-1916), a private-school headmaster, writer, and IRB man who was to lead the 1916 uprising, voiced such sentiments in a typically vague and high-flown — and some have said blasphemous — way, in the last pamphlet he wrote.

The gentry. . . have uniformly been corrupted by England and the merchants and middle-class capitalists have, when not corrupted, been uniformly intimidated, whereas the common people have for the most part remained unbought and unterrified. It is, in fact, true that the repositories of the Irish tradition, as well the spiritual tradition of nationality as the kindred tradition of stubborn physical resistance to England, have been the great, splendid, faithful, common people — that dumb multitudinous throng which sorrowed during the penal night, which bled in '98, which starved in the Famine; and which is here still — what is left of it — unbought and unterrified. Let no man be mistaken as to who will be lord in Ireland when Ireland is free. The people will be lord and master. The people who wept in Gethsemane, who trod the sorrowful way, who died naked on a cross, who went down into hell, will rise again glorious and immortal, will sit on the right hand of God, and will come in the end to give judgment, a judge just and terrible. . . .

The Sovereign People (March 1916), in P.H. Pearse, *Political Writings and Speeches* (Dublin, 1924) p. 345.

V Home Rule and rebellion in the north, 1910-14

44 John Redmond: Dollar dictator

The Liberal government of 1905-9 secured the cooperation of the Irish party by 'governing according to Irish ideas', which meant extending full consultation to Redmond and Dillon in matters of public patronage but otherwise differed little in practice from the Tory policy of 'killing home rule with kindness'. Even the ill-fated attempt to set up an administrative council in 1907, vetoed by the Irish party, had its origins in the devolution scheme evolved under Wyndham's administration. The Liberals, faced increasingly with resistance to their measures from the House of Lords, were reluctant to put an Irish issue in the forefront of their programme. The Lords' rejection of the 1909 budget seemed a much more attractive battleground. But by-election trends indicated clearly that the massive overall majority of 1906 was unlikely to recur, that the Liberal party would need, at the least, Irish support to win a number of crucial seats in British constituencies and, quite possibly, the support of Irish party MPs to form a working majority in the House of Commons. Thus John Redmond could address Liberal cabinet ministers (and Irish-American financial backers) with an authority not possessed by an Irish leader since Parnell in 1886. A copy of the following letter found its way to the prime minister, Asquith, who declared a few days later that a future Liberal government would be entirely free to deal with the Irish question along the lines of full legislative home rule.

John Redmond to John Morley   27 November 1909

The political conditions in Ireland are such that unless an official declaration on the question of home rule be made, not only will it be impossible for us to support Liberal candidates in England, but we will most unquestionably have to ask our friends to vote against them. . . . as you know very well, the opposition of Irish voters in Lancashire, Yorkshire and other places, including Scotland, would mean the loss of many seats.

Declarations of individual candidates in favour of home rule are of no use to us. We cannot acquiesce in the present situation being continued. There is a large majority in the government and in the House of Commons in favour of home rule, and yet their hands are tied by reason of the fact that the home rule issue was deliberately withdrawn from the consideration of the electors at the last election.

We must, therefore, press for an official declaration which will show clearly that the home rule issue is involved in the issue of the House of Lords by declaring that the government shall be free to deal with it, not on the lines of the Council Bill, but on the lines of national self-government, subject to imperial control, in the next parliament. . . .

> Bodleian Library, Asquith Papers, Ms. 36 f. 1.

45   Ulstermen prefer the Kaiser, 1911?

Two general elections, in January and December 1910, could not dislodge the Irish party from its new position of strength in relation to its Liberal allies. An attempt to reach a settlement by means of a bi-partisan agreement between the major British parties, occasioned by the death of Edward VII, came to nothing. So that when the year 1911 opened, a government programme was clear at last. The House of Lords, under threat of the mass creation of Liberal peers by George V, was to pass a Parliament Bill reducing its power of veto to a temporary stay of two years, leaving the way clear for Irish home rule to be brought forward in 1912. The Unionist party continued to oppose home rule altogether, although its only real strength in Ireland lay in Ulster. The Liberals and the Irish party went ahead with their plans on the assumption that any resistance would be party political, both in character and in essence. It soon became clear, however, that statements such as the press interview given by a prominent Ulster Unionist MP, Captain James Craig (1871-1940) was not the bluff which it was at first taken for.

Neither Mr Redmond nor the English people has any conception of the deep-rooted determination of the sturdy men and women of Ulster, or of the silent preparations that are being made to meet by armed resistance the encroachment on their civil and religious liberties that would naturally follow the establishment of a parliament in Dublin.

Further, there is a spirit spreading abroad which I can testify to from my personal knowledge—that Germany and the German Emperor would be preferred to the rule of John Redmond, Patrick Ford [editor of the American newspaper, *Irish World*] and the Molly Maguires. That sentiment has been doubtless strongly augmented by the number of kidnapping cases that have recently come to light consequent upon the Church of Rome decree *(Ne Temere)* put into full force with rigour in Ireland, but successfully resisted in Germany. . . .

. . .There are a very large number of people in other parts of the United Kingdom who are unwilling or unable to believe that Ulster will, if forced, adopt Lord Randolph Churchill's advice: 'Ulster will fight, and Ulster will be right.' Such steps will be taken when the proper moment arises as will convince those unbelievers and the whole of the British public that if the need arises armed resistance of the most determined character will be resorted to sooner than submit to the dominance of the Church of Rome which any parliament in Dublin would spell to the people of Ulster.

> Transcription from the *Morning Post,* 9 January 1911

46   Willoughby de Broke: Every white man

Their very adoption of the name 'Unionist' after 1886 acknowledged a measure of commitment on the part of English Conservatives. But the scale and intensity of their opposition to home rule between 1911 to 1914 was something new. Historians have seen this trend variously as part of the 'Ulster bluff', as determination to prevent dismemberment of the United Kingdom, and as a cynical exercise by a thrice-defeated political party. Evidence can be found to lend support to all these interpretations. But for many Conservatives, like the backbench English peer Lord Willoughby de Broke (1869-1923), the 'Ulster struggle' took on a symbolic significance. De Broke had taken an active part in the ineffective resistance to the Parliament Bill in 1911. It seemed to him that the traditional values of the British Empire were being swept away by radicals who held power only with the support of Irish nationalists. In this context Ulster, where Protestant and 'loyal' feelings had assumed such militancy and cut across class barriers, became an ideal issue and location for a defiant stand. This extract is from a speech made by de Broke at Dromore, Co. Down, in September 1912.

The Unionists of England were going to help Unionists over here, not only by making speeches. Peaceable methods would be tried first, but if the last resort was forced on them by the Radical government, the latter would find that they had not only Orangemen against them, but that every white man in the British Empire would be giving support, either moral or active, to one of the most loyal populations that ever fought under the Union Jack.

> Transcription from the *Belfast Newsletter,* 27 September, 1912

47 Bonar Law: No length of resistance. . .

The third Home Rule Bill at last saw the light of day on 11 April 1912. Two days earlier an estimated 100,000 Ulster Protestants had marched past the platform in military formation at a protest demonstration in Belfast's Balmoral grounds. Sir Edward Carson (1854-1935), the Dublin-born lawyer who became leader of the Irish Unionist group in the Conservative party in 1910, made it clear both that he associated himself with the armed resistance spoken of by Craig and that, apparently, he intended to use that resistance to thwart nationalism altogether — 'if Ulster succeed, home rule is dead', he declared in the House of Commons in June 1912. A few months earlier, the sophisticated but seemingly lethargic Arthur Balfour had been replaced as Tory leader by Andrew Bonar Law (1858-1923), a Scots Canadian with Ulster family connections who gave full endorsement to the style and tone of the Ulster resistance. Law and Carson were the main platform speakers at the Balmoral demonstration. In July, Law went even further in his commitment to the Ulster cause, at a mass meeting held in the grounds of Blenheim Palace, family seat of the Duke of Marlborough.

. . .In our opposition. . . we shall not be guided by the considerations or bound by the restraints which would influence us in an ordinary constitutional struggle. . . . They may, perhaps they will, carry their home rule bill through the House of Commons, but what then? I said the other day in the House of Commons and I repeat here that there are things stronger than parliamentary majorities.

. . .Before I occupied the position I now fill in the party I said that, in my belief, if an attempt were made to deprive these men [Ulster Unionists] of their birth-right — as part of a corrupt parliamentary bargain — they would be justified in resisting such an attempt by all means in their power, including force. I said it then, and I repeat it now with a full sense of the responsibility which attaches to my position, that, in my opinion, if such an attempt is made, I can imagine no length of resistance to which Ulster can go in which I should not be prepared to support them, and in which, in my belief, they would not be supported by the overwhelming majority of the British people.

Transcription from *The Times,* 29 July 1912

48 Ulstermen humbly rely on their God, 1912

To underline further the strength of Ulster Protestant feeling, and to achieve an even greater show of numbers, the local Unionist leaders declared 28 September 1912 to be 'Ulster Day', on which about 450,000 men and women signed a document or supporting declaration based in concept on the seventeenth-century Scottish Covenant. Carson signed with a silver pen. Some lesser political lights signed in their own blood.

ULSTER'S SOLEMN LEAGUE AND COVENANT

Being convinced in our consciences that Home Rule would be disastrous to the material well-being of Ulster, as well as of the whole of Ireland, subversive of our civil and religious freedom, destructive of our citizenship, and perilous to the unity of the Empire, we, whose names are underwritten, men of Ulster, loyal subjects of His Gracious Majesty King George V, humbly relying on the God Whom our fathers in the days of stress and trial confidently trusted, do hereby pledge ourselves in solemn Covenant throughout this our time of threatened calamity to stand by one another in defending for ourselves and our children our cherished position of equal citizenship in the United Kingdom and in using all means which may be found necessary to defeat the present conspiracy to set up a home rule parliament in Ireland. And in the event of such a Parliament being forced upon us we further and mutually pledge ourselves to refuse to recognize its authority. In sure confidence that God will defend the right, we hereto subscribe our names. And further we individually declare that we have not already signed this Covenant. God Save the King.

> Transcription from *The Times*, 20 September 1912

49   Winston Churchill: A combination of rancour and fanaticism

Even before the third Home Rule Bill was introduced, the Liberal cabinet had privately resolved to consider special treatment for Ulster if it became necessary and, Asquith reported to the king, intended making 'careful and confidential inquiry. . . as to the extent and character of the Ulster resistance'. Whether that special treatment would take the form merely of some local autonomy within an Irish framework, or whether it would mean exclusion of Ulster from the settlement, whether it would be permanent, indefinite, or strictly temporary, was not made clear. At all events, there was probably no bargaining advantage to be gained from premature concessions, and certainly no prospect of securing Irish party support for them in the absence of extreme duress. It was not until the unrevised Home Rule Bill had made its second journey through the Commons in 1913 that modification was seriously discussed between the parties. A letter from Winston Churchill (1874-1965), then First Lord of the Admiralty, in August 1913 typifies the cautious way in which the matter was being broached with the Nationalists. Churchill was the first member of the government to take up the question of Ulster, and was shortly to threaten resignation from the cabinet if Ulster was coerced. There is some evidence to suggest that he may even have been considering Ulster as an issue over which he might return to the Conservative party, which he had deserted nine years earlier on the question of free trade.

Winston Churchill to John Redmond   31 August 1913

. . .I do not believe there is any real feeling against home rule in the Tory party apart from the Ulster question, but they hate the government, are bitterly desirious of turning it out, and see in the resistance of Ulster an extra-parliamentary force which they will not hesitate to use to the full.

I have been pondering a great deal over this matter, and my general view is just what I told you earlier in the year — namely, that something should be done to afford the characteristically Protestant and Orange counties the option of a moratorium of several years before acceding to the Irish parliament. . . . Much is to be apprehended from a combination of the rancour of a party in the ascendant and the fanaticism of these stubborn and determined Orangemen. . . .

NLI Redmond Papers

50   The bishop of Raphoe: A queer autonomy

The partition of Ireland was not a solution that had ever before been seriously countenanced. But a letter to *The Times* in favour of compromise from a veteran home rule ruler and Liberal elder statesman, Lord Loreburn, in September 1913, and a public speech by Churchill a few days later, brought discussion into the open. The bishop of Raphoe, Patrick O'Donnell (1856-1927), the Irish party's most active supporter within the ranks of the Catholic hierarchy, was quick to call attention to the position of the Catholic minority in northeast Ulster. Even under a scheme for giving 'Ulster' separate treatment within the general jurisdiction of a home rule government, let alone any proposal for omitting Ulster from home rule altogether, he argued, the situation would be intolerable for nationalists. Interestingly enough, however, in the light of later developments, he placed the unity of the Irish party above any attempt to create a distinct voice for nationalist Ulster — a voice which in the long run might have been less of a challenge to Ulster unionism than to the official nationalist leadership.

Bishop of Raphoe to John Redmond   9 October 1913

. . .There is no length to which any of us would refuse to go to satisfy the Orangemen at the starting of our new government, provided Ireland did not suffer seriously, and provided also the Nationalist minority in the N.E. did not suffer badly. But it is not hard for Mr Churchill to realize that, under the bill as it stands, the set of Protestants who patently need no protection are the Ulster Unionists, and that, with the home rule of the bill, the Catholic and Nationalist minority in the N.E. corner remain under the domination in all local things which they have endured so long, until the spirit of freedom sets things right, as it would in a few years. But he may not see the point that nothing could justify cutting this minority off from their claims under the bill, and deliberately leaving them under a harrow that might be worse than what they have endured.

Autonomy in education, etc., for the N.E. corner would be queer autonomy for them.

On matters of this kind there is a good deal of feeling that the Nationalists of Ulster should form a special committee, organize, and speak out, and insist on being represented as fully as the Orangemen at any conference. My own view has been that we in the interests of home rule should avoid forming a second camp in Ulster. . . .

NLI MS. 15, 217(4): Redmond Papers

51   John Redmond: Ireland is a unit

In private correspondence amongst themselves, the leaders of the Irish party acknowledged frankly that if the government offered, and persuaded the Unionists to submit to, home rule for Ireland with the option of exclusion for the four counties with Protestant majorities—Antrim, Armagh, Down and Londonderry—it would be difficult for them to object. But no such firm offer had been made, and in the meantime, Redmond, as he did in a speech at Limerick on 12 October 1913, could do no more than hint at the possibility of some local autonomy for Ulster within home rule.

Irish Nationalists can never be assenting parties to the mutilation of the Irish nation; Ireland is a unit. It is true that within the bosom of a nation there is room for diversities in the treatment of government and of administration, but a unit Ireland is and a unit Ireland must remain. . . . The two-nation theory is to us an abomination and a blasphemy. . . .

As cited in: D.Gwynn, *The Life of John Redmond* (Geo. J. Harrap, London, 1932), p. 232

52   Patrick Pearse: We may shoot the wrong people

The organization and drilling of 100,000 members of the UVF was becoming a source of concern not only to the government, but to other interests as well. The two years of debate which had occupied the entire attention of the Irish party leaders caught the imagination of active nationalists less than did the activities of the Ulstermen. In November 1913 a history professor at the new University College, Dublin, Eoin MacNeill (1867-1945), published an article in the Gaelic League newspaper under the heading 'The North began'. It purported to welcome the UVF as a rejection by a group of Irishmen of British leadership, but on a more practical level it proposed the establishment of an 'Irish Volunteer Force' along similar lines. MacNeill was not known as an extreme nationalist, but was soon approached discreetly by others who were, as a result of which he summoned a huge meeting in Dublin on 25 November 1913 when the new body was founded. For the Irish party leaders this apparent emulation of Carson's departure from constitutionalism seemed nothing other than embarrassing. But too many of their own supporters were involving themselves in it for a straight denunciation to be advisable. Accordingly they sailed anxiously with it until June 1914, when they felt in a position to deliver an ultimatum to the leadership of the movement and gain half the places on the provisional committee for 'Mr Redmond's nominees'. A revived IRB was secretly very active within the new Volunteer movement, its membership increased by the addition of Irish language enthusiasts like Patrick Pearse, a former moderate raised by the possibilities of the new movement to a pitch of revolutionary excitement.

I have come to the conclusion that the Gaelic League, as the Gaelic League, is a spent force; and I am glad of it. I do not mean that no work remains for the Gaelic League, or that the Gaelic League is no longer equal to work; I mean that the vital work to be done in the new Ireland will be done not so much by the Gaelic League itself as by men and movements that have sprung from the Gaelic League or have received from the Gaelic League a new baptism and a new life of grace. The Gaelic League was. . . a prophet and more than a prophet. But it was not the Messiah. I do not know if the Messiah has yet come, and I am not sure that there will be any visible and personal Messiah in this redemption: the people itself will perhaps be its own Messiah, the people labouring, scourged, crowned with thorns, agonizing and dying, to rise again immortal and impassible. . . .

If we had not believed in the divinity of our people, we should in all probability not have gone into the Gaelic League at all. We should have made our peace with the devil, and perhaps might have found him a very decent sort; for he liberally rewards with attorney-generalships, bank balances, villa residences, and so forth, the great and the little who serve him well. Now, we did not turn our backs upon all these desirable things for the sake of *is* and *tá*. We did it for the sake

of Ireland. In other words, we had one and all of us. . . an ulterior
motive in joining the Gaelic League. . . . Our Gaelic League time was
to be our tutelage: we had first to learn to know Ireland, to read the
lineaments of her face, to understand the accents of her voice; to re-
possess ourselves, disinherited as we were, of her spirit and mind, re-
enter into our mystical birthright. . . .

To every generation its deed. The deed of the generation that has
now reached middle life was the Gaelic League: the beginning of the
Irish Revolution. Let our generation not shirk *its* deed, which is to
accomplish the revolution. . . .

I am glad, then, that the North has 'begun'. I am glad that the
Orangemen have armed, for it is a goodly thing to see arms in Irish
hands. I should like to see the AOH armed. I should like to see the
Transport Workers armed. I should like to see any and every body of
Irish citizens armed. We must accustom ourselves to the thought of
arms, to the sight of arms, to the use of arms. We may make mistakes
in the beginning and shoot the wrong people; but bloodshed is a
cleansing and a sanctifying thing, and the nation which regards it as
the final horror has lost it manhood. There are many things more
horrible than bloodshed; and slavery is one of them.

> *The Coming Revolution* (November 1913), in
> P.H. Pearse, *Political Writings and Speeches*
> (Dublin, 1924), pp. 91-9.

53   The impact of a new university

The founding of the National University and its constituent University College,
Dublin, in 1908 established a new academic and student body in the capital
alongside that of the predominantly Unionist Trinity. Some of the influences
in the new college, like that of the professor of national economics, T.M.
Kettle — an ex-Irish party MP who later met his death as an officer in the
British army — were moderate ones. But the prevailing tone of the more politically conscious students was 'Irish-Ireland'. They remembered less the Irish
party's role in the creation of their university than the subsequent opposition of
its leaders to the implementation of compulsory Irish for matriculation. They
were at best independent of Irish party thinking, and were to provide the basis
of an officer corps for the Irish Volunteers in 1916.

Since the gigantic meetings, organized by students some years ago, on
behalf of Irish as an essential subject in the matriculation of the
National University, no event of a kindred significance has called forth
the public response of students of University College as did the opening

public meeting of the Irish Volunteers.

. . .practically every male student of University College, whose movements were not restricted by a special discipline, attended at the inception of the 'Irish Volunteers'. To the meeting at the Rotunda about three hundred and fifty students went—a large proportion of them marching as a body. And this number may be taken as fairly close to the total aggregate of male students. . . .

> *The National Student*, IV, ii (December 1913), cited in: F.X. Martin (ed.), *The Irish Volunteers, 1913-15* (Jas, Duffy & Co. Ltd., Dublin, 1963), pp. 120-1.

54 Sir Edward Carson: Ulster has a strong right arm

In 1912-13 Irish Nationalist leaders affected not to take the Ulster Volunteer Force very seriously. It performed its drill with dummy rifles and its leaders were out-of-office politicians. But in March 1914 seventy British army officers stationed at the Curragh camp, Co. Kildare, extracted an agreement from the Secretary of State of War that the army would not be used to enforce home rule in Ulster. In the circumstances Asquith's subsequent rebuttal was unconvincing. A few weeks later a shipload of 20,000 German rifles from Hamburg was landed at the Ulster port of Larne by Major Fred Crawford (1861-1952) and distributed overnight to UVF units throughout the province. Carson and the local Unionist leaders were fully aware of the plan in advance. But as the public posture of Unionist and Nationalist became more combative and overtly military, the trend behind the scenes was increasingly towards compromise. It was clear that the Irish party leaders would not in fact insist on full and total inclusion of all nine Ulster counties in the home rule scheme at once, although they were still a long way from accepting the exclusion of six or nine counties for an indefinite period. But Carson on the other hand at last moved back publicly from a position of root-and-branch opposition to Irish home rule of any kind.

Ulster looms very largely in this controversy, simply because Ulster has a strong right arm, but there are unionists in the south and west who loath the bill just as much as we Ulster people loath it, whose difficulties are far greater, and who would willingly fight, as Ulster would fight, if they had the numbers. Nobody knows the difficulties of these men better than I do. Why, it was only the other day some of them ventured to put forward as a business proposition that this bill would be financial ruin to their businesses, saying no more, and immediately they were boycotted, and resolutions were passed, and they were told that they ought to understand as Protestants that they ought to be thankful and grateful for being allowed to live in peace among the people who are there. Yes, we can never support the bill which hands these people over to the tender mercies of those who have always been their bitterest enemies. We must go on whatever happens, opposing the bill to the end. That we are entitled to do; that we are bound to do. But I want to speak explicitly about the exclusion of Ulster. . . . If the exclusion of Ulster is not shut out, and if at the same time the prime minister says he cannot admit anything contrary to the fundamental principles of the bill, I think it follows that the exclusion of Ulster is not contrary to the fundamental principles of the bill. . . .

On the other hand I say this, that your suggestions — no matter what paper safeguards you put, or no matter what other methods you may attempt to surround these safeguards with for the purpose of raising what I call 'your reasonable atmosphere' — if your suggestions try to compel these people to come into a Dublin parliament, I tell you I shall regardless of personal consequences, go on with these people to the end with their policy of resistance.

HC Deb. 5th series, vol. 58, cols. 175-6 (11 February 1914)

VI Conscription and rebellion in the south, 1914-18

55 The one bright spot, August 1914

During the late spring and summer of 1914 negotiations continued. From 21 to 24 July an eight-man conference of Liberal, Irish party, Conservative and Unionist leaders met at Buckingham Palace. They discussed details of which counties might be excluded from the settlement and possible mechanisms for excluding them, but they could find no way round the crucial issue of whether the exclusion was to be temporary or permanent. What the next step might have been is not clear, although the emulation of the Larne gun-running on a smaller scale by the Irish National Volunteers at Howth, Co. Dublin, on 26 July—leading to an incident in Dublin in which soldiers fired on a crowd, killing three and wounding thirty-eight—did not bode well for future peace. Many feared that the continued growth of the rival volunteer forces could only end in civil war. The sudden and, in the short view, unexpected involvement of Britain in a European conflict, announced by Sir Edward Grey to the House of Commons on 3 August 1914, brought new priorities to the situation. Redmond, without consulting his colleagues, declared Ireland's immediate support for the war and pledged the cooperation of the Irish National Volunteers in the defence of Ireland.

I hope the House will not consider it improper on my part, in the grave circumstances in which we are assembled, if I intervene for a very few moments. I was moved a great deal by that sentence in the speech of the Secretary of State for Foreign Affairs in which he said that the one bright spot in the situation was the changed feeling in Ireland. In past times, when this Empire has been engaged in these terrible enterprises, it is true—it would be the utmost affectation and folly on my part to deny it—the sympathy of the Nationalists of Ireland, for reasons to be found deep down in centuries of history, has been estranged from this country.

Allow me to say, sir, that what has occurred in recent years has altered the situation completely. . . and today I honestly believe that the democracy of Ireland will turn with the utmost anxiety and

sympathy to this country in every trial and every danger that may over-
take it. . . .

I say to the Government that they may tomorrow withdraw every
one of their troops from Ireland. I say that the coast of Ireland will be
defended from foreign invasion by her armed sons, and for this
purpose armed Nationalist Catholics in the South will be only too glad
to join arms with the armed Protestant Ulstermen in the North. Is it
too much to hope that out of this situation there may spring a result
which will be good, not merely for the Empire, but good for the future
welfare and integrity of the Irish nation?

> HC Deb. 5th series, vol. 65, cols. 1828-9
> (3 August 1914)

56   John Redmond: Recruiting sergeant

Redmond's speech on 3 August 1914 appears to have been a unilateral gesture,
independent of any pledge from the government. But during September
Asquith pursued a course which met the immediate concerns of the Irish party,
and effectively postponed the home rule crisis for the time being. The Home
Rule Act was placed 'on the statute book', but further legislation suspended its
operation until the end of the war, and until an additional measure could be
implemented to settle the Ulster difficulty. Two days after the passing of this
agreement, on 20 September, Redmond made an apparently unplanned
appearance at a Volunteer parade at Woodenbridge, near his home in Co.
Wicklow, and called for unqualified enlistment in the British army. Irish
nationalists, he now argued, should be prepared to fight for the Allied cause in
the front line of the conflict, and not just in Ireland itself.

The duty of the manhood of Ireland is twofold. Its duty is, at all costs,
to defend the shores of Ireland against foreign invasion. It is a duty
more than that, of taking care that Irish valour proves itself on the
field of war as it has always proved itself in the past.

The interests of Ireland — of the whole of Ireland — are at stake in
this war. The war is undertaken in defence of the highest principles of
religion and morality and right, and it would be a disgrace for ever to
our country, and a reproach to her manhood, and a denial of the
lessons of her history, if young Ireland confined their efforts to
remaining at home to defend the shores of Ireland from an unlikely
invasion, and shrunk from the duty of proving on the field of battle
that gallantry and courage which has distinguished our race all
through its history.

I say to you, therefore, your duty is twofold. I am glad to see such magnificent material for soldiers around me, and I say to you, 'Go on drilling and make yourselves efficient for the work, and then account yourselves as men, not only in Ireland itself, but wherever the firing-line extends, in defence of right, of freedom, and of religion in this war.

> Transcription from D. Gwynn, *The Life of John Redmond* (London, 1932), pp. 391-2

57   The means and ends of volunteering

By the summer of 1914 the Irish National Volunteers had become, nominally, a very large body indeed — perhaps as many as 180,000 men — although the proportion of these who were effectively trained, equipped or armed was small by comparison with the UVF. The guiding spirit of the movement, *pace* Redmond's intervention in June, was revolutionary: frank hostility to England, and a less frank affectation that the INV and the UVF were pulling essentially in the same direction. But at the grass-roots level, different factors operated: on one level, especially in the north, members of the INV felt that they might somehow or other 'fight for home rule'; on another level there were many, especially southern Protestants with military experience, who though it realistic to come to terms with the inevitability of home rule, to provide 'responsible' leadership for a potentially formidable force, and who saw in Redmond's speech of 3 August a bridge to their Catholic neighbours and ex-tenants. The only lasting importance of this development was the negative impact it had on the popularity of the INV, for it lent credence to the Sinn Fein charge that the Irish party was out to 'conscript the people'. This correspondence from the files of the Inspector-General gives some indication of the difficulties brought to the nationalist movement by its new accretions.

Major S.C. Hickman to Col. Maurice Moore   Newmarket-on-Fergus, Co. Clare

(a) 13 August 1914

I am not sure if it was you I used to know in the good old soldiering days, anyhow I will write you a few lines. . . . Though I have hitherto done nothing in the Irish National Volunteer movement, it is not because I have not approved of it, I always have. . . . I may tell you from the start that I am very much on the home rule side — but I want unity in Ireland. . . .

In this county the I.N. Volunteer scheme is badly done I think — in fact not done at all — if I could take up the job and organize it a bit here I am willing to do so. I have done twenty years in the R[oyal] H[orse] A[rtillery] my reserve service expired a little time ago, and though I would give my eyes to go with the army and have offered my services, of course there is no chance — can't put back the clock alas!

(b) 16 September 1914
After seeing the report of a meeting of the County Board of the I.N. Vols. in Ennis — and that they seemed to wish for an inspecting officer of their own choosing, I sent you a wire to appoint whoever they wanted in my place — it is better so. . . . I could not stand taking orders from some of the people who appear to be in authority on the County Board. I am very sure you would not care to be under their orders. . . .

I confess I am a bit afraid of the whole thing — if it is to be run by some people I hear about here, good fellows in their own way — but it wants a different class of man at the head, or it seems to me the movement may lead to great trouble in the future. I was undertaking the job to work under you and be a sort of restraining force as well as working it — but from what I gather that seems impossible. The idea among the country people is that the Nat. Vols. are to be trained, and armed with American rifles, and then be ready to fight Ulster any day! And the way people talk encourages all this too much I think. . . . I feel awfully ashamed of us all in the south not enlisting in the Irish Division, and this movement has a lot to do with it. . . .

NLI Maurice Moore Papers, Ms. 10547/5

58   The Volunteer split

The founders of the Irish Volunteers ('National' only crept into the movement's name under Redmondite influence) had only accepted Redmond's intervention through fear that his denunciation would destroy them. But it was clear, even before the war started, that the body was a heterogeneous grouping of attitudes, unlikely to be capable of effective action. Redmond's recruiting speech at Woodenbridge provided an ideal opportunity for the original Volunteer leadership to break with him by making an appeal to national sentiment which also held obvious attractions for Volunteers with no taste for enlistment in the army. The following manifesto was accordingly issued on 24 September 1914, immediately splitting the movement into Irish Volunteers (about 10,000 members, mostly strongly committed to militant nationalism) and National Volunteers (many times greater in number, but with a large proportion of merely nominal members).

TO THE IRISH VOLUNTEERS

Ten months ago a Provisional Committee commenced the Irish Volunteer movement with the whole purpose of securing and defending the Rights and Liberties of the Irish people. The movement on these lines, though thwarted and opposed for a time, obtained the support of the Irish Nation. When the Volunteer Movement had become the main factor in the Irish position, Mr Redmond decided to acknowledge it and to endeavour to bring it under his control.

Three months ago he put forward the claim to send twenty-five nominees to the Provisional Committee of the Irish Volunteers. He threatened, if the claim was not conceded, to proceed to the dismemberment of the Irish Volunteer Organization.

. . .The Provisional Committee, while recognizing that the responsibility in that case would be altogether Mr Redmond's, decided to risk the lesser evil and to admit his nominees to sit and act on the Committee. . . .

Mr Redmond addressing a body of Irish Volunteers on last Sunday, has now announced for the Irish Volunteers a policy and programme fundamentally at variance with their own published and accepted aims and objects, but with which his nominees are, of course, identified. He has declared it to be the duty of the Irish Volunteers to take foreign service under a Government which is not Irish. He has made this announcement without consulting the Provisional Committee, the Volunteers themselves, or the people of Ireland, to whose service alone they are devoted.

. . .Those who, by virtue of Mr Redmond's nomination, have heretofore been admitted to act on the Provisional Committee accordingly cease henceforth to belong to that body. . . .

At the next meeting of the Provisional Committee we shall propose. . . . To oppose any diminution of the measure of Irish self-government which now exists as a statute on paper, and which would not now have reached that stage but for the Irish Volunteers. . . . To repudiate any undertaking by whomsoever given, to consent to the legislative dismemberment of Ireland; and to protest against the attitude of the present Government, who, under the pretence that 'Ulster cannot be coerced', avow themselves prepared to coerce the Nationalists of Ulster. . . . To declare that Ireland cannot, with honour or safety, take part in foreign quarrels otherwise than through the free action of a National Government of her own; and to repudiate the claim of any man to offer up the blood and lives of the sons of

Irishmen and Irishwomen to the service of the British Empire while no National Government which could speak and act for the people of Ireland is allowed to exist. . . .

> As cited in: F.X. Martin (ed.) *The Irish Volunteers, 1913-15* (Jas Duffy & Co. Ltd., Dublin, 1963) pp. 152-4

59   Mortal men and pocket patriots

The split in the Volunteers was for some while less clear-cut at local level than it was centrally. Local officers might find their decisions reversed by the men; companies where neither Irish party nor Sinn Fein partisanship was strong might be genuinely undecided; real confusion and misunderstanding also existed. Now that Redmond had come out for full army recruiting, it was difficult to see any immediate political purpose which the National Volunteers could serve. Their real function was to keep as many men as possible out of the ranks of the rival Irish Volunteers, and so a flurry of activity and organization was necessary. Many Irish party MPs, like Redmond's brother William who was later killed at the front, took an active part at this stage. The second extract is an interesting sidelight on the mechanics of grass-roots nationalism.

(a) Col. Maurice Moore to William Redmond M.P.   19 October 1914

> . . .There are many Volunteers who don't know much about the matters in dispute and if they parade for us at all will join in all right afterwards. They are not Sinn Feiners, but don't want to go off to fight in Belgium, and your speech will probably have the desired effect.

(b) Father M. Gilligan, C.C. to National Volunteer Headquarters, Dublin   21 April 1915

> . . .Volunteer companies in some places have broken up and in other places been seriously injured through the self-interest of publicans. They have managed in many places to get themselves appointed commanders and then have the drilling carried out at back or front of their premises. I know of one case where the publican—a very prominent man in the county—marched the men from the drilling ground through the village and gave them the 'dismiss' in front of his premises—needless to say there is no Volunteer company in that parish now, and it was not the split that broke it up either. . . . I had to fight the same difficulty in my own parish.

Bung [D.P. Moran's name for the liquor trade] has captured and controlled the Gaelic Athletic Association for his own benefit. Will he be allowed to do the same thing with the Volunteers? He is very patriotic, but in many cases his patriotism is in his pocket.

NLI Maurice Moore Papers, Ms. 10547/5

60 Two views on the state of Ireland, 1914

Before the end of 1914, recruiting and the general question of support for the war had replaced home rule as the central issue in Irish politics. At first recruiting in Dublin, Belfast and the larger towns was maintained at a reasonable level. But the Irish Volunteers, and the general movement known as 'Sinn Fein' — although that term embraced a trend of opinion considerably wider than the Sinn Fein party proper — found in 'England's war' a potentially more effective propaganda weapon than extreme nationalism had possessed for more than a generation. This correspondence between one of the Irish party leaders and the Under-Secretary, chief public official in the Irish administration, reflects the concerns which now dominated the situation.

(a) John Dillon MP to Sir Matthew Nathan   28 November 1914

This war coming just before we finally secured home rule has created a position of terrible difficulty and embarrassment for us, and up to the beginning of this month the War Office and other government authorities have done nothing but add to our difficulties. Yet we have retained the confidence and the leadership of about twenty to one of the nationalists of Ireland and secured their goodwill to England in this war. And according to my information we have completely paralysed the attempts of the Germans to secure the cooperation of the Irish in America in influencing American opinion against England. I do not believe that the Sinn Feiners and pro-Germans are making any headway against us in Ireland.

But because certain Tory newspapers, and rabid anti-Irish Unionists in the House of Commons, clamour for coercion measures, the government are about, I fear, to embark on that dangerous course. . . . My strong feeling is — and I speak only for myself in this matter — that so far from helping us, or promoting recruiting, the suppression of these wretched, scurrilous rags will only increase our difficulties and raise fresh obstacles in the path of recruiting from the ranks of Irish nationalists.

Had it not been for the perversity of the War Office in treating with contempt any suggestion we made, a very large number of nationalists would have entered the New Army before now.

There is a considerable movement in favour of recruiting since the Irish brigades were really put in working order, and I think that movement would be largely strengthened by other measures, if the War Office could be got to adopt them.

But I greatly fear that the suppression of the papers, with the consequences which will probably follow, may have a very evil influence on the whole situation.

(b) Sir Matthew Nathan to John Dillon   30 November 1914

. . .From my very short experience in this country I believe Irishmen *are* affected by what they hear and read, probably more than more phlegmatic peoples. When you and Mr Redmond hold anti-hatred meetings in the country I am quite sure you pull out people from the Sinn Fein ranks. But the Sinn Fein leaders are very active; they seem always on the move and, so far as I can judge from the reports I receive, to be constantly getting new recruits. Their cleverly worded and insidiously scattered papers spread all over the country and in the distribution of leaflets they and their American allies have the field practically all to themselves. I sometimes wish there had been a stronger newspaper and leaflet 'reconciliation' campaign and wonder whether the strength of the hatred party has not been underestimated by the regular press in Ireland.

I lay no special stress on the recruiting aspect of the question because I am doubtful whether this is much affected by the Sinn Fein movement. A peasant proprietor or tenant population has a natural tendency 'to watch the harvest ripen, its herds increase' rather than to go out and fight like the labourer who does so without giving up anything. Besides, those who are wavering between 'reconciliation' and 'hatred' are probably not the sort of men to come as recruits should they decide on reconciliation. But the more of them that are known to decide on hatred, the greater the inducement for a foreign army to come over to Ireland. . . .

Bodleian Library, Nathan Papers, Ms. 451 f. 218, Ms. 462 f. 191.

61   Ireland prefers the Kaiser, 1915?

In May 1915 the last Liberal government came to an end when criticism of its conduct of the war forced Asquith to form a coalition administration. Redmond was offered a cabinet place, but replied that 'the principles and history of the party I represent make the acceptance of your offer impossible'. Carson's status in his party was such that he could not be passed over, nor did he share Redmond's difficulties over acceptance. In these circumstances the Irish party's objections to his inclusion have something of a dog-in-the-manger quality about them. And yet its dilemma was a hopeless one, for acceptance of office by any of its leaders would almost certainly have wrecked the party, while it seemed clear that one of the main tasks of the coalition government would be to implement military conscription in Britain and, it had to be assumed, in Ireland as well. The outburst of the bishop of Killaloe (Michael Fogarty, 1859-1955) coming from a member of the Catholic hierarchy previously sympathetic to the Irish party, is indicative of the changing climate of opinion in nationalist Ireland.

(a) John Dillon MP to Sir Matthew Nathan   28 May 1915

. . .A *great deal* of mischief has already been done—from the recruiting point of view—in this country by the formation of the coalition government, and the inclusion of Carson. If you are consulted as to the question of conscription—I think you should represent *strongly* that any attempt to enforce conscription in Ireland will have *most serious* and deplorable results.

> Bodleian Library, Nathan Papers, Ms. 451, f. 268

(b) Bishop of Killaloe to John Redmond MP   3 June 1915

The English have got all they wanted from Ireland, and don't care two pence about her feelings. Such is our reward for her profuse loyalism and recruiting. The people are full of indignation, but are powerless. . . .

As far as Ireland is concerned, there is little to choose between Carsonism and Kaiserism, of the two the latter is a lesser evil: and it almost makes me cry to think of the Irish Brigade fighting not for Ireland but for Carson and what he stands for—Orange ascendancy here.

Home rule is dead and buried and Ireland is without a national party or national press. The *Freeman* is but a government organ and the national party but an imperial instrument. What the future holds in store for us God knows—I suppose conscription with a bloody feud between people and soldiers. I never thought that Asquith would have consented to this humiliation and ruin of

Irish feeling. There is a great revulsion of feeling in Ireland.

NLI Redmond Papers, Ms. 15188/5

62   Problems of recruiting, 1915

Rising prices, low wages, underemployment and relatively attractive War Office separation allowances (payable to wives) for family men, encouraged voluntary recruiting in Irish towns during the first year or so of the war. In rural areas, however, the situation was different. Although that large Irish class known as 'farmers' sons' was to a great extent agricultural labour surplus to requirements in a strictly economic sense, and therefore ideal recruiting material, in practice higher prices for farm produce provided more family income to keep such men at home, and more incentive to farm intensively. As the pace of voluntary recruiting inevitably slackened once the willing were creamed off, recruiting authorities began to look for ways round this difficulty.

Circular Letter from the Central Council for the Organization of Recruiting in Ireland   11 August 1915

. . .Steps so far taken have failed to attract considerable numbers of recruits from the farming and commercial classes in Ireland. This failure is, we believe, reacting unfavourably upon recruiting among the labouring classes who naturally resent the abstention of others who should share the burden of the war.

We are satisfied that a much larger number of recruits could be obtained from the classes named were it not for their reluctance to enter upon their training with recruits from the labouring classes. This class prejudice is probably much more pronounced in Ireland than elsewhere in the United Kingdom.

The abstention of the classes named has undoubtedly produced a further and serious obstacle to general recruiting — in so far that anti-war propaganda has made special headway among farmers' sons and commercial [i.e. shop] assistants. The most certain way to counteract this tendency is to attract recruits from their ranks.

NLI Maurice Moore Papers, Ms. 10561/1

63   Problems of the Irish party, 1916

Many members of the Irish party, most notably John Dillon, attributed a fair measure of blame for the war to Britain's foreign policy under Sir Edward Grey, and never consented to appear on recruiting platforms. Once home rule had been put 'on the statute book' and shelved, however, John Redmond and some others in the party committed themselves to wholehearted support for the British and 'Imperial' war effort. Both Redmond's brother and his son became wartime army officers. In March 1916, after conscription had been introduced in Britain, Redmond invited all the party's MPs to attend a conference with a view to stimulating Irish recruiting. Some of the replies he received give an interesting impression of the state of the various localities on the eve of the Easter Rising.

William Doris MP to John Redmond MP   Westport, Co. Mayo
                                              8 March 1916

. . .As to this western part of the county, I fear we have very little chance of getting recruits, and the calling of public meetings for the purpose would only show our weakness in this respect. On all questions (but this important question of the hour) the vast majority of the people are with the Party.

Most of our young fellows emigrate as they grow up and the small landowners will not listen to a suggestion that any of their few remaining sons should enlist. The Protestant farmers' sons in this district are even more hopeless slackers than our own people. Our shop assistants—mostly small farmers' sons—became such extreme nationalists all in a moment that they could not dream of 'fighting for England', and they are now regarded as Sinn Feiners. . . .

The landlord party here (Lord Sligo and co.) took control of the recruiting movement, and thus gave the 'extreme patriots' a further pretext for opposing it—'Just imagine Doris, the old Land Leaguer, on Lord Sligo's platform', etc.

The leading disturbers and pro-Germans here are a few disappointed placehunters. If Dublin Castle gave them the appointments they looked for we would have very little pro-Germanism in the Westport district. I fear I would not be of any assistance at your conference, but if you think otherwise you have only to let me know.

NLI Redmond Papers, Ms. 15262/3

64   The Republic declared, 1916

Events in Dublin during Easter week 1916 were to knock the bottom out of Irish recruiting altogether. The week-long rising, in which somewhat over 400 (the majority civilian and crown forces) were killed and about 1,000 wounded, took the Irish party and the government by surprise. The Irish administration continued, until the last minute, to accept the Irish party view that to take strong action against 'the Sinn Fein element' would only 'create martyrs'. Thus the Irish Volunteers were able to train and drill quite openly from 1914 right up until the Rising, the majority of them, including their nominal chief-of-staff Professor Eoin MacNeill, in the belief that their purpose was defensive and that they would act only if it was necessary to resist suppression. This was an ideal arrangement for the secret IRB group within the movement, who were able to plan a rising, and indeed publicly announce mobilization for 'manoeuvres', in circumstances where the government had decided on avoidance of provocation as its first priority. In the final event things ran less smoothly for the Volunteers — the German ship bringing arms for the country areas was captured, and due to misunderstanding (only a small part of which was wilful) the country outside Dublin almost entirely failed to rise. The Volunteers in Dublin acted *en masse* however, now under the direction of their real IRB leaders, augmented by the republican socialist Connolly, acting as a self-styled provisional government. Of the other signatories to the proclamation, Pearse, MacDonagh and Plunkett were teachers and poets, Ceannt was also a Gaelic League activist, MacDermott had worked for some years as an organizer for Sinn Fein, while Clarke was a much older man who had served fifteen years in Portland prison for dynamite offences.

Poblacht na h-Eireann
The Provisional Government of the Irish republic to the people of Ireland

Irishmen and Irishwomen: In the name of God and of the dead generations from which she receives her old tradition of nationhood, Ireland, through us, summons her children to her flag and strikes for her freedom.

Having organized and trained her manhood through her secret revolutionary organization, the Irish Republican Brotherhood, and through her open military organizations, the Irish Volunteers, and the Irish Citizen Army, having patiently perfected her discipline, having resolutely waited for the right moment to reveal itself, she now seizes that moment, and, supported by her exiled children in America and by gallant allies in Europe, but relying in the first on her own strength, she strikes in full confidence of victory.

We declare the right of the people of Ireland to the ownership of Ireland, and to the unfettered control of Irish destinies, to be sovereign and indefeasible. The long usurpation of that right by a foreign people and government has not extinguished the right, nor can it ever be extinguished except by the destruction of the Irish people. In every generation the Irish people have asserted their right to national freedom and sovereignty; six times during the past three hundred years they have asserted it in arms. Standing on that fundamental right and again asserting it in arms in the face of the world, we hereby proclaim the Irish republic as a sovereign independent state, and we pledge our lives and the lives of our comrades-in-arms to the cause of its freedom, of its welfare, and of its exaltation among the nations.

The Irish republic is entitled to, and hereby claims, the allegiance of every Irishman and Irishwoman. The republic guarantees religious and civil liberty, equal rights and equal opportunities to all its citizens, and declares its resolve to pursue the happiness and prosperity of the whole nation and of all its parts, cherishing all the children of the nation equally, and oblivious of the differences carefully fostered by an alien government, which have divided a minority from the majority in the past.

Until our arms have brought the opportune moment for the establishment of a permanent national government, representative of the whole people of Ireland, and elected by the suffrages of all her men and women, the Provisional Government, hereby constituted, will administer the civil and military affairs of the republic in trust for the people. We place the cause of the Irish republic under the protection of the Most High God, whose blessing we invoke upon our arms, and we pray that no one who serves that cause will dishonour it by cowardice, inhumanity, or rapine. In this supreme hour the Irish nation must, by its valour and discipline, and by the readiness of its children to sacrifice themselves for the common good, prove itself worthy of the august destiny to which it is called.

Signed on behalf of the provisional government,

THOMAS J. CLARKE, SEAN MACDIARMADA, THOMAS MACDONAGH, P.H. PEARSE, EAMONN CEANNT, JAMES CONNOLLY, JOSEPH PLUNKETT.

Transcription from *The Times,* 1 May 1916

65   The Republic smashed

The Rising, restricted in the event to the hopeless defence of a few bastions, lasted only as long as it took the authorities to flood the city with troops. After a week Pearse surrendered on behalf of the Irish Volunteers, and martial law was declared throughout the country. The seven signatories of the proclamation of the republic and eight other men were shot following summary courts martial between 3 and 12 May. Another 75 death sentences were commuted to terms of imprisonment, including that passed on Eamon de Valera (1882-1975), whilst of the remaining 81 who faced courts martial 10 were found not guilty and 71 received prison sentences ranging from six months' hard labour to penal servitude for life. In addition, 1867 unconvicted prisoners were interned at Frongoch, in north Wales, or at other camps and prisons in England. By June 1917 all had been released, convicted and unconvicted, including 11 who had received life sentences.

The available evidence does not seriously weaken the traditional view that the Rising — or rather the executions and general aftermath, for the rising itself was visibly unpopular with the mass of Dubliners — was primarily responsible for stimulating the great upsurge of militant nationalist feeling which swept Ireland in 1916-18. John Dillon's bitter speech to the House of Commons, disliked and despised as it was by English Unionists and even moderate Liberals, reflects accurately the change which overtook Irish national feeling, even down to the alarmism and exaggeration over the harsh events which were taking place.

. . .I asked the Prime Minister, first of all, whether he would give a pledge that the executions should stop. That he declined to give. Secondly, I asked him whether he could tell whether any executions had taken place in Ireland since Monday morning; the last we had official notification of before I left there. The reply of the Prime Minister was 'No, Sir, so far as I know, not'. On Monday twelve executions had been made public. Since then, in spite of the statement of the Prime Minister, I have received word that a man named Kent had been executed in Fermoy, which is the first execution that has taken place outside Dublin. The fact is one which will create a very grave shock in Ireland, because it looks like a roving commission to carry these horrible executions all over the country. . . .

[On 26 April a well-known Dublin intellectual, Francis Sheehy-Skeffington, and two journalists were arrested in the street and, though not implicated in the rising in any way, shot without trial on the orders of a demented captain of the Royal Irish Rifles]. . . . All Dublin was ringing with this affair for days. It came to our knowledge within two or three days after the shooting. And are we to be told that this is the excuse for what has occurred? A more lurid light on military law in Ireland could not possibly be imagined than that a man is to be shot in Portobello Barracks — it must have been known to at least 300 or 400 military men, the whole city of Dublin knew it, his poor wife was denied all knowledge of it until her husband was lying buried in the barrack yard for three or four days — and the military authorities in Dublin turn round and say they knew nothing whatever about it until the 6th of May. How on the face of these facts, which I shall explain more fully in a few moments, can we blame the population of Dublin if they believe, as they do believe, that dozens of other men have been summarily shot in the barracks?

. . .It is the first rebellion that ever took place in Ireland where you had a majority on your side. It is the fruit of our life work. We have risked our lives a hundred times to bring about this result. We are held up to odium as traitors by those men who made this rebellion, and our lives have been in danger a hundred times during the last thirty years because we have endeavoured to reconcile the two things, and now you are washing out our whole life work in a sea of blood. . . .

Here are some of the facts that I know to be true, and I want to put it to the house of commons, do you approve of this action? One of the practices going on in the barracks is that these unhappy persons, and they have taken numbers of them, are threatened with instant death in order to force them to become informers. They are given half-an-hour of life, and then put up against a wall, and several of them have given evidence against their comrades. Is that approved of by the house of commons without any trial? Do they approve of that form of torture, because it really is torture?

. . .The great bulk of the population were not favourable to the insurrection, and the insurgents themselves, who had confidently calculated on a rising of the people in their support, were absolutely disappointed. They got no popular support whatever. What is happening is that thousands of people in Dublin, who ten days ago were bitterly opposed to the whole of the Sinn Fein movement and to the rebellion, are now becoming infuriated against the government on account of these executions, and, as I am informed by letters received this morning, that feeling is spreading throughout the country in a most dangerous degree. . . .

> HC Deb. 5th series, vol. 82, cols. 935-48 (11 May 1916)

66 The power of the press

The *Freeman's Journal* was virtually the Irish party's official daily newspaper. It reported the speeches of party leaders and the business of branches in shattering detail, and its editorials came increasingly to reflect party policy. But the paper's style and presentation took little heed of the journalistic innovations being made by Northcliffe's popular press. The *Irish Independent*, owned by a leading Dublin businessman, William Martin Murphy (1844-1921), was Ireland's largest-selling daily paper, but it tended to reflect the independent nationalist views of Murphy's friend T.M. Healy

(1855-1931) and his associate in the All-for-Ireland League, William O'Brien. Although it was bitterly hostile to the Rising — Murphy had been the main object of Larkin's and Connolly's strike activity in Dublin in 1913 — the *Independent's* criticism of the official party line gave important help to rival movements.

Frank Barrett to John Redmond MP   Cork, 12 October 1916

May I draw your attention to a most vital consideration. Circulation of the *Freeman's Journal* in this city is about 80 copies. Circulation of the *Irish Independent* well over 1,500. I believe the same thing prevails right throughout Ireland. It is a great pity that something cannot be done to reduce the size of the *Freeman* and also its price to one halfpenny. The *Independent* has done, and is doing, a lot of damage to the great nationalist movement of which you are the great leader. Its 'taproom logic' has weakened and poisoned the minds of many of your supporters, who foolishly buy it daily, for its war news and general news in a brief form, such as they dish up, Halfpenny papers are the papers of today. . . .

NLI Redmond papers, Ms. 15262/5

67 The state of Ireland, 1916: Amnesty the key?

The Rising had made nonsense of the Redmondite and government preoccupation with recruiting problems in Ireland. In a desperate effort to salvage the situation, Lloyd George instituted talks during May and June 1916 with both Ulster Unionist and Irish party leaders in the hope of implementing home rule at once. But reconciliation foundered once more on the question of whether the exclusion of Ulster should be permanent or temporary. In the long run the only significant feature of the episode was that Redmond and his Belfast colleague Joseph Devlin (1871-1934) persuaded a large gathering of Ulster nationalists to agree voluntarily to the temporary exclusion of six counties from the settlement. The Irish party could thus be branded with some degree of justification, if not with entire fairness as 'partitionist' by its republican rivals, and Ulster nationalists treated as 'acquiescent' by British governments. Attempts at settlement having failed, Irish party leaders had to look elsewhere for ways of demonstrating their efficacy to the electorate.

John Redmond MP to H.H. Asquith   30 November 1916

The condition of Ireland, though still far from satisfactory, has vastly improved within the last two months, and that improvement has been due, amongst other causes, to the release of over a thousand of the interned prisoners, and the confident expectation, which has been

spread by us, that the government contemplated a policy of conciliation, involving the removal of martial law and military rule, the
release of the remainder of the interned prisoners. Recent events and
widely spread statements in the press have confirmed that impression,
and if, in this matter of the interned prisoners, the popular expectations are disappointed the result will be a fresh outbreak of bitterness
and exasperation, which may undo all the good effected during the
last two months.

The effect of a refusal to release these men will be most dangerous to
the position and influence of the National party in Ireland, and will be
pointed to by all those in Ireland who are hostile to constitutional and
parliamentary action as a fresh proof that the British government
attach no weight to the wishes of the Irish people expressed through
their parliamentary representatives.

An amnesty movement is already on foot, and, in the event of a
refusal to release the prisoners, it will inevitably rapidly assume
immense proportions. We shall feel it necessary to support this
movement with all our influence. It will also be supported actively by
the Catholic Church in Ireland. Great meetings and processions will
be organized, and the difficulties of the government in Ireland will be
immensely increased.

After months of furious and angry agitation the prisoners will, of
course, be released, when infinite mischief has been done, and the
release can have no healing effect on the Irish situation, but would be
hailed by Sinn Feiners and extremists as one more proof that violent
agitation is the only argument to which the British government will
listen.

In the course of an amnesty movement a platform will be afforded
to all the bitterest enemies of the Irish party, and of any agreed Irish
settlement, to make inflammatory and bitter speeches, passions will be
excited, old race-hatred lashed to fury, and there will be the gravest
danger of bloody collision between the people and the police and
military.

I feel that it is unnecessary for me to enlarge on the effect of such a
condition of things in Ireland, on foreign opinion, and on the conduct
of the war. Exaggerated and highly coloured accounts of hostile and
bitter speeches in Ireland will be scattered all over the world, and no
censorship will be able to prevent the circulation of such reports. . . .
If now Ireland is to be thrown into a fresh tempest of anger and agitation by the refusal of the government to release 560 untried men at the
request of the representatives of the overwhelming majority of the

Irish people, the feeling in the dominions, and in the United States, which has recently shown signs of improvement, will be intensified against Great Britain. . . .

In conclusion, I feel it right to say that I am under no delusion as to the dangers of the Irish situation, or as to the attitude which will be adopted by these prisoners when released. But I and my colleagues feel strongly that they can do much more harm as prisoners in Frongoch than at liberty in Ireland.

NLI Redmond Papers, Ms. 15262/9

68   The state of Ireland, 1917: Abstention the key?

By Christmas 1916 all the Rising internees had been released. At a by-election in remote West Cork an unofficial candidate who pledged himself to the Irish party was successful against two independent nationalists, one of whom claimed to be a Sinn Feiner. But this was to be the Irish party's last shred of real electoral hope. The victory at North Roscommon, in February 1917, of papal Count George Plunkett (1851-1948), father of one of the men executed in 1916, over an official Irish party candidate, stimulated the development of a real political movement out of the ashes of 1916 and marks the beginning of the visible collapse of the Irish party. Plunkett's policy was 'abstention from Westminster', though its significance at this stage was less as a policy than as a touchstone of the new 'republican' nationalism, differentiating it clearly from the waning orthodoxy. The Irish party appeared to be politically bankrupt. Maurice Moore (1854-1939), Inspector-General of the now-defunct National Volunteers, took a pessimistic, but essentially correct view of the situation.

Col. Maurice Moore to John Dillon, MP   4 March 1917

I have been about the country, specially in Mayo, and have had an opportunity of discussing the political situation with very many people; with Priests, Party followers, Independents and Sinn Feiners, both there and in Dublin. I feel that it is right to inform you on this matter, even if the information is disagreeable. For many reasons I am in a better position to hear the real views of the people than members of the party or their agents.

In the first place practically all the young men are Sinn Feiners in more or less degree. Your speeches and actions ought to have mitigated hostility, but they have not; the prisoners and Sinn Feiners believe that the late arrests were instigated by the Party and that the speeches in the House were merely bluff. They are hostile both to the policy, the members and leaders of the Party, and would change all if possible.

The older and more responsible men, as an example of whom I might take the Parish Priests, are gravely dissatisfied with the party policy; they desire much more vigorous action both by *vote* and speech against any government that refuses Irish demands: They are not hostile to the leaders, whose past services they remember, but they would like to see them more active and determined — *not in talk only*. They have lost faith in the Home Rule Bill, and demand control over all taxation, and over trade, customs, and excise, and an abolition of concurrent legislation; these are three main items.

Both the young men, and the older men to whom I have referred, have lost confidence in the rank and file of the party, and will certainly change it at the next election. Local men, who were formally popular are regarded with aversion; this is a sudden and unexpected revulsion of feeling, but quite understandable when one considers the strong national feelings that have taken hold of the people.

There are some farmers who stick by the Party remembering past favours, and some shopkeepers; but both these classes are wavering and becoming amenable to the pressure of opinion. You may remember the same change gradually working in 1879 and '80.

In one parliamentary division I discussed matters with ten out of fifteen parish priests, and without exception they took the views I have reported above. I am informed the other five are not exceptions. Many of the curates go further.

This is a serious state of affairs and no speech-making in Parliament will change it, though *your* speeches might under other circumstances have been effective. If something decisive be not done the revolution may go to the extreme of changing the whole party, leaders and all.

As to what policy would be approved there is a difference of opinion, and the majority of the people are undecided. Any policy adopted will I think be attacked by some of the violent Sinn Fein papers, but the bulk of the people would, I think, agree to a really live hostility to the Government. What that is to be is worthy of consideration; no policy is suitable to every emergency; circumstances alter and policy with them. Independent opposition, party support, obstruction, rebellion, Carson's Ulster bluff, passive resistance, each is appropriate to a set of circumstances, and each has been effective in its time, and each is subject to grave difficulties at other times. I have never been an advocate for abstention from Parliament; it has not hitherto been a suitable weapon, but it may be now.

It is necessary to attract the eyes of Europe and America, and induce the Colonies to act for us. It would put England in a false position, and the Colonial Conference is approaching. If it is to be done at all it should be done with dramatic effect. The coming debate on Wednesday gives the opportunity; consider what would be the effect of 80 members walking out of the House together, after Lloyd George's speech postponing action.

The Sinn Fein proposal to bring the matter before the Peace Conference may be impracticable, but there is nothing impossible about the Imperial Conference. Some such suggestion was made by Lloyd George's settlement proposal, and moreover the Irish trade amendment can hardly be discussed without raising the question of self-government.

The danger is that it is very difficult to resume parliamentary action if objectionable legislation is threatened. It would certainly be necessary for the whole party to return to Dublin, and call together a conference of persons representative of all Ireland — not deputies from party organizations — but Chairmen of county councils, mayors and chairmen of town councils, representatives of trades, manufacturers, labour, professions, journalists and so on; some three hundred in all, and keep them in conference for a week at a time; recalling them as often as possible.

This policy will not be acceptable to cautious men; but the present dangers are imminent and an alternative is difficult to find.

NLI Maurice Moore Papers, Ms. 10561/9

69   Irish-America: A new desertion every day

The Easter Rising caught the imagination of Irish-America in a way that the Irish party had been unable to do since the home rule policy had begun to crumble in 1913. With constituency associations in Ireland collapsing and the *Freeman's Journal* close to bankruptcy, Redmond and Dillon were in desperate need of new financial resources. When America entered the war in April 1917 it was decided to ask another senior MP, T.P. O'Connor (1848-1929), to make an extended American tour in the hope that the allied war effort might have created new sympathies amongst Irish-Americans. Although O'Connor remained away for a year, and achieved a modicum of success in fund-raising, his initial impression reflected accurately enough the true facts — the bonds between constitutional nationalism and Irish-American opinion, which Parnell had forged forty years before, were now broken.

T.P O'Connor MP to John Redmond MP   Washington DC
9 July 1917

I have found my task more difficult than ever I anticipated. Feeling here about the executions and England was far more violent even than in Ireland. Indeed, it became clear to me before I was twenty-four hours in New York that the Irish here — at least of the masses — had just got back to the old position; and had learned nothing and forgotten nothing since 1846. We were scarcely in the hotel when a manageress, a big Irishwoman, announced to Hazelton [Nationalist MP] that he wasn't an Irishman at all; spoke of Tirpitz to me as the grandest man of the War because he had done the most injury to England. Then every post brought me abusive letters, some signed, some not; the language in some of them was coarse beyond imagination. The *Gaelic American* made an even more blackguardly attack, and the *Irish World,* though not so personal as the *Gaelic American,* was fierce enough, calling me the Benedict Arnold of the Irish movement.

M.J. Ryan [President of the United Irish League of America], to whom we sent a telegram on our arrival, merely replied that he had suggested to Jordan [UIL Secretary] that he should come and see us; since then not a word from Ryan. All these things brought home to me clearly that for the moment we were down and out so far as great masses of the people were concerned; and that if I had thought of attempting a public meeting it would have ended in disorder. Some women interrupted even the memorial service for poor Willie [Redmond] in New York.

I found it also a miscalculation that the entrance of America into the war would have put any stop to the Clan-na-Gael activities. It hasn't that effect in the least yet, though it may by and by. The campaign against me is active and widespread, apart from the newspapers. . .

My main work at the present moment is propaganda through the Press. . . . I have reason to hope that this active propaganda will do good; our side of the question has never been put; and the only purely Irish papers that are read by our people are against us. I have no reason to doubt that the majority of clerical opinion is either hostile to the War or not very enthusiastic. None of them have come to see me yet. [Cardinal] Gibbons, I should say, is the only one whole-heartedly with the Allies. . . .

P.S. I feel almost like James II — a new desertion every day.

NLI Redmond Papers, Ms. 15215/2

70   Volunteers and wire-pullers

The message of the North Roscommon result was hammered home by another by-election defeat for the Irish party in South Longford early in May—this time at the hands of an imprisoned Volunteer. The Irish party no longer offered inspiration to the nationalist electorate, and as a result it began also to lose more calculating supporters. But there was as yet no organized alternative party to turn to, only an assortment of pre-war Sinn Feiners, Irish Volunteers (whose leaders were still mostly in prison), and others, held together by a general feeling of *ex post facto* support for the Rising and a vague policy of withdrawal from Westminster. Count Plunkett, father of a martyr and of two other Volunteers, though elderly and lacking any political experience, filled the vacuum for several months. In Cork city and county, where for years William O'Brien and his moderate All-for-Ireland League had managed to keep most of the parliamentary seats out of the hands of the Irish party, the situation in 1917 was especially complicated.

Mary MacSwiney to Count Plunkett   Cork City, 30 May 1917

. . .I am very puzzled by the invitation. . . which has. . . not emanated from the usual Irish Volunteer sources, but from certain local politicians, who will only be prepared to act as politicians. You will, I am sure, forgive me for the sake of our common cause, for telling you that here in Cork it is necessary to be particularly careful of political wire-pulling. You are a 'trump-card' at present, you know. There are all over the country many earnest and convincing and, in their way, sincere politicians who would like to play that 'trump-card' and win; but I assure you the only friends it is safe to trust the organi-zation of an independent Ireland to must be sought—in Cork—in the ranks of the Volunteers and Cumann na mBan. You will not find them so pushing, or perhaps on the surface so capable, but you will find that both in the city and the county of Cork they are trusted because they are known to be honest. Unless your executive is composed mainly of them and controlled by them it cannot succeed. Any man who was ever prominent here either as an O'Brienite or a Redmondite will not command the confidence of the county. You would see that for your-self if you knew how high party feeling has risen here and what bitter-ness still exists. Both parties are watching, and if there is any attempt at an O'Brienite capture of the new movement it is damned at once. . .

NLI Count Plunkett Papers, Ms. 11383/6

71   Irish-Ireland revived

The release of all convicted Volunteers, including Eamon de Valera, in June 1917 coincided exactly with his nomination for another by-election vacancy in

East Clare, adjacent to his native county of Limerick. Still no formal organization has been found to give full coherence to the new political spirit, but that such a spirit existed was amply confirmed — both by the welcome given to the returned convicts as they passed through Dublin, in contrast to the lukewarm reception experienced by the internees earlier — and more especially by the shattering victory of de Valera in East Clare, with over 71 per cent of the poll in a straight fight with an Irish party candidate. The following brief comments from D.P. Moran's *Leader* convey some impression of the new spirit.

(a) . . . The new movement, miscalled Sinn Fein, is really the Irish-Ireland movement reinforced and stimulated by the Maxwell [military] regime, and by the new value given to small nations as a result of the world war. . . .

22 September 1917

(b) . . . What the Irish Party are up against today is not a policy but a protest. It serves their logic-chopping purposes to assume that they are up against a policy, and then they proceed to ask what is the policy. . . . The new movement at present has not reached the stage of political definiteness. . . . [It is]. . . a national insurrection. . . .

29 September 1917

(c) . . . The Irish language and Irish industry were, we believe, planks in the United Irish League — it is all a question of the verb to do rather than, if we may put it so, the verb to plank. . . .

3 November 1917

72 Sinn Fein: The doctrine of suppressed sovereignty

Sinn Fein ('Ourselves') had been founded as a political party by a Dublin journalist, Arthur Griffith (1872-1922), in 1905. Its goal of a dual monarchy for Britain and Ireland, on the Austro-Hungarian model, and its policy of achieving this through complete withdrawal from British institutions and the unilateral establishment of an alternative structure, attracted little serious attention. Only its name made any impact, for the anti-Redmondite Irish Volunteers of 1914-16, whose real policy was in fact the apparently very different one of securing an independent republic by military means, were erroneously dubbed 'Sinn Fein Volunteers' by police, press and people. Sinn Fein thus took no part in the 1916 rising, although Griffith and some of his associates were interned nonetheless. Differences in temperament and emphasis between Sinn Fein and the Volunteers were considerable. But the unco-ordinated election successes in 1917 brought the various leaders into closer cooperation, and placed a premium on the early resolution of differences. At Sinn Fein's tenth annual convention in October 1917 its constitution was revised in such a way as to satisfy the Volunteers, and Griffith made way for de Valera as president. The aims of the movement were declared to be 'the international recognition of Ireland as an independent Irish republic', after which 'the Irish people may by referendum freely choose their own form of government'. How this was to be achieved is not entirely clear: talk of another rising was played down, and more publicity given to Griffith's plan for an appeal to the international peace conference which was expected to follow the war.

Ireland's claim to be at the Peace Conference was based on a doctrine of international law, the doctrine of suppressed sovereignty. They could not in Ireland secure belligerent rights unless they became, *de facto,* master of the country. As Bulgaria's claim was put forward on the doctrine of suppressed sovereignty, Ireland's claim was also good. . . . Their case was strong and their case must be heard. It could only be heard on two conditions. The first was that they destroy the representation that at present existed in the English Parliament. The very existence of that representation in the English Parliament denied Ireland's claim to sovereign independence. . . . In addition, they must have in Ireland before that Conference met, and the sooner they had it the better, a constitutional assembly chosen by the whole people of Ireland which could speak in the name of the people of Ireland. . . .

Cork Examiner, 26 October 1917

73   Volunteers and land-grabbing

The strategic niceties debated between de Valera and Griffith could have made little impact on most Irishmen. But during the winter of 1917-18 a number of schemes of varying degrees of ingenuity were devised to translate 'ourselves alone' into terms more appealing to the common man. Talk of a famine caused by the mass export of Irish farm produce to England was met by imaginative publicity stunts such as the impounding of consignments of pigs at the dockside by Volunteers. On a wider scale, graziers were encouraged to obey the Department of Agriculture's order to till at least ten per cent of their land by decisions of local Sinn Fein clubs to march out and plough up their grass. The memoirs of a policeman who later became sympathetic to Sinn Fein describe one such episode in early 1918. Shortly afterwards the Sinn Fein standing committee acted firmly to stifle such class-conscious and socially divisive operations, but not before they had provided an effective boost to party recruitment in western grazing districts.

When. . . the Volunteers began to divide ranches the British government had to sit up and take notice. It was well for the Volunteers and Sinn Fein that it did so, as otherwise there would have been chaos in the country.

My first experience of land division was at a farm in a place called Toberanania, about a mile from Ballintogher village. The local Sinn Fein club decided to divide a farm among 'deserving small farmers' in the district. Since all the farmers around were 'deserving' and 'small' they all turned up on the appointed day at the farm due for division. The local secretary, who was himself a 'small' farmer, got up on a cart and announced that he was about to divide the farm. 'Hands up', he said, 'all who want an addition to their farms'. Every hand went up. I was half tempted to put up my own hand so as not to feel odd in that great forest of hands. As there were only about eighty acres to be divided it would have required a miracle almost equal to that of the loaves and fishes to satisfy that crowd of land-hungry men and women. It was at that moment that the secretary showed real leadership. 'Ladies and gentlemen', he said, 'we did not anticipate so many applications and, as you are all aware, our one ambition is to see that everybody is satisfied. We have decided to take all the names and each case will get our personal and sympathetic attention. In the meantime we shall confine ourselves to marking out the plots with the ploughs and taking over the farm in the name of the Irish Republic.' The cheering in response to this announcement could be heard miles away and after the secretary had made a few concluding remarks all present, except the police, shouted in chorus 'Up the Republic', and 'Down with British tyranny'. A few ploughmen then went into action and ploughed single furrows in a very large field to mark off divisions of land. As most of the land in question was of poor quality and too swampy for the horses, the division of the rest of it was deferred to that day week when another 'monster' meeting was to be held at the same time and place. Fortunately for the leader, he was safely behind the bars of Sligo jail that day week. When he came out some months later he was met by the bands and acclaimed a local hero. In the meantime the division of Toberanania farm was postponed indefinitely.

J.A. Gaughan, *Memoirs of Constable Jeremiah Mee, RIC* (Anvil books, Dublin, 1975), pp. 51-2

74   The one bright spot, June 1918

The reorganization and expansion of Sinn Fein was the most significant
political development in Ireland between the rising and the end of the
European war. Efforts by the Irish party and the government to find a way of
taking the steam out of the new republicanism met with no success. Lloyd
George's attempt to buy time by transferring responsibility for a settlement
back onto Irish shoulders, through the Irish Convention of 1917-18, in practice
meant time for Sinn Fein to reorganize and expand its popular support. The
Convention met in Trinity College, Dublin, under the chairmanship of Sir
Horace Plunkett from July 1917 until May 1918. Its participating membership
of about ninety consisted of an assortment of Irish party and Ulster Unionist
MPs, local councillors, peers and landlords representing southern Unionist
opinion, and leading clergymen of the main denominations. Sinn Fein
condemned the whole affair, and even John Dillon remained sceptically on the
sidelines. In the final phase of the debate both sides split: Redmond and a
minority of his Irish party colleagues reached agreement with the southern
Unionist group to implement home rule without partition, though also without
control of customs and associated duties or defence, but were thwarted by the
total opposition of the Ulster Unionists and the refusal of the majority of the
nationalists to cooperate without Ulster's agreement. By the time that the
Convention ended in total failure, Redmond had been dead for several weeks.

More important from the point of view of Irish public opinion was the
government's passage in April 1918 of a Military Service Bill giving the government discretionary power to impose conscription in Ireland by order-in-
council without further debate. Shortly afterwards almost all the Sinn Fein
and Volunteer leaders were re-interned on the basis of their alleged involvement in a highly improbable 'German plot' for another rising. The impact of
these events was described by Hugh Law (d. 1943), a Protestant landowner
from Donegal, one of the more moderate Irish party MPs.

. . .Moreover, alas! over every proposal, even the best, hangs the
shadow of conscription. By a tragic accident (for such I must suppose
it) the Report of the Convention appeared in the Irish press on the
same day as the announcement of the Cabinet's resolve to extend the
military service acts to Ireland: and the Prime Minister has indicated
his intention of associating with the 'tender' of a new home rule bill an
Order-in-Council bringing these Acts into operation. Conceive the
plight of the Irish ministry whose first task it will be to cooperate in
enforcing conscription!

No-one who has not been in Ireland during the past six weeks can
possibly realize how passionate is the resentment which has been
aroused. Those who blame the Roman Catholic bishops and the
parliamentary party for the share they have taken in the anti-

conscription movement have little sense of realities. If these had not intervened to regularize and moderate popular action, there might well have been bloodshed; and this, not in certain specially disturbed areas, but all up and down the country. My own constituency [West Donegal] has for at least a quarter of a century been completely free from agrarian or other troubles. During the sixteen years I have represented it in the House of Commons, I cannot recall a single instance of boycotting, intimidation, or similar outrage. Yet there, as elsewhere, I know that men were, and are, ready to take to the hills or die fighting in their homes rather than be compelled to join the Army. The tension is extraordinary, and the wildest stories find belief. Thus the visit of a single RAMC officer to a disused workhouse which it was thought might serve for a convalescent home at once produced a rumour that 500 soldiers had arrived in the district to commence a drive for conscripts; and quick on its heels came the statement that these were Gurkhas, specially trained to hunt men through the mountains and kill them with knives. To Englishmen it may well seem incredible that fellow-subjects of theirs should credit their rulers with intentions such as are here implied. Nevertheless, it is not only peasants who believe that the aim of an influential section here and in Ireland is not so much to gain recruits for the Army as to find a pretext for a pogrom in which the troublesome aspirations of Ireland after self-government may be once and for all quenched in blood, and the work half-done by Cromwell completed.

To this pass has a country come which in August 1914, was the 'one bright spot on the horizon'. . . .

Contemporary Review, Vol. cxiii, p. 606 (June 1918)

VII   The creation of two new states

75   Manifesto to the Irish people, 1918

The war came to an end without the implementation of conscription in Ireland. But from April until October 1918 the threat had been close enough to serve Sinn Fein as a formidable propaganda weapon until the very last days of the war. The general election of December, following only six weeks after the termination of hostilities returned Lloyd George and his coalition convincingly to power in Britain as 'the men who won the war'. But in Ireland the same pace of events was to the advantage of Sinn Fein: their resistance to conscription was remembered, while their policy of an 'appeal to the peace conference' could not yet be put to the test. The Irish party was annihilated at the polls, winning only six seats, five of which were in Ulster (and four of those as the result of a pact with Sinn Fein to avoid losing the seats to Ulster Unionists). Sinn Fein, whose election manifesto appears below, won seventy-three seats and immediately set about establishing Dail Eireann as a republican constituent assembly.

MANIFESTO TO THE IRISH PEOPLE

The coming general election is fraught with vital possibilities for the future of our nation. Ireland is faced with the question whether this generation wills it that she is to march out into the full sunlight of freedom, or is to remain in the shadow of a base imperialism that has brought and ever will bring in its train naught but evil for our race.

Sinn Fein gives Ireland the opportunity of vindicating her honour and pursuing with renewed confidence the path of national salvation by rallying to the flag of the Irish Republic.

Sinn Fein aims at securing the establishment of that Republic.
1   By withdrawing the Irish representation from the British parliament and by denying the right and opposing the will of the British government or any other foreign government to legislate for Ireland.
2   By making use of any and every means available to render impotent the power of England to hold Ireland in subjection by military force or otherwise.

3   By the establishment of a constituent assembly comprising persons chosen by Irish constituencies as the supreme national authority to speak and act in the name of the Irish people, and to develop Ireland's social, political and industrial life, for the welfare of the whole people of Ireland.

4   By appealing to the Peace Conference for the establishment of Ireland as an independent nation. At that conference the future of the nations of the world will be settled on the principle of government by consent of the governed. Ireland's claim to the application of that principle in her favour is not based on any accidental situation arising from the war. It is older than many if not all of the present belligerents. It is based on our unbroken tradition of nationhood, on a unity in a national name which has never been challenged, on our possession of a distinctive national culture and social order, on the moral courage and dignity of our people in the face of alien aggression, on the fact that in nearly every generation, and five times within the past 120 years our people have challenged in arms the right of England to rule this country. On these incontrovertible facts is based the claim that our people have beyond question established the right to be accorded all the power of a free nation.

Sinn Fein stands, less for a political party than for the nation; it represents the old tradition of nationhood handed on from dead generations; it stands by the Proclamation of the Provisional Government of Easter, 1916, reasserting the inalienable right of the Irish people to achieve it, and guaranteeing within the independent nation equal rights and equal opportunities to all its citizens.

Believing that the time has arrived when Ireland's voice for the principle of untrammelled national self-determination should be heard above every interest of party or class, Sinn Fein will oppose at the polls every individual candidate who does not accept this principle.

The policy of our opponents stands condemned on any test, whether of principle or expediency. The right of a nation to sovereign independence rests upon immutable natural law and cannot be made the subject of a compromise. Any attempt to barter away the sacred and inviolate rights of nationhood begins in dishonour and is bound to end in disaster. The enforced exodus of millions of our people, the decay of our industrial life, the every-increasing financial plunder of our country, the whittling down of the demand for the 'Repeal of the Union', voiced by the first Irish Leader to plead in the Hall of the Conqueror to that of Home Rule on the Statute Book, and finally the contemplated mutilation of our country by partition, are some of the ghastly results of a policy that leads to national ruin. . . .

The present Irish members of the English parliament constitute an obstacle to be removed from the path that leads to the Peace Conference. By declaring their will to accept the status of a province instead of boldly taking their stand upon the right of the nation they supply England with the only subterfuge at her disposal for obscuring the issue in the eyes of the world. By their persistent endeavours to induce the young manhood of Ireland to don the uniform of our seven-century old oppressor, and place their lives at the disposal of the military machine that holds our nation in bondage, they endeavour to barter away and even to use against itself the one great asset still left to our nation after the havoc of centuries. . . .

As cited in: D. Macardle, *The Irish Republic* (4th edn., 1951), pp. 919-20

76   All legitimate methods of warfare

When the revolutionary Dail — in fact little more than one-third of it, since the majority were either in prison or on business elsewhere — met on 21 January 1919 it declared Ireland to be an independent republic, issued a 'democratic programme' of social and economic policies along the broad lines of Patrick Pearse's later thought, and appointed de Valera, Griffith and Count Plunkett to present Ireland's claim at the Versailles peace conference. But despite the efforts of John Devoy and his associates in America, and of a leading Sinn Feiner in Paris itself, neither President Wilson nor the other allied leaders could be persuaded to admit the Irish delegation to the conference table. Many, possibly the majority, of the Sinn Fein electorate had no clear idea of what alternative strategy the party might adopt, other than passive resistance to the British administration. An editorial which appeared in the revived Volunteer journal indicated more clearly than did the publications of the Dail what the immediate future was to hold.

The principle means at the command of the Irish people is the Army of Ireland, and that Army will be true to its trust. . . . If they are called on to shed their blood in defence of the new-born Republic, they will not shrink from the sacrifice. For the authority of the nation is behind them, embodied in a lawfully constituted authority whose moral sanction every theologian must recognize, an authority claiming the same right to inflict death on the enemies of the Irish State, as every free national government claims in such a case. Dail Eireann, in its message to the Free Nations of the World, declares a 'state of war' to

exist between Ireland and England, a fact which has been recognized
and acted on by the Volunteers almost from their inception; it further
declares that that state of war can never be ended until the English
military invader evacuates our country.

We have thus a clear issue laid down, not by any body that could be
termed 'militarists' or 'extremists', but by the accredited representatives of the Irish people met in solemn session, in a document
drawn up with the utmost care and a full sense of responsibility, and
unanimously adopted.

The 'state of war', which is thus declared to exist, renders the
National Army the most important national service of the moment. It
justifies Irish Volunteers in treating the armed forces of the
enemy—whether soldiers or policemen—exactly as a National Army
would treat the members of an invading army. It is necessary that this
point should be clearly grasped by Volunteers.

Every Volunteer is entitled, morally and legally, when in the
execution of his military duties, to use all legitimate methods of
warfare against the soldiers and policemen of the English usurper, and
to slay them if it is necessary to do so in order to overcome their resistance. He is not only entitled but bound to resist all attempts to disarm
him. . . .

An t-Óglach, 31 January 1919

77 Shirkers and malcontents

In the early stages of the war of independence, during the first half of 1919, it
was not always clear that the various components of the republican movement
were working together as cohesively as hindsight had tended to suggest.

(a) The conscription danger brought a large accession of strength to
our ranks. Many of the newcomers were undoubtedly men whose
eyes had been opened to the necessity of the Irish Volunteers by
this moment of national peril and who joined to take their part in
the defence of the Irish people. Some, it is to be feared, were
influenced by more selfish consideration, and were affected more
by the sense of personal peril than the danger to the nation. . . we
have no time for shirkers or slackers. . . .

An t-Óglach, February, 1919

(b) Michael Collins to Austin Stack   17 May 1919

You will be interested to hear that all precedents have been abolished by the new standing committee [of Sinn Fein]. . . . The policy now seems to be to squeeze out anyone who is tainted with strong fighting ideas or I should say I suppose ideas of the utility of fighting. Of course any [sic] of the Dail ministers are not eligible for the standing committee and only a third of the entire number may be members of the Dail. The result is that there is a standing committee of malcontents, and their first act is to appoint a pacifist secretary and announce the absence of H[arry] B[oland]. Our own people give away in a moment what the Detective division has been unable to find out in five weeks.

NLI Ms. 5848

78 Stirring up a hornet's nest

The 'first shots' in the military campaign were fired by a small group of Volunteers in Co. Tipperary in January 1919. Apparently with the deliberate intention of bringing about a regular guerilla campaign they ambushed a routine delivery of dynamite to Soloheadbeg quarry, near Tipperary town, shooting dead the two unsuspecting constables who guarded it. It was the first of a number of such incidents in 1919, resulting in the deaths of 14 policemen and soldiers during the year. A rather smaller number of civilians died at the hands of crown forces during the same period. Irish clerical and nationalist opinion at this stage drew a clear line between the earnest endeavours of Sinn Fein and Dail Eireann to secure national independence, and the murders being perpetrated by small groups of Volunteers 'acting on their own initiative'. As time went on it became apparent that no such easy distinction could be made. Dail ministers like Michael Collins (1890-1922) combined their key roles in the collection and distribution of the very large Republican Loan funds that were being raised in Ireland and America with the direction of what was becoming a systematic and cohesive guerilla war. In 1920, 232 police and soldiers were killed, and later still 24 Volunteers were shot or hanged for murder, almost all of them between February and May 1921. From early 1920 onwards the mass importation of British soldiers, a new, ruthless Auxiliary Force and large numbers of 'black and tans' (Englishmen recruited into the Royal Irish Constabulary to replace the mass of Irishmen who were resigning) to deal with the worsening security situation led to repression and reprisals amongst the civilian population which effectively solidified nationalist opinion behind the IRA. In August 1919 relations between the Dail and the IRA were put on a more formal basis, and although many churchmen continued to denounce Volunteer operations, and non-military members of the Dail remained uneasy about developments, it was clear that the military campaign was what counted. Thus events which, in 1919, had seemed to many to be rather squalid or brutal episodes, assumed a more heroic stature as prospects of success loomed nearer, a stature which the nationalist framework of politics did not allow to diminish even many years afterwards.

SOLOHEADBEG MEMORIAL
Commemorating the Ambush at Soloheadbeg,
21 January 1919. . . .
Unveiled by the President of Ireland
SEAN T. O CEALLAIGH
On Sunday, 22nd January, 1950. . . .

There is a saying: 'Where Tipperary leads all Ireland follows.' This saying is well borne out by what followed the lead given the country at Soloheadbeg on Tuesday, 21 January, 1919, the day on which the first Dail Eireann unanimously adopted the Declaration of Irish Independence. On that date an engagement took place between members of the Irish Volunteers and an armed enemy party, resulting in two RIC constables being shot dead and their equipment and arms, and the explosives they were escorting, captured. . . .

It is our proud claim for Soloheadbeg, that it was the first deliberate planned action by a select party of the Irish Volunteers (shortly to be recognized as the Irish Republican Army) renewing the armed struggle, temporarily suspended, after Easter Week 1916. . . .

The men who took part in the Solohead Ambush broke so far with tradition that they refused to fly the country after their coup. This course was urged upon them, but they determined to remain and carry on the fight against the enemy wherever and whenever they could, and with ever-increasing intensity. Their lead was an incentive to the rest of the country, and before long the British were finding that they had stirred up a hornet's nest. The rescue of Sean Hogan at the Station of Knocklong in the following May further increased the morale of the IRA by showing what a few ill-armed men could achieve when they were imbued with the determination to do or die. In collaboration with the Dublin Brigade the war was brought into the streets of Dublin, including the abortive attack on the then Lord Lieutenant at Ashtown in December, 1919, which had, nevertheless, the effect of further stepping up the national morale. Barrack attacks, ambushes and raids on enemy communications followed, in all of which the Tipperary Volunteers took a leading part, leading up to the formation of regular Flying Columns in each area. . . .

D. Breen, *My Fight for Irish Freedom* (Anvil Books, (Dublin), 1964), pp. 182-3

79   The Lisburn pogrom, 1920

In Ulster the IRA campaign was inevitably more restricted and 'defensive'. The violent episodes in the south nonetheless produced a Protestant mob backlash in the north which was most pronounced in July and August 1920, and in the early months of 1922. In Belfast, Catholics and their sympathizers in the Labour movement were driven from the Protestant-dominated (and best paid) employment in shipbuilding and engineering, and the fragile non-sectarian industrial unity established during a major strike in 1919 was broken. Old-established patterns of residential segregation were reinforced and extended, as refugees from outlying districts (150 families on one day in August 1920) flooded into the main Catholic district of the Falls. Particularly bad incidents — indiscriminate attacks on Catholic houses and business premises, leading to wholesale evacuation — occurred in Banbridge, Co. Down and Lisburn, Co. Antrim after two police officers, natives of the towns, were killed by the IRA. Fred Crawford, the UVF gun-runner of 1914, described in his diary the aftermath of the Lisburn episode, in which 273 homes were burned out.

. . .I took Adair up to Lisburn to see the state it was. It reminded me of a French town after it had been bombarded by the Germans as I saw in France 1916. We visited the ruins of the Priests' house on chapel hill it was burnt or gutted and the furniture all destroyed. When coming down the avenue I found a small pair of manicure scissors that had been thro the fire. I kept them as a souvenir of the event. We called at Mr Stephensons and had tea there Mrs Thompson his sister was also with him. They told me of some very hard cases of where Unionists had lost practically all they had by the fire of the house of a Catholic spreading to theirs, and also of some very decent respectable families of long standing loosing [sic] everything also. But when one thinks of the brutal cold blooded murder of Inspector Swanzie [sic for Swanzy] one does not wonder at the mob loosing [sic] its head with fury. . . . It has been stated that there are only four or five RC families left in Lisburn others say this is wrong that there are far more. Be that as it may there certainly are practically no shops or places of business left to the RC's. . . .

P.J. Buckland, *Irish Unionism 1885-1923: a documentary history* (PRONI, Belfast, 1973), p. 445

80   The demography of partition

The Home Rule Act of 1914, which had been suspended for the duration of the war, never in fact came into operation. A new Government of Ireland Act was passed into law in 1920, providing on the one hand for a wider devolution of legislative powers (though not sufficient even to slow down or divide the Sinn Fein/IRA campaign for independence), but on the other for a partition of the country. Two devolved legislatures were to be established, one in Dublin, the other in Belfast. In the south the elections of May 1921 for 'the House of Commons of Southern Ireland' were (apart from the 4 Dublin University seats) an uncontested walkover for Sinn Fein, whose 124 representatives ignored the Act and instead constituted themselves as the second Dail Eireann. In the north, however, this partition with devolution was 'reluctantly' accepted by the Unionists as a 'final concession': elections for a 52-seat 'House of Commons' returned 40 Unionist members, together with 6 Sinn Feiners and 6 Nationalists, all of whom abstained, and a government was set up with Sir James Craig as 'Prime Minister of Northern Ireland'. The Northern Parliament's area of jurisdiction was limited to six of the nine Ulster counties (Antrim, Armagh, Down and Londonderry, which had clear Protestant majorities, and Fermanagh and Tyrone, where Catholics were slightly in the majority), which together made up the largest possible area in which Protestants could command an overwhelming majority. Unionists in the three 'abandoned' Ulster counties of Cavan, Donegal and Monaghan (where the Protestant proportion was below a quarter) who had been included in the Ulster Covenant of 1912, manipulated the demographic arguments as best they could, but to no avail.

. . .It was represented that a Parliament for the nine Counties would have a Nationalist and Sinn Fein majority. Mr Moles, MP, had the hardihood to state that it would consist of 33 Nationalists and 31 Unionists. It was pointed out to him in vain that the population of Ulster was:-

Protestants	890,880
Roman Catholics	690,816
Leaving a Protestant Majority of	200,064

and that it was impossible a majority of 200,000 should not be able to return a majority of members.

It was further shown that at the last Election [December 1918] for the nine Counties, when the number of members to be elected was 38, the members returned were

Unionists	23
Nationalists	15
Unionist Majority	8

and that Election was held on the PRESENT FRANCHISE.

It was further pointed out that the new bill gives Ulster 64 members

and that if there had been 64 at the last election the numbers would
have been

Unionists	38
Nationalists	26
	—
Giving a Unionist majority of	12

All was in vain. Mr Moles persisted in his estimate but gave no
reasons for it except that the result of the last municipal election in
Belfast was not satisfactory to certain interests there. It was insinuated
that the Unionist working men of Belfast could not be depended on as
heretofore, and therefore we must be cast out. This is a libel on the
Unionist Labour voters in Belfast. To those who are acquainted with
municipal affairs in Belfast it is not surprising that Labour should
assert itself in elections for the Corporation, but to infer from that fact
that the sturdy working men of Belfast are not as staunch Unionists as
ever they were is not only unjust but untrue. After all why should not
Unionist labour be represented in the Belfast Corporation, and even in
the Ulster Government, and why are we to be abandoned lest that
should happen?

. . .An argument that has been used is that the three Counties
contain a majority of Nationalists and Sinn Feiners. That is true. But
so does Derry City, Fermanagh County, Tyrone County, South
Armagh, South Down and the Falls Division of Belfast. Yet no one
proposes to exclude them. The truth is that it is impossible to fix upon
any exclusively Unionist area. There are more Unionists in the
Southern [i.e. Irish Free State] area than there are Nationalists in the
three Counties and no provision whatever is made for them. In their
case we are told minorities must suffer, but that doctrine seems to be
ignored where the minority is a Nationalist one. . . .

> *Ulster and Home Rule: No Partition of
> Ulster,* Statement by Delegates for Cavan,
> Donegal and Monaghan, PRONI
> Montgomery Papers, D. 627/435

81   The Anglo-Irish Treaty, 6 December 1921

The IRA's guerilla war against crown forces was halted by a truce early in July
1921. After an exchange of views and manoeuvres between the British Prime
Minister, Lloyd George, and Eamon de Valera as leader of Sinn Fein and
'President of the Irish Republic', teams of negotiators—the British led by
Lloyd George, the Irish by Arthur Griffith and IRA leader Michael

Collins—met in London throughout most of the autumn, and on 6 December signed 'Articles of Agreement for a Treaty between Great Britain and Ireland'. Southern Ireland, the 26-county area, was to have full dominion status, rather than the limited devolution of the 1920 Act. If the Parliament of Northern Ireland opted to keep the six counties out of the new scheme, as it undoubtedly would, then Article 12 provided for a boundary commission with powers to modify the partition line—although to what extent was left undefined.

1   Ireland shall have the same constitutional status in the community of nations known as the British Empire as the Dominion of Canada, the Commonwealth of Australia, the Dominion of New Zealand, and the Union of South Africa, with a parliament having powers to make laws for the peace and good government of Ireland and an executive responsible to that parliament, and shall be styled and known as the Irish Free State.
2   Subject to the provisions hereinafter set out the position of the Irish Free State in relation to the imperial parliament and government and otherwise shall be that of the Dominion of Canada. . . .
4   The oath to be taken by members of the parliament of the Irish Free State shall be in the following form: I. . . do solemnly swear true faith and allegiance to the constitution of the Irish Free State as by law established and that I will be faithful to H.M. King George V, his heirs and successors by law in virtue of the common citizenship of Ireland with Great Britain and her adherence to and membership of the group of nations forming the British Commonwealth of nations.
5   The Irish Free State shall assume liability for the service of the public debt of the United Kingdom as existing at the date hereof and towards the payment of war pensions as existing at that date in such proportion as may be fair and equitable, having regard to any just claims on the part of Ireland by way of set off or counter-claim. . . .
7   The government of the Irish Free State shall afford to his majesty's imperial forces:
    (a) in time of peace such harbour and other facilities as are indicated in the annex hereto, or such other facilities as may from time to time be agreed between the British government and the government of the Irish Free State; and
    (b) in time of war or of strained relations with a foreign power such harbour and other facilities as the British government may require for the purposes of such defence as aforesaid. . . .
11   Until the expiration of one month from the passing of the act of parliament for the ratification of this instrument, the powers of the parliament and the government of the Irish Free State shall not be

exercisable as respects Northern Ireland, and the provisions of the Government of Ireland Act, 1920, shall, so far as they relate to Northern Ireland, remain of full force and effect, and no election shall be held for the return of members to serve in the parliament of the Irish Free State for constituencies in Northern Ireland, unless a resolution is passed by both houses of the parliament of Northern Ireland in favour of the holding of such elections before the end of the said month.

12   If before the expiration of the said month, an address is presented to his majesty by both houses of parliament of Northern Ireland to that effect, the powers of the parliament and government of the Irish Free State shall no longer extend to Northern Ireland, and the provisions of the Government of Ireland Act, 1920 (including those relating to the Council of Ireland), shall so far as they relation to Northern Ireland, continue to be of full force and effect, and this instrument shall have effect subject to the necessary modifications.

Provided that if such an address is so presented a commission consisting of three persons, one to be appointed by the government of the Irish Free State, one to be appointed by the government of Northern Ireland, and one who shall be chairman to be appointed by the British government shall determine in accordance with the wishes of the inhabitants, so far as may be compatible with economic and geographic conditions, the boundaries between Northern Ireland and the rest of Ireland, and for the purposes of the Government of Ireland Act, 1920, and of this instrument, the boundary of Northern Ireland shall be such as may be determined by such commission. . . .

17   By way of provisional arrangement for the administration of Southern Ireland during the interval which must elapse between the date hereof and the constitution of a parliament and government in accordance therewith, steps shall be taken forthwith for summoning a meeting of members of parliament elected for constituencies in Southern Ireland since the passing of the Government of Ireland Act, 1920, and for constituting a provisional government, and the British government shall take the steps necessary to transfer to such provisional government the powers and machinery requisite for the discharge of its duties, provided that every member of such provisional government shall have signified in writing his or her acceptance of this instrument. But this arrangement shall not continue in force beyond the expiration of twelve months from the date hereof.

18   This instrument shall be submitted forthwith by his majesty's government for the approval of parliament and by the Irish signatories

to a meeting summoned for the purpose of the members elected to sit in the House of Commons of Southern Ireland. . . .

Articles of Agreement for a Treaty between
Great Britain and Ireland [Cmd. 1560], 1921
Sess. II, i. 75

82 A republican alternative: 'Document No. 2'

The five Irish negotiators had signed the Treaty under threat of 'immediate and terrible war' by Lloyd George if they refused. They were not given an opportunity to return to Dublin for last-minute consultations, and they did not take advantage of the telephone for communication. The Treaty which they put before the Dail for approval thus proclaimed neither a sovereign republic nor, with any degree of certainty, a united Ireland. De Valera found that the checks which he had built into the negotiating arrangements had been by-passed. He refused to be committed to so large a concession, and opposed the Treaty in the Dail. But he had been aware since the summer truce that some degree of compromise would be necessary, and in the course of debate brought forward his alternative plan, known as 'Document No. 2'. In its attempt to reconcile republicanism with the British Commonwealth, through the device of external association, it foreshadowed the arrangements which India and other new states have been able to make in more recent years. Interestingly, it also accepted the basic Treaty position on Ulster. But de Valera already knew that such a formula would not be acceptable to the British government, and in the circumstances the main function of Document No. 2 was to provide the most conciliatory rallying-ground on which all the republican opponents of the Treaty could gather during the months of dispute that followed.

That inasmuch as the 'Articles of Agreement for a treaty between Great Britain and Ireland', signed in London on December 6th, 1921, do not reconcile Irish National aspirations and the Association of Ireland with the Community of Nations known as the British Commonwealth and cannot be the basis of an enduring peace between the Irish and the British peoples, DAIL EIREANN, in the name of the Sovereign Irish Nation, makes to the Government of Great Britain, to the Governments of the other States of the British Commonwealth, and to the peoples of Great Britain and of these several States, the following proposal for a Treaty of Amity and Association which, DAIL EIREANN is convinced, could be entered into by the Irish people with the sincerity of goodwill. . . .

1   That the legislative, executive, and judicial authority of Ireland shall be derived solely from the people of Ireland.

2   That, for purposes of common concern, Ireland shall be associated

with the States of the British Commonwealth, viz:- The Kingdom of Great Britain, the Dominion of Canada, the Commonwealth of Australia, the Dominion of New Zealand, and the Union of South Africa.

3   That when acting as an associate the rights, status, and privileges of Ireland shall be in no respect less than those enjoyed by any of the component States of the British Commonwealth. . . .

6   That, for purposes of the Association, Ireland shall recognize His Britannic Majesty as head of the Association.

7   That, so far as her resources permit, Ireland shall provide for her own defence by sea, land and air, and shall repel by force any attempt by a foreign Power to violate the integrity of her soil and territorial waters, or to use them for any purpose hostile to Great Britain and the other associated States.

8   That for five years, pending the establishment of Irish coastal defence forces, or for such other period as the Governments of the two countries may later agree upon, facilities for the coastal defence of Ireland shall be given to the British Government as follows:

(a) In time of peace such harbour and other facilities as are indicated in the Annex hereto, or such other facilities as may from time to time be agreed upon between the British Government and the Government of Ireland;

(b) In time of war such harbour and other naval facilities as the British Government may reasonably require for the purposes of such defence as aforesaid. . . .

13   That Ireland shall assume liability for such share of the present public debt of Great Britain and Ireland, and of payment of war pensions as existing at this date as may be fair and equitable, having regard to any just claims on the part of Ireland by way of set-off or counter-claim, the amount of such sums being determined in default of agreement, by the arbitration of one or more independent persons, being citizens of Ireland or the British Commonwealth. . . .

16   That by way of transitional arrangement for the Administration of Ireland during the interval which must elapse between the date hereof and the setting up of a Parliament and Government of Ireland in accordance herewith, the members elected for constituencies in Ireland, since the passing of the British Government of Ireland Act in 1920 shall, at a meeting summoned for the purpose, elect a transitional Government to which the British Government and Dail Eireann shall transfer the authority, powers, and machinery requisite for the discharge of its duties, provided that every member of such transition

Government shall have signified in writing his or her acceptance of this instrument. But this arrangement shall not continue in force beyond the expiration of twelve months from the date hereof.

17   That this instrument shall be submitted for ratification forthwith by His Britannic Majesty's Government to the Parliament at Westminster, and by the Cabinet of Dail Eireann to a meeting of the members elected for the constituencies in Ireland set forth in the British Government of Ireland Act, 1920, and when ratifications have been exchanged shall take immediate effect. . . .

ADDENDUM
NORTH-EAST ULSTER

Resolved:

That, whilst refusing to admit the right of any part of Ireland to be excluded from the supreme authority of the parliament of Ireland, or that the relations between the parliament of Ireland and any subordinate Legislature in Ireland can be a matter for treaty with a government outside Ireland, nevertheless, in sincere regard for internal peace, and in order to make manifest our desire not to bring force or coercion to bear upon any substantial part of the province of Ulster, whose inhabitants may be unwilling to accept the national authority, we are prepared to grant to that portion of Ulster which is defined as Northern Ireland in the British Government of Ireland Act of 1920, privileges and safeguards not less substantial than those provided for in the Articles of Agreement for a Treaty between Great Britain and Ireland signed in London on December 6th, 1921.

Transcription from The Times, 5 January
1922

83   Cathal Brugha: A draught of poison

Cathal Brugha, *angl.* Charles Burgess (1874-1922), was, like Patrick Pearse, of partly English origin. As Minister of Defence in the revolutionary Dail, he came into frequent contact with Michael Collins, the effective leader of the IRA, and was said to be very jealous of him. Brugha was an irreconcilable republican, who was to die a few months later in a gun-battle with Free State forces. His contribution to the debate on the Treaty illustrates both the attitude of the extreme republican group towards distinctions which others saw primarily as questions of terminology, and the way in which Document No. 2 held the opponents of the Treaty together.

Now Mr Griffith has referred to the difference between this Treaty of his and the alternative that we have as being only a quibble; and yet the English government is going to make war, as they say they will, for a quibble. The difference is, to me, the difference that there is between a draught of water and a draught of poison. If I were to accept this Treaty and if I did not do my best to have it defeated I would, in my view, be committing national suicide; I would be breaking the national tradition that has been handed down to us through the centuries. We would be doing for the first time a thing that no generation thought of doing before — wilfully, voluntarily admitting ourselves to be British subjects, and taking the oath of allegiance voluntarily to an English king. . . .

. . .We are prepared to enter into an agreement, an association with the British Commonwealth of Nations as it is usually called, on the same or similar lines as that on which one business firm enters into association with another, or several others. . . . Now, by entry into a combination, no firm sacrifices its independence as a firm. We are prepared, on the same terms, to enter into an association with the British Commonwealth of Nations, and for the purpose of that combination we are prepared to recognize the English government as the head of the combination. . . . Now by entering into such arrangements we are not going into the British Empire; neither do we take any oath whatsoever; and there will be no representative of the British crown in the shape of a governor-general in Ireland. We are entering into that arrangement, into this association, as external associates. . . .

> *Dail Eireann, Treaty Debates,* pp. 325-34 (7 January 1922)

84   Sean MacEntee: Partition perpetuated

Most of the opposition to the Treaty in Dail Eireann, like that of de Valera and Brugha, focused on the question of sovereignty. The only critic to place his emphasis elsewhere, on the Ulster question, was Sean MacEntee (b.1889) — himself a Belfast man, although his later ministerial career was to be in southern politics.

I am opposed to this Treaty because it gives away our allegiance and perpetuates partition. By that very fact that it perpetuates our slavery; by the fact that it perpetuates partition it must fail utterly to do what it is ostensibly intended to do — reconcile the aspirations of the Irish people to association with the British Empire. When did the achievement of our nation's unification cease to be one of our national aspirations?

MR MILROY: I desire to ask this Deputy if he is prepared to coerce all these northern counties to come in?

MR MacENTEE: I am not responsible for policy in this Dail. If I were I might be prepared to lay a programme before you, but until I am sitting with a Government of the Republic it is not open to any man to ask me what I would do in such a case. . . .

Mr Milroy stated that the economic advantages of the case in connection with the six counties were such that, sooner or later, they would be compelled to resume association with the rest of Ireland. Does Mr Milroy. . . tell me that material or economic facts are the determining factors in nationality? Would he have said that when we were asking the people of Ireland to risk their economical welfare on the question of nationality three years ago? Ah! he would not, and if I had said that to him he would have regarded it as insulting. I say there is more in nationality and history than mere materialism; and I say because there are more than these things in history and nationality, this Treaty is the most dangerous and diabolical onslaught that has ever been made upon the unity of our nation, because, Sir, by the very effort in it we are going to be destructive of our own nationality. . . .

. . .the provisions of this Treaty mean this: that in the North of Ireland certain people differing from us somewhat in tradition, and differing in religion, which are very vital elements in nationality, are going to be driven, in order to maintain their separate identity, to demarcate themselves from us, while we, in order to preserve ourselves against the encroachment of English culture, are going to be driven to demarcate ourselves so far as ever we can from them. I heard something about the control of education. Will any of the Deputies who stand for it tell me what control they are going to exercise over the education of the Republican minority in the North of Ireland? They will be driven to make English, as it is, the sole vehicle of common speech and communication in their territory, while we will be striving to make Gaelic the sole vehicle of common speech in our territory. And yet you tell me that, considering these factors, this is not a partition provision. Ah! Sir, it was a very subtle and ironic master-stroke of English policy to so fashion these instruments that, by trying to save ourselves under them, we should encompass our own destruction. . . .

The Minister for Finance [Michael Collins], referring again to the problem of secessionist Ulster, more or less washed his hands of the whole matter when he said: 'Well, after all, what are we to do with these people?' Well I am not responsible for policy, but of all the things I may have done, this one thing I would not do: I would not let them go. I would not traffic in my nation's independence without, at least, securing my nation's unity. I would not hand over my country as a protectorate to another country without, at least, securing the right to protect my countrymen.

> *Dail Eireann, Treaty Debates,* pp. 152-8 (22 December 1921)

85   Michael Collins: Find a better way

Collins's defence of the Boundary Commission idea demonstrated the essential ambiguity which lay behind the seeming flexibility of the approach: on the one hand the Protestant north would not be coerced; on the other hand the apparent plight of northern Catholics should give no cause for long-term concern because the Boundary Commission would shortly secure the unity of the country.

. . .We have stated we would not coerce the northeast. We have stated it officially in our correspondence. I stated it publicly in Armagh and nobody has found fault with it. What did we mean? Did we mean we were going to coerce them or we were not going to coerce them? What was the use of talking big phrases about not agreeing to the partition of our country. Surely we recognize that the northeast corner does exist, and surely our intention was that we should take such steps as would sooner or later lead to mutual understanding. The Treaty has made an effort to deal with it, and has made an effort, in my opinion, to deal with it on lines that will lead very rapidly to goodwill and the entry of the northeast under the Irish parliament (applause). I don't say it is an ideal arrangement, but if our policy is, as has been stated, a policy of non-coercion, then let somebody else get a better way out of it. . . .

> *Dail Eireann, Treaty Debates,* p. 35 (19 December 1921)

86   Thomas Moles: An Irish Thermopylae

The city of Derry had in 1921 a Catholic proportion of fifty-six per cent (which in more recent years has increased to sixty-six per cent). Its outskirts were but a mile or two east of the proposed partition line and its historic centre lay on the western bank of the river Foyle, the 'natural' frontier in the area. If the Boundary Commission was to operate at all on the lines which the pro-Treaty

Sinn Feiners predicted, Derry would be the crucial test. But the city was equally important to the political mythology of Unionism, which Ulster speakers in the Westminster debate on the Treaty provisions lost no time in making clear.

Mr T. MOLES: . . .Let me now look at another matter. The city of Derry is historic ground. It enshrines memories that no Ulsterman, no man who loves his country, ought ever to forget. The very dust of its churchyard heaves with the immortal dead. The apprentice boys who made a stand in Derry created an Irish Thermopylae as noble and historic as the old, and they are buried there. Our cathedral is there. There too are the walls behind which a famished garrison fought disease and fought the enemy and held high the lamp of freedom and kept its flame pure and bright. There is no Ulsterman who would surrender a yard of them. The thing is impossible. It would outrage every sentiment and every feeling we have ever cherished and respected, and I tell you that if an attempt be made to deprive us of Derry you will succeed only when you have prevailed over a conquered community and a divided country. . . .

HC Deb. 5th series, vol. 149, cols. 340-1 (16 December 1921)

87 Republicans and the rules of warfare

On 7 January 1922 the Dail voted to approve the Treaty by the moderate margin of 64 votes to 57. De Valera had resigned the Presidency of the Republic on the previous day, and was replaced by Arthur Griffith. Collins meanwhile took a parallel role as 'Chairman of the Provisional Government of the Irish Free State' under the Treaty. In practice the two men worked together, but the myth of an independent republic going into voluntary liquidation as the result of a Treaty freely concluded with Great Britain, was maintained. Equally the Anti-Treaty party denied the right of any group to 'abolish the republic'. The split in the Dail was soon paralleled by a split in the IRA, just as it was beginning to expand its numbers and take over occupation of barracks from the retiring British forces. In April the Anti-Treaty IRA forces occupied the Four Courts and other buildings in Dublin, in defiance of Free State authorities. The politicians endeavoured to find a peaceful way round this dangerous situation, notably by means of a Collins-de Valera election pact to maintain the existing balance of forces in the new Free State parliament (or 'third Dail' to the Anti-Treatyites). But the intervention of Labour and a Farmers' Party, both of which recognized the Free State, upset this balance to the Republicans' disadvantage. Thus the new assembly consisted of 58 Pro-Treatyites and 34 other supporters of the Treaty, ranged against 36 Anti-Treatyites.

The military wing of the Republican forces, the Anti-Treaty IRA, had meanwhile sought its own form of reunion by means of a concerted attack on the north. A forty square mile section of Co. Fermanagh was held against British forces for a week in an attempt to draw the Free State leaders back into conflict with Britain over Ulster. But while Collins was for a while ready to connive at Anti-Treaty IRA activity against the north as a diversionary tactic, outward neutrality was maintained until, following his June election success, he took advantage of British assistance to drive the Anti-Treaty forces from their Dublin bastion. IRA activity in the north came to a virtual halt as civil war spread through the southern and western counties of the Free State. Notwithstanding the death of Griffith and the killing of Collins in an ambush during August, the control of towns and communications was quickly reasserted by superior Free State forces. More than 500 died in July and August however, and guerilla incidents continued in face of stern repression.

The following letter from the Chief of Staff of the Army Council of the (Anti-Treaty) IRA, sent to the Speaker of the Provisional Parliament in November 1922, maintained the myth of the inviolable republic. Shortly after the letter a Pro-Treaty member of parliament was shot dead in a Dublin street, whereupon the Provisional Government ordered the execution of four imprisoned Anti-Treaty IRA leaders without trial.

Sir,

The illegal body over which you preside has declared war on the soldiers of the Republic and suppressed the legitimate Parliament of the Irish Nation.

As your 'Parliament' and Army Headquarters well know, we on our side have at all times adhered to the recognized rules of warfare. In the early days of this war we took hundreds of your forces prisoners, but accorded to them the rights of Prisoners-of-War and, over and above, treated them as fellow-countrymen and former comrades. Many of your soldiers have been released by us three times although captured with arms on each occasion. But the prisoners you have taken you have treated barbarously, and when helpless have tortured, wounded and murdered them.

We have definite proof that many of your Senior Officers including members of your 'Parliament' have been guilty of most brutal crimes towards the IRA prisoners and have reduced your soldiers to a state of savagery in some areas.

Finally you are now pretending to try IRA prisoners before your make-believe courts. You have already done to death five after such mock ceremonials. You now presume to murder and transport the soldiers who have brought Ireland victory when you, traitors, surrendered the Republic twelve months ago.

Next to the members of your 'Provisional Government' every member of your body who voted for this resolution by which you pretend to make legal the murder of soldiers is equally guilty. We therefore give you and each member of your body due notice that unless your army recognizes the rules of warfare in the future we shall adopt very drastic measures to protect our forces.

Transcription from the *Irish Independent,* 3 December 1922

88   Legion of the Rearguard

The guerilla war continued into the spring of 1923, with the Anti-Treaty forces driven increasingly into remote mountain districts. They returned to the tactics of the war against Britain, but this time with decreasing support from the local communities on which they depended. The bitterness engendered during these months was possibly greater than at any time during the war of independence. The number of executions — 77 in six months compared to 24 under the British administration over a slightly longer period — lends support to this view. At last, following the death of the IRA chief of staff in April 1923 de Valera, who as political leader of the Republican movement had commanded little influence during the war, was able to call on his forces to conceal their arms and stand down.

Soldiers of the Republic, Legion of the Rearguard. . . . The Republic can no longer be defended successfully by your arms. . . military victory must be allowed to rest for the moment with those who have destroyed the Republic. . . . Much that you set out to accomplish is achieved. You have saved the nation's honour and kept open the road of independence. You have demonstrated in a way there is no mistaking that we are not a nation of willing bond-slaves. Seven years of intense effort have exhausted our people. Their sacrifices and their sorrows have been many. If they have turned aside and have not given you that active support which alone could bring victory in this last year, it is because they saw overwhelming forces against them and they are weary and need a rest. . . . A little time and you will see them recover and rally again to the standard. . . .

As cited in E. Neeson, *The Civil War in Ireland* (The Mercier Press, Cork, 1966) p. 75

89 Eoin MacNeill: Economic and geographical considerations

The Boundary Commission provided for in the Treaty came into existence, at the request of the Free State government, in the summer of 1924. Richard Feetham, a justice of the South African supreme court, was appointed as chairman by the British government, who also nominated an Ulster representative, J.R. Fisher, when the Northern Ireland government declined to do so. The Free State government nominated its Minister for Education, Eoin MacNeill, a distinguished Gaelic scholar and a native of Co. Antrim. First meetings were held in November 1924, and hearings continued throughout border areas during the following winter, spring and summer. Notwithstanding the appointment of MacNeill, a political minister, the whole emphasis of the Commission was judicial rather than political. The Commissioners bound themselves not to take their respective governments into confidence, and while there is evidence that Fisher largely disregarded this, MacNeill appears to have been punctilious in the extreme, keeping his governmental colleagues entirely in the dark. At last, in November 1925, a detailed leak of the proposed award appeared in the *Morning Post* newspaper. Although formal confirmation of the proposals did not become publicly available until the opening of the public records in 1968, the press leak was substantially correct: the Commission's award was limited to minor adjustments and rationalizations of the long border, reducing its length from 280 to 229 miles. In all it was suggested that 180,000 acres containing 31,000 people be transferred to the Free State (notably in south Armagh), but that 50,000 acres in east Donegal and elsewhere, containing 7,500 people, be transferred to Northern Ireland. Taken in conjunction with the sharply limited scope of the Commission, the actual loss of territory was more than the Free State government could accept. MacNeill resigned from the Commission, and the Free State leaders negotiated a new settlement with the British government, renouncing their claim to a boundary revision in exchange for absolution from their outstanding financial obligations to Britain under the Treaty. MacNeill had not proved a very effective commissioner, but his unpublished memoir, written some years later, outlines his difficulties clearly.

As regards the partition clause, Article 12 of the Treaty, there has been a great deal of misunderstanding. The same clause appears word for word in what was known as 'Document No. 2', which Mr de Valera put forward as the proper substitute for the actual Treaty during the debate about it. From the first I regarded this clause as very faulty in some respects. . . .

The clause provides that the amendment of the boundary should be in accordance with the will of the inhabitants but only so far as this would appear compatible with economic and geographical considerations. The will of the inhabitants was ascertainable, but the economic and geographical considerations were left entirely to be decided by the commission in accordance with any opinion that its members might happen to hold. Moreover it was evident that the decision of the commission, if it came to any, would be dominated by the voice of the chairman representing the British government. . . .

One thing I was able to observe for myself in the course of the proceedings was that the chairman was very deeply impressed by the evidence brought forward on two points. One of these was the conduct of the 'B Specials' [a part-time police force attached to the Royal Ulster Constabulary, exclusively Protestant, which was used extensively during the troubles], the other was the gerrymandering of the [Ulster] constituencies. . . . I specially recommended that the Free State government should have recourse to the League of Nations which had made the protection of minorities a prominent part among its objects. Nothing was done in this way. My own opinion is that the government made the mistake of thinking that good relations could be promoted by avoiding drawing attention to objectionable features on the British side.

> MacNeill Papers, cited in F.X. Martin & F.J. Byrne (eds.), *The Scholar Revolutionary*, (Jas. Duffy & Co. Ltd., Dublin, 1973) pp. 269-72

90   Republicans and the golden chariot of English finance

A three-party political system emerged quickly in independent Ireland, and has remained remarkably stable. Cumann na nGaedheal (as the Pro-Treaty party became in 1923), perhaps inevitably in view of its origins, has been the most cautious, moderate and 'pro-British' of these parties. It lost power for the first time in 1932 and re-emerged, after a short period of crisis and flirtation with Italian-style fascism in the form of the Blueshirt movement, essentially unchanged as Fine Gael. Its subsequent periods in office were only made possible by coalition with the Labour party, a moderate reformist body which has remained very much the third party in the state. The Anti-Treaty Republicans followed the civil war with a period of parliamentary abstention, but their main stream entered the Dail as Fianna Fail in 1927, winning power in 1932. During this period the party placed more emphasis on industrial development, and hence on protection against British products, than its predecessors had done, and a tariff war with Britain lasted from 1933 to 1938. In 1936 it produced a new External Relations Act, ending the Free State, but maintaining external association with the British Commonwealth and in the following year a new constitution, which recognized the 'special position of the Catholic church' within the state. Its basis of support had by now widened

considerably from its western and small-farm origins, but in winning control of
the centre of the political stage and becoming the 'natural majority' party it
had disappointed many republicans, social radicals and anti-clericals. The
IRA, sometimes operating with Sinn Fein as a political wing, provided a more-
or-less permanent focus for this array of dissidents, though always resisting
efforts to turn it into 'Free State party number four'. Not all IRA opinion was
left-wing but, except in the north where resistance to partition was sometimes
enough, the old Connollyite synthesis of the national and class struggles offered
the only really coherent republican critique of the orthodox political parties.
One statement of this position was made in the majority resolution of the short-
lived Republican Congress movement of 1934.

. . .2   Our freedom can only be achieved by the destruction of the
imperialist puppet states in the North and South. Whoever stands in
the way of a free united republic for all Ireland is an ally of British
imperialism. Incessant struggle on every field must expose the
hypocrisy and anti-working class bias of those who stand for anything
less.
3   The success of such a struggle can be guaranteed by the leadership
of the well organized, disciplined forces of the working class, leading
the whole mass of the impoverished and badly oppressed sections of
the toilers in the towns and of the small farmers in the country. . . .
4   We have learnt by the sad betrayals of middle-class leaders in the
past that the working class must be the leaders if our republican ideals
are to succeed. The Irish working class is the only class that cannot be
bought by the economic concessions of the British imperialists,
because the satisfaction of its full demands is impossible within the
confines of any system under which it remains subject to wage-earning
and profit-making exploitation.
5   The main body of capitalist and financial interests in the country,
based on the exploitation of the working class, is in alliance with the
imperial state. These allies of British imperialism sacrifice the
interests of the nation to their own immediate interests. Instead of
organizing against British imperialism they organize for it.
6   While it is true that certain sections of Irish capitalists develop an
opposition to the British Empire for the purpose of securing the
exploitation of the Irish market in their own interest, it is equally true
that this opposition can always find terms of settlement *within the
Empire,* and the reality of the danger of Irish capitalism attempting to
make its compromise with imperial interests the basis of a national
settlement was clearly shown by the general acquiescence in
Document No. 2 by the anti-Treaty section of Dail Eireann.

7   Only by uprooting capitalism, the whole system of exploitation from which imperialist domination flows, only by bursting the economic chains which bind us to the golden chariot of English finance, only by establishing a new political and economic system of society can we assure ourselves of freedom from English domination. . . .

Republican Congress, 29 September 1934

91   The Republic declared, 1948

The External Relations Act of 1936 signalled an effective end to Ireland's involvement in the affairs of the British Commonwealth. Two years later, as part of the tariff war settlement, Britain surrendered control of the Irish naval bases which she had held under the Treaty, thus making it possible for the Irish government to adopt a neutral foreign policy. The wartime Fianna Fail governments withstood both the sporadic efforts of the IRA to embroil them with the Nazis and the more serious pressures applied in an attempt to enlist them in the Allied cause.

The continuation of partition was presented as the moral justification for neutrality, but public emphasis on this issue rebounded on Fianna Fail in the immediate postwar period in the shape of Clann na Poblachta, a new political party — constitutional, but radical, republican and antipartitionist — which won ten crucial seats in the 1948 general election. Fianna Fail was thus replaced by an Inter-Party government consisting of the formerly pro-Commonwealth and somewhat conservative Fine Gael, the rival Labour and National Labour parties, and Clann na Poblachta, along with some smaller groups. It was this improbable coalition which surprised the world, in the autumn of 1948, by at last declaring an Irish Republic and formally renouncing its membership of the British Commonwealth. This speech by the coalition leader, John A. Costello (1891-1976), on the second reading of the Republic of Ireland Bill, sets out the case for his government's action. The weakness of the arguments relating to partition indicate the relatively low priority of that issue in the practical politics of the new republic.

This Bill will end, and end forever, in a simple, clear and unequivocal way this country's long and tragic association with the Institution of the British Crown and will make it manifest beyond equivocation or subtlety that the national and international status of this country is that of an independent republic. It is necessary for me to state what I believe to be the effect of this Bill as clearly and as emphatically as possible so that there can be no arguments in the future, no misunderstandings, no suggestions that lurking around the political structure of this state there is some remnant or residue of that old institution and that politicians might be able to seize upon that for their own purposes, for the purposes of vote-catching or for the purposes of evoking again the anti-British feeling which has been fruitful ground on which politicians have played for many years past. . . .

. . .Nothing that can be done by this measure will in any way be a retrograde step in our relations with that country. Our people pass freely from here to England. We have trade and commerce of mutual benefit to each other. We have somewhat the same pattern of life, somewhat the same respect for democratic principles and institutions. The English language in our Constitution is recognized as the second official language of this nation. But we have still stronger ties than even those. Our missionary priests, nuns and brothers have gone to England and have brought the faith there, and are giving no inadequate contribution to the spiritual uplift which is so necessary in the atheistic atmosphere of the world today. We have our teachers there, lay and religious; we have our doctors and professional men there; we have our working men and our craftsmen and our girls who have gone over to earn a living there.

. . .But no people can be expected willingly and permanently to accept as part of their political institutions the symbol of the British Crown, when fidelity to the Catholic faith, the faith of the vast majority of our Irish people, was throughout the years regarded as disaffection and disloyalty to the British Crown, when love of country became treason to the British Crown, when every attempt to secure personal rights and national liberty was deemed rebellion against the Crown. . . .

. . . In the Dail debates of 20 June 1947 the question was put: 'Who is our head of State?'. . . Mr McGilligan said:

'With regard to the Constitution, I have often queried whether or not we had an individual known as the head of the State. The Minister for Posts and Telegraphs is so bemused about the situation that he thinks the President is the head of the State. He told me so in a recent debate. I do not think he would claim that he is that. If we had a Head of State in this country—

THE TAOISEACH [Mr de Valera]: We have.

MR McGILLIGAN: I say 'no'.

THE TAOISEACH: The President is the head of the State.

MR McGILLIGAN: The President is not the head of the State.

THE TAOISEACH: He is.'

I am pointing out to the Dail and to the people of the country the kind of thing that was bringing us into disrepute, the kind of thing we want to stop by this Bill.

As regards the question: were we a member of the Commonwealth of Nations or not? — that was a matter of acute controversy also. On 11 July 1945. . . . Mr [James] Dillon raised the point as follows:

'MR DILLON: Are we a republic or are we not, for nobody seems to know?

THE TAOISEACH [Mr de Valera]: We are, if that is all the Deputy wants to know.

MR DILLON: This is a republic. That is the greatest news I have heard for a long time. Now we know where we are. . . .'

Apparently then, as a result of all that we had reached the point where everybody said we were not a member of the Commonwealth of Nations. That is the answer to those who are asking us why we are leaving the Commonwealth of Nations. We are not leaving it because we left it long ago. In my view we left it in 1936. . . .

What about partition? What about its [the Bill's] effect on partition? When this Bill has passed, every section of this community in Ireland, every section of this Irish people, can unite with all their energies directed and not distracted towards a solution of this last political problem. . . . You have only to look at the map, or to ask any soldier to look at the map, to realize how the unity of Ireland would serve the cause of the maintenance of peace. Look at what it would mean to the cause of peace in this country; look at what a bulwark a united country would be to any menacing horde that might threaten the peace of the world. . . .

> *Dail Debates,* cxiii, 347-90 (24 November 1948)

92   Eamon de Valera: The case for introducing religion

The republican support which Fianna Fail lost by entering and taking office in Free State politics had no apparent impact on its political fortunes. Under the leadership of Eamon de Valera (to 1959) and his successors, the party was out of office for scarcely a decade in the following half-century. Far more important than militant support lost was Catholic respectability gained. A party whose leaders had frequently been denied the sacraments during the civil war period was able, during the 1930s, to build a bridge between the Catholic church and anti-treatyite nationalism which removed its opponents' advantage in this respect. The keystone in this arch was the special position of the Catholic church established by the Constitution of 1937, but the groundwork had been prepared over a number of years.

In 1931 a committee of Mayo County Council had opposed the appointment of a Protestant to the post of county librarian. The Cumann na Gaedheal government, notwithstanding its reputation as a guardian of Catholic interests, found itself in the position of defending the choice of the Local Government Appointments Commission which it had set up to control jobbery. De Valera, as leader of Fianna Fail, was not slow to identify his party with the uncompromising Catholic position. The Protestant librarian was found an equivalent post elsewhere but the incident, which was by no means an isolated one, seemed to confirm the prejudices of Northern Ireland Protestants concerning their southern neighbour.

I believe that every citizen in this country is entitled to his share of public appointments, and that there should not be discrimination on the ground of religion, discrimination, mind you, in the sense that because a person was of a particular religion, religion should not be made an excuse for denying a person an appointment for which he or she was fully qualified. Then there comes the question, what are qualifications? If I thought that the principle that the librarian in a Catholic community should be Catholic was a new principle, introduced merely to deny a Protestant an appointment, I would vote against it, but I know from my youth that it is not so. So does the Minister for Local Government, and so does every Catholic Deputy in this House. They know, if they have been instructed in the matter at all, that the guardianship of education has been jealously looked after, so far as Catholics are concerned. So far as education is concerned they made tremendous sacrifices in order to see that Catholic children were educated in accordance with Catholic principles. There is, however, even more than education in it, and the Minister knows it. On the occasion to which I refer the reason that I was going to speak was because the appointment was in connection with a doctor. Now, I say deliberately that it is not because we want to use religion as an excuse that this matter is raised by Catholics in the country. If they are raising it, it is because everybody knows that at the moment of death Catholics are particularly anxious that their people should be attended by Catholic doctors. I say that if I had a vote on a local body, and if there were two qualified people who had to deal with a Catholic community, and if one was a Catholic and the other a Protestant, I would unhesitatingly vote for the Catholic. Let us be clear and let us know where we are. . . .

If this librarian were simply a sort of clerk, who attended to somebody who came in and handed out a book which that person asked for, then I would not have any hesitation in saying that it was not an educational position, and that there was no reason whatever for introducing religion in that case. . . but if the librarian goes round to the homes of the people trying to interest them in books, sees the children in the schools and asks these children to bring home certain books, or asks what books their parents would like to read; if it is active work of a propagandist educational character — and I believe it must be such if it is to be of any value at all and worth the money spent on it — then I say the people of Mayo, in a county where, I think — I forget the figures — over 98 per cent of the population is Catholic, are justified in insisting upon a Catholic librarian.

Dail Debates, vol. 39, cols. 516-518 (17 June 1931)

93 National Health: An issue of the gravest moral and religious importance

From the 1920s to the 1950s, if not beyond, the status and influence of the Catholic church in the Irish State appeared to be increasing. The proportion of priests in the population increased steadily also, from 1:879 in 1911 to 1:558 in 1961. Catholic social teaching, part of a wide international movement in the church, made a deeper and more lasting impact in Ireland than perhaps anywhere in the western world. Only the readiness of most serious politicians in the period to acknowledge the special authority of the Catholic church on a wide range of social issues avoided the bitter church-state controversies which had troubled many European countries a half-century earlier.

Marital and medical matters had for long been areas of special concern for the Catholic church. Divorce is not permitted in the Irish Republic, and the importation of contraceptives, even for private use, remained illegal until the 1970s. The most serious conflict in this area was over the 'mother and child' health scheme in 1950-1. Introduced by the Clann na Poblachta Health Minister in the Inter-party government, Dr Noel Browne, the scheme sought to provide free state medical care for mothers and for children up to the age of sixteen. The Catholic hierarchy informed the Taoiseach, John A. Costello, of its opposition to the scheme in the following letter, dated 10 October 1950. The matter remained private for some months, but Dr Browne failed to reach an accommodation and resigned in April 1951 when his own cabinet colleagues withdrew their support. He immediately released the relevant correspondence to the press, and the material was later published as a propaganda pamphlet by the Ulster Unionist party.

Fianna Fail legislation in 1953 eventually provided free health care on a means-tested basis for the poorest section of the population, and offered subsidized provision for which the majority of others were eligible. The most striking feature of the episode was the wide interpretation of Catholic moral teaching employed by the hierarchy, and the alacrity with which all components of the Inter-party government acceded to its views.

The Archbishops and Bishops of Ireland, at their meeting on October 10th, had under consideration the proposals for Mother and Child health service and other kindred medical services. They recognize that these proposals are motivated by a sincere desire to improve public health, but they feel bound by their office to consider whether the proposals are in accordance with Catholic moral teaching.

In their opinion the powers taken by the State in the proposed Mother and Child Health Service are in direct opposition to the rights of the family and of the individual and are liable to very great abuse. Their character is such that no assurance that they would be used in moderation could justify their enactment. If adopted in law they would constitute a ready-made instrument for future totalitarian aggression.

The right to provide for the health of children belongs to parents, not to the State. The State has the right to intervene only in a subsidiary capacity, to supplement, not to supplant.

It may help indigent or neglectful parents; it may not deprive 90 per cent of parents of their rights because of 10 per cent necessitous or negligent parents.

It is not sound social policy to impose a state medical service on the whole community on the pretext of relieving the necessitous 10 per cent from the so-called indignity of the means test.

The right to provide for the physical education of children belongs to the family and not to the State. Experience has shown that physical or health education is closely interwoven with important moral questions on which the Catholic Church has definite teaching.

Education in regard to motherhood includes instruction in regard to sex relations, chastity and marriage. The State has no competence to give instruction in such matters. We regard with the greatest apprehension the proposal to give to local medical officers the right to tell Catholic girls and women how they should behave in regard to this sphere of conduct at once so delicate and sacred.

Gynaecological care may be, and in some other countries is, interpreted to include provision for birth limitation and abortion. We have no guarantee that State officials will respect Catholic principles in regard to these matters. Doctors trained in institutions in which we have no confidence may be appointed as medical officers under the proposed services, and may give gynaecological care not in accordance with Catholic principles.

The proposed service also destroys the confidential relations between doctor and patient and regards all cases of illnesses as matter for public records and research without regard to the individual's right to privacy.

The elimination of private medical practitioners by a State-paid service has not been shown to be necessary or even advantageous to the patient, the public in general or the medical profession.

The Bishops are most favourable to measures which would benefit public health, but they consider that instead of imposing a costly bureaucratic scheme of nationalized medical service the State might well consider the advisability of providing the maternity hospitals and other institutional facilities which are at present lacking and should give adequate maternity benefits and taxation relief for large families.

The Bishops desire that your Government should give careful consideration to the dangers inherent in the present proposals before they are adopted by the Government for legislative enactment and, therefore, they feel it their duty to submit their views on this subject to you privately and at the earliest opportunity, since they regard the issues involved as of the gravest moral and religious importance.

> Transcription from: *The Irish Times,*
> 12 April 1951

94   The bishop of Clogher on the duties of teachers

By and large politicians were so cautious in their handling of church-state questions that any potential conflicts which did surface were the outcome of initiatives by third parties. Thus when an international soccer match was scheduled between Ireland and Yugoslavia in Dublin in 1955, the archbishop of Dublin's chancellor complained at this recognition of a regime which had oppressed Catholics generally, and maltreated an archbishop in particular. The Ministry of Defence withdrew its offer of a band for the occasion, and the state-controlled radio station cancelled its plans for a commentary (the match went ahead as planned, before a good crowd). The only clear example of state resistance to church pressure has been Fianna Fail's passage of the Intoxicating Liquor Bill of 1959 in face of hierarchical opposition to Sunday opening.

In education, the Catholic church has customarily played a very active role. The 'non-Catholic' atmosphere of Ireland's oldest and best-endowed university, Trinity College, Dublin, caused it to be closed to Catholic students in the Dublin archdiocese by archiepiscopal ban until 1970. In the schools, Catholic social teaching influenced the requirement between 1934 and 1952 that all women resign their posts upon marriage. In elementary school education, where the state has long acknowledged the Church's special interest, it was the teachers' trade union — itself overwhelmingly Catholic in membership — which occasionally pressed matters to a confrontation.

Only a few days after the Irish Minister for Education had been expressing his satisfaction at the concord existing between church and state over education in Ireland, an attack has been made upon his Department and upon the Irish National Teachers' Organization by Dr O'Callaghan, bishop of Clogher, at a confirmation service in his diocese on June 5th.

The bishop's accusation was that the teachers want to take the schools out of the hands of the church, to give them over to the state. His suspicions were apparently aroused by hearing that the teachers were anxious that their schools should in future be cleaned, lighted and heated by the local authorities. This suggested to him that the teachers were becoming snobs. Why should a caretaker be required to clean out a school 'for these lords who are coming in for a few hours?' The teachers should remember that 'they are ordinary people like the rest of us, and that it is not beyond any of us to take the dust off our desks or to light our fires.'

The bishop's words are symptomatic of the conflict that exists between the teachers and the managers of the Irish primary schools. Teachers are paid by the Department of Education, but they are selected by the school manager, who is the parish priest (or the rector, in the case of Protestant schools). The system was designed as a compromise between the claims of church and state. . . .

Times Educational Supplement, 13 June 1952

95 'These embankments of Irish'

Irish had ceased to be the working language of the majority of the Irish people even before the introduction of a publicly-supported school system in 1831. By 1911 the number of Irish-speakers in the population had fallen to less than eighteen per cent. The Irish revolutionary elite of 1916-22 had almost all entered political life initially through the Gaelic League, and so both the major parties in the new state were intensely committed to the revival of the 'national' language. All these leaders saw a close connection between language and national identity, and for many of them the restoration of Irish as the language of the state, or the creation of genuine bilingualism, was a serious goal. The schools were the focus of this policy. Whereas in 1922 less than half the national (i.e. primary) school teachers were qualified to teach through the medium of Irish, by 1937 the vast majority were so qualified. Between 1928 and 1954 most infant classes were taught entirely in Irish. After 1932 the Fianna Fail government attempted to increase the pace of change, and by the end of its long first tenure of office in 1948 probably more than half the class-time of all elementary school children was devoted to Irish language study. In academic secondary schools Irish became a compulsory element in the School Leaving Certificate (in 1959 over one-third of total Certificate failures were due entirely to failure in Irish). In 1973 the Fine Gael Minister for Education reduced Irish to voluntary status in the Certificate, but school grants still depend on the bulk of their pupils taking courses in the subject. In 1961 twenty-seven per cent of the population aged three years and over claimed competence in the language.

In recent years popular opinion appears to have been hostile, if not to the language revival itself, at least to the policy of using the schools as the spearhead of the movement. The Irish National Teachers' Association has expressed concern about its negative effects on general educational achievement since the 1930s. Thomas Derrig, Education Minister (with one brief gap) from 1932 to 1948, had little time for parental opinion, and sought to place the issue on a higher moral plane (a). De Valera, himself a former mathematics teacher, took a similar view (b). No official enquiry into the educational impact of the language policy has ever been implemented, but a private survey, carried out in the early 1960s by a Catholic priest/educationalist with the cooperation of the Irish Department of Education, tended to confirm the earlier doubts of parents and teachers (c).

(a) We in this country are threatened to be engulfed by the seas of English speech washing our shores, so to speak, not alone from one side, but from the other, not alone through the newspapers, but through films and through the radio. I do not know how anybody can maintain that the unequal struggle can be maintained by the protagonists of Irish, unless we try to regard this as a matter in which we must have wholehearted effort. . . . We are trying to set up these embankments of Irish, these dykes, in order to keep out the tide of anglicization and it is a very urgent matter indeed that we should get these embankments up.

Dail Debates, lxxxvii, 761-2 (2 June 1942)

(b) . . . If we want the second language, if we want to do Irish as well, do not imagine that we can do it in the same time. . . . When children go through the whole of the school course, you cannot expect that at the end of the fourth or fifth year they will have the same facility in reading or writing English as pupils who would be concerned with only the English language. That is the test that parents apply today. The ordinary parent, who does not know Irish, and who wants to test the child, just puts out his chest and says: 'When I was your age I was able to read the sixth book'.

Mr D. Morrissey: Is that not the test which will also be applied by the ordinary employer of the child?

The Taoiseach: I will deal with that aspect of the matter and, if Deputies so desire, I will go into all the details. I think it is time we got to close grips with this subject. We ought not to beat about the bush. I say that you cannot in the same time do all the things that formerly we did in arithmetic, over and above the essentials. Certain non-essential things must be cut off. We must have time for doing Irish, first of all, by cutting off the unnecessary things in arithmetic. It will be necessary, of course, for a boy to know ordinary multiplication, addition, subtraction, division and simple decimals. If you cut off the extra things we used to do you will have sufficient time for the extra thing which has come in — Irish.

We shall have to be satisfied with a less high standard in English. There is no other way out of it. So far as the schools are concerned, you cannot have the same high standard if you are doing Irish as we had before; it is unreasonable to expect it. At the same time that is not saying that the child is not as well educated. . . .

Dail Debates lxxxiii, 1094-5 (27 May 1941)

(c) The incentives put forward for learning Irish are cultural and political only, and they do not appear to inspire any sense of urgency in the majority of Irish people. Their children live in an English-speaking environment and depend for their knowledge of Irish almost entirely on their teachers. Thus, unlike bilingual children in the USA, Irish children are asked to acquire a second language which is not the language of the world they live in.

The Irish child differs in another way from his counterpart in countries such as France or Sweden, where a second language is sometimes taught in primary schools. Irish national schools as we have seen devote 42 per cent of the available time over the first six years to Irish, and only 22 per cent to English. Whereas in other countries the proportion devoted to the second language is very much less than that devoted to the mother tongue.

It is a serious matter that native-English speakers who are taught arithmetic in Irish should be retarded in arithmetic as a result. But this is not so serious as the effect of the general policy for the restoration of the Irish language on attainment in English. . . . The effect on English attainment, on the other hand, is very grave indeed, since all Irish national school children whose mother tongue is English (over 96 per cent of national school children) are involved. Many of them leave school with no more than a primary education, so it is doubtful if they will have an opportunity of catching up on their counterparts in Great Britain whose attainments in English, after all, few would regard as satisfactory. Those amongst Irish children who go forward to various forms of secondary education are less well prepared than they might be to follow secondary school courses in which the reading of books in English will form a major part of their work. On the credit side they have a reasonably good knowledge of Irish for children who have learned the language in school only; but this is not to say that the aim of restoring the Irish language is nearer to realization today than at the turn of the century when Douglas Hyde founded the Irish [*sic* for Gaelic] League. . . .

J. Macnamara, *Bilingualism and Primary Education: A Study of Irish Experience* (Edinburgh University Press, Edinburgh, 1966), pp. 135-8

96 'The fiercest literary censorship this side of the Iron Curtain'

Equally sustained efforts have been made since the inception of the Free State to insulate the Irish people from the mainstream of Anglo-American cultural influence in other ways (even when the purveyors of such influence have themselves been Irish), most notably by literary censorship. A Committee of Enquiry on Evil Literature was set up by the Cumann na Gaedheal government in 1926, primarily to consider what might be done about excluding salacious British magazines and newspapers from the Free State. The Censorship of Publications Act, passed in 1929, created a Censorship Board which could recommend to the government the banning of any book which its part-time unpaid members considered obscene or indecent, or which advocated birth-control. In 1946 the Censorship Act transferred the initial banning power directly to the Censorship Board, and authorized customs officials to seize any incoming literature which they thought the Board should see.

In practice the Board from its earliest days interpreted its brief very widely, banning a large number of works of international literary repute as well as the predictable batches of pornography. It was scarcely surprising that the writer Robert Graves, a frequent victim of the Board, described its operations as 'the fiercest literary censorship this side of the Iron Curtain' (*Irish Times*, 22 June 1950). In 1967 some flexibility was introduced by limiting all bans to a twelve-year period (renewable). In recent years Board policy has been more liberal, and recent Irish governments have endeavoured to make the country an attractive tax-haven for writers. But the long predominance on the Board of the thinking which denied some of the following, (a) and (b), to Irish readers was not quickly forgotten by the state's critics, internal or extenal. Like the laws against divorce and contraception, strict censorship has survived for so long partly because the proximity of the United Kingdom and the open border have acted as a safety-valve: the forbidden items and services have in practice been fairly readily obtainable outside the state by those with sufficient money and energy.

One of the most vigorous attempts to discredit the Censorship Board was made in the Irish Senate in November/December 1942, when attention was focused on the Board's banning of certain books, including *The Tailor and Ansty*, a rabelaisian novel set in rural Cork by an Englishman, Eric Cross, and *The Laws of Life*, a medical book by a Catholic gynaecologist, Dr Halliday Sutherland, published by the leading Catholic publishing house, Sheed and Ward. In 1941 the Board had banned *The Laws of Life* altogether, even though the second edition (published in 1936) had appeared with the *permissu superiorum* of the Catholic archbishop of Westminster. The Senate motion of 'no confidence' in the Censorship Board was defeated by 34 votes to 2.

(a) Some books banned by the Censorship Board in the 1930-46 period

FARRELL, James T.	Studs Lonigan (17 July 1936)
FAULKNER, William	7 titles, inc. Sanctuary and As I Lay Dying (27 October 1931) (17 December 1935)
FRANCE, Anatole	A Mummer's Tale (27 November 1936)
FREUD, Sigismund	Collected Papers (vol. II) (11 August 1944)
GOGARTY, O. ST John	Going Native (23 January 1942)
GRAVES, Robert	Claudius the God and His Wife Messalina (25 September 1936) I, Claudius (25 September 1936) Wife to Mr Milton (11 August 1942)
GREENE, Graham	Brighton Rock (14 February 1939)

	It's a Battlefield (11 February 1938)
	Stamboul Train (18 October 1938)
HEMINGWAY, Ernest	A Farewell to Arms (31 March 1936)
	Fiesta (12 September 1941)
	For Whom the Bell Tolls (10 June 1941)
	To Have and Have Not (11 February 1938)
HUXLEY, Aldous	After Many a Summer (9 February 1940)
	Antic Hay (12 August 1930)
	Brave New World (8 March 1932)
	Brief Candles (11 July 1930)
	Eyeless in Gaza (1 September 1936)
	Point Counter Point (13 May 1930)
ISHERWOOD, Christopher	Goodbye to Berlin (13 June 1939)
MAUGHAM, Somerset	6 titles, inc. Cakes and Ale (7 Nov 1930)
MEAD, Margaret	Coming of Age in Samoa (15 August 1944)
	Growing Up in New Guinea (15 Aug 1944)
MOORE, George	A Storyteller's Holiday (20 January 1933)
MORAVIA, Alberto	Wheel of Fortune (11 March 1938)
O'CASEY, Sean	I Knock at the Door (16 May 1939)
	Pictures in the Hallway (8 May 1942)
	Windfalls (4 December 1934)
O'CONNOR, Frank	Dutch Interior (12 July 1940)
O'FAOLAIN, Sean	Bird Alone (1 September 1936)
	Midsummer Night Madness (22 April 1932)

PROUST, Marcel	Remembrance of Things Past: Vol. 9 (The Captive) Pt. 1 (9 April 1943) Vol. 10 (The Captive) Pt. 2 (9 April 1943) Vol. 11, Pt. 2 (Sweet Cheat Gone) (9 April 1943) Vol. 12 (Time Regained) (9 April 1943)
STEINBECK, John	The Grapes of Wrath (9 February 1940) To a God Unknown (16 August 1935)

(b) Some books banned in the 1946-66 period

AMIS, Kingsley	Lucky Jim (16 April 1954) That Uncertain Feeling (20 June 1956)
BECKETT, Samuel	Watt (20 October 1954) Molloy (20 January 1956)
DOLCI, Danilo	To Feed the Hungry (12 June 1962)
FORESTER, C.S.	The African Queen (20 June 1951)
GIDE, André	Fruits of the Earth (15 February 1951)
HELLER, Joseph	Catch 22 (13 November 1962)
HEMINGWAY, Ernest	Across the River and into the Trees (17 November 1950) The Sun Also Rises (14 November 1952)
HYDE, H. Montgomery	Roger Casement (9 June 1964)
KAZANTZAKI, Nikos	Zorba the Greek (10 October 1952)
KENYATTA, Jomo	Facing Mount Kenya (19 June 1953)
KOESTLER, Arthur	The Age of Longing (15 May 1953) Arrow in the Blue (13 February 1953)
McCARTHY, Mary	The Group (21 January 1964)

MANN, Thomas	The Holy Sinner (1 August 1952)
	The Black Swan (19 November 1954)
	The Confessions of Felix Krull (18 Nov '55)
MOORE, Brian	Wreath for a Redhead (19 December 1952)
	The Lonely Passion of Judith Hearne (11 February 1958)
MURDOCH, Iris	The Flight from the Enchanter (15 June 1956)
	A Severed Head (20 February 1962)
NABOKOV, Vladimir	Laughter in the Dark (17 November 1950)
	Lolita, vols. I and II (20 January 1956)
SPARK, Muriel	The Bachelors (23 December 1960)
SARTRE, Jean Paul	The Age of Reason (21 March 1947)
	The Diary of Antoine Roquentin (14 June 1949)
	Intimacy and other stories (28 July 1950)
	Iron in the Soul (13 October 1950)
	The Chips are Down (Les Jeux Sont Fait) (15 June 1951)
THOMAS, Dylan	Adventures in the Skin Trade (21 October 1955)
	A Prospect of the Sea and other stories and prose writings (17 February 1956)
UPDIKE, John	Rabbit, Run (20 February 1962)

M. Adams, *Censorship: The Irish Experience* (Dublin, Sceptre Books, 1968), pp. 240-9

(c) MR KEHOE: . . . I challenge anyone to read it and to lay it down without a feeling of profound depression that any man posing as a litterateur, coming here from England, should go along to collect garbage and father it on somebody as evidence that the Irish people are depraved. Perhaps they are depraved — so are people in all countries — but why should a man from England come over to portray them and make capital out of it? Have we no spirit that we do not rise up in revolt against this sort of thing?

Again, I say, that anyone who reads *The Tailor and Ansty* will come away profoundly saddened that such filth should be imposed on an unsuspecting people, with all our old stories transmogrified, added to, and shown in a different light altogether from the atmosphere in which they are heard — traipsed out in that subtle way which comes so easily to the born litterateur — and made to appear quite differently in the published volume from what they would appear in the rude context of their birthplace. It is not a pleasant thing for a literary man to do that. Our standards are not the standards of the modern world. We may have our faults, but we should endeavour to keep our standards aloft and remain faithful to them to the end. . . .

> *Seanad Debates,* vol. xxvii, cols. 40-1 (18 November 1942)

(d) PROFESSOR MAGENNIS [Chairman of the Censorship Board]. . . . Engaged couples, under the economic pressure who cannot afford to marry, and yet unable to resist the carnal urge, might be tempted to use this. This first edition, providing a calculation as to how to determine the infertile periods becomes what I called it at the time we were reporting to the Minister — the fornicator's *vade mecum* or, if you like, the harlot's handbook. That is what it would become if circulated indiscriminately published, with those words — that 'the Catholic Church permits the use of the safe period'.

> *Ibid.* cols. 149-50 (2 December 1942)

(e) PROFESSOR TIERNEY: . . . Another point that I dislike about the whole debate on this unfortunate book [*The Tailor and Ansty*] is the tendency to debate it from the standpoint that on our side is virtue and Erin and on the other side the Saxon and guilt, or something of that sort. There is a tendency to throw a white sheet over ourselves and pretend that we are the purest, finest, most lovely people in the world. I do not think, speaking as one person, that it shows a proper, Christian spirit to adopt that attitude of almost pharisaical pretence. It is because there is so much of that attitude about that the discussion on this whole censorship question has assumed the rather absurd proportions it has assumed. You have it all over the country. . . .

The other case is that much discussed case of the *Laws of Life*, and we are all very indebted to Senator Magennis for the long account that he gave of the circumstances that led to its banning. Having listened to him with great attention and respect, I still cannot agree that it was wise on the part of the Minister to accept the advice of the Censorship Board and to ban the book. I quite admit the copy that was banned did not bear the *permissu superiorum* and that there was a definite misunderstanding about that, and I am naturally prepared to concede to Senator Magennis the point he made as to the changes between the two issues. None the less, the fact remains that for our Irish Censorship Board and our Government to censor, as in its general tendency indecent and obscene, a book published by one of the best known and most respected Catholic publishing firms in the world, and published, no matter in what circumstances, with the *permissu superiorum* of the Westminster Archdiocese, was certain to raise some scandal and to give rise to grave doubts in the minds of many people, not only in the minds of people whose profession in life is the writing of obscene literature or any kind of literature, but in the minds of ordinary Christian people, especially of Catholics both here and in other countries. Though we may have our own peculiar standard of virtue — as is so often asserted in this debate — we are not so immune from the whole wide world as that we can afford lightly to indulge in actions like that and not expect to suffer for those actions. . . .

Ibid. cols. 263-5 (3 December 1942)

VIII   Defensive ascendancy in Ulster, 1922-68

97   Unionism and Labour

The absence of class consciousness from Ulster Protestant politics had for long been the despair of Nationalists and the delight of Unionists. The advance of trade union organization in Ireland from 1916 onwards, coupled with the outbreak of social revolution in a number of European cities in the following three years, rather shook the faith of the Unionist party in the permanence of this situation. A widespread strike in Belfast in the early months of 1919 seemed to confirm that the city was in danger of going the way of 'Red Clydeside' if not worse. In an attempt to stave off the expected socialist challenge, the Unionist leaders had established an Ulster Unionist Labour Association in 1918, under the chairmanship of J.M. Andrews, a large textile employer. This body shortly secured the election of three working-class Unionists for Belfast seats in the Westminster parliament, but made no apparent impact on party policy nor — in the long run — on its personnel. Until the reappearance of sectarian rioting in 1920 however, socialism continued to constitute something of a threat to the Unionist party in Belfast, as the following letter from a leading Unionist organizer (who later became Minister for Home Affairs) indicates.

Dawson Bates to Sir Edward Carson   30 June 1919

The question of extending the area of the work of this [Ulster Unionist Labour] Association has given Andrews and myself a great deal of concern. You know the circumstances which led to the formation of this Association (of which you are President), and which ultimately led to three Labour [Unionist] members being selected for the City of Belfast.

The two principal Unionist organizations which exist at the present time in Ulster are the Parliamentary [constituency] Associations and the Orange Institution. Having regard to the fact that members of both these organizations comprise all classes, it is obvious that it is a practical impossibility that matters outside the question of the Union should be the subject of discussion and action. Therefore, no subjects, except those directly affecting the Union, are discussed. The working people in Belfast have felt for a very considerable time past that means should be placed at their disposal whereby domestic matters could be discussed by them under Unionist auspices. As you are aware the Trade Unions are practically precluded from discussing political matters other than those affecting Labour Questions, but while this is strictly accurate, at the same time many of the Unions are controlled by officials who hold home rule views. The result has been that frequently the opinions of the working classes in Belfast on the question of the Union are misrepresented in England and elsewhere. The absence of such means as I have indicated above frequently leads to the younger members of the working classes joining Socialist and extreme organizations run by the Independent Labour Party, where they are educated in views very different to those held by our body. The defect has to a very large extent been made good by the Ulster Unionist Labour Association, but at the same time it is felt that having ordinary meetings, such as they have about once a month, is not sufficient. In other words, the Association will have to extend its sphere of operations.

The matter has been discussed at several of the Meetings of the Association, and finally on Saturday last a Resolution was passed, of which I enclose a copy, which puts the matter in a nutshell. If the Resolution is given effect to, it means the formation of four working-men's Clubs in Belfast, on the lines of the Working-men's Conservative and Liberal Clubs in England. These Clubs will be kept linked with the Ulster Unionist Labour Association, and, consequently, with the Ulster Unionist Party.

I have had many talks with Andrews on this subject, and I think if this arrangement could be carried out it would do an incalculable amount of good. On the other hand, if nothing is done the Association will die, because its members will feel that it is not sufficiently progressive to meet an admittedly felt want.

Andrews you will naturally understand feels in his position, as Chairman of the Association and one of the Honorary Secretaries of the Ulster Unionist Council—in addition to being an Employer of labour himself—a good deal of responsibility, and he would not be a party to extending the sphere of the existing Association without your approval.

As you are aware, there are many employers in Belfast who take the view that Andrews goes too far on labour questions, but, on the other hand, the vast bulk of thinking employers, and those who have the interests of the Empire at heart, realize that Andrews' actions have been most beneficial. . . .

PRONI Carson Papers, D. 1507/1/3/41

98   The Craig-Collins Pact, 30 March 1922

Following the elections of May 1921 for the House of Commons of Northern Ireland, the Unionist party began the development of a state machinery. By the end of the year it had assumed responsibility for law enforcement in the province and a new regular force, the Royal Ulster Constabulary, was in the process of formation. But the Treaty ended a patchy IRA truce, while the inter-communal hostility between Catholics and Protestants — which had resulted in savage outbreaks of rioting and intimidation of Catholics from employment in 1920 — was an additional dimension to the northern problem. A large, armed special constabulary force, consisting of full-time 'A' men and part-time 'B' men, was formed by the Northern government. This caused disquiet in some political circles in Britain, for its paramilitary nature appeared to conflict with the Northern government's right to raise police but not military forces. Inevitably, since the purpose of the force was to defend the existence of the new state, its membership was exclusively Protestant and so, equally inevitably, it appeared to be a re-emergence of the old UVF of the previous decade, now with official sanction. Arguments that such arrangements made for peace by keeping the Protestant militants under disciplined control were countered by widespread Catholic allegations of misconduct by the Specials themselves, especially the part-time 'B' men.

For Collins and the new Provisional government in the Free State, the situation was complicated. They had no wish to see the Northern state succeed and, struggling vainly to reconcile their anti-treaty IRA colleagues in the south, could scarcely be expected to give priority to squashing the northern IRA. On the other hand Protestant violence against Catholics in the north, more or less indiscriminate, at times exceeded the level of IRA activity, especially in Belfast during the early months of 1922. However much he might have expected the Boundary Commission to settle the long-term problems of northern Catholics, Collins could not disclaim all short-term responsibility for their safety. Equally it was imperative for Craig to show that his government could stabilize the north. He and Collins therefore came together in London on 30 March 1922, under the aegis of the British government, to sign a pact. It was intended only as a short-term measure, and was never effectively implemented, but it remains the only explicit attempt to implement 'minority protection' in Ulster prior to the experiments of the 1970s.

Heads of agreement between the Provisional Government and Government of Northern Ireland:
1   Peace is today declared.

2   From today the two Governments undertake to cooperate in every way in their power with a view to the restoration of peaceful conditions in the unsettled areas.

3   The police in Belfast to be organized in general in accordance with the following conditions:

    (1)   Special police in mixed districts to be composed half of Catholics and half of Protestants, special arrangements to be made where Catholics or Protestants are living in other districts. All specials not required for this force to be withdrawn to their homes and their arms handed in.

    (2)   An Advisory Committee, composed of Catholics, to be set up to assist in the selection of Catholic recruits for the Special police.

    (3)   All police on duty, except the usual secret service, to be in uniform and officially numbered.

    (4)   All arms and ammunition issued to police to be deposited in barracks in charge of a military or other competent officer when the policeman is not on duty, and an official record to be kept of all arms issued, and of all ammunition issued and used.

    (5)   Any search for arms to be carried out by police forces composed half of Catholics and half of Protestants, the military rendering any necessary assistance.

4   A Court to be constituted for the trial without jury of persons charged with serious crime, the Court to consist of the Lord Chief Justice and one of the Lords Justices of Appeal of Northern Ireland. . . .

5   A Committee to be set up in Belfast of equal numbers Catholic and Protestant with an independent Chairman, preferably Catholic and Protestant alternately in successive weeks, to hear and investigate complaints as to intimidation, outrages, etc., such Committee to have direct access to the heads of the Government. The local Press to be approached with a view to inserting only such reports of disturbances, etc., as shall have been considered and communicated by this committee.

6   IRA activity to cease in the Six Counties, and thereupon the method of organizing the special police in the Six Counties outside Belfast shall proceed as speedily as possible upon lines similar to those agreed to for Belfast.

7   During the month immediately following the passing into law of the Bill confirming the constitution of the Free State. . . there shall be

a further meeting between the signatories to this agreement with a view to ascertaining:

(a) Whether means can be devised to secure the unity of Ireland.

(b) Failing this, whether agreement can be arrived at on the boundary question otherwise than by recourse to the Boundary Commission outlined in Article 12 of the Treaty.

9 In view of the special conditions consequent on the political situation in Belfast and neighbourhood, the British Government will submit to Parliament a vote not exceeding £500,000 for the Ministry of Labour of Northern Ireland to be expended exclusively on relief work, one-third for the benefit of Roman Catholics and two-thirds for the benefit of Protestants. The Northern signatories agree to use every effort to secure the restoration of the expelled workers. . . .

Transcription from *The Times,* 31 March 1922

99   The passage of the Local Government Bill, 1922

The system of proportional representation by single transferable vote was implemented for local government elections in Ireland in 1920. The result in the north was to weaken the Unionist party, by giving more weight to dispersed and previously ineffectual Nationalist votes, and by allowing the appearance of third parties. The Belfast Labour party had done unexpectedly well in the city in 1920 at the expense of the Unionists, while Nationalists and Sinn Feiners had won control of Fermanagh and Tyrone county councils, Derry city council (for the first time) and a number of smaller units. After May 1921 the Catholic-controlled councils attempted to ignore the newly-created Northern parliament and continue their allegiance to the revolutionary Dail in Dublin. Local government thus took its place beside law and order as an area in which the Unionist regime felt it imperative to establish its authority. The first step in this direction was to end the PR system of election, and in doing so the Northern Ireland cabinet, though provoking a constitutional crisis, established a very favourable precedent for the development of its relationship with the British government.

(a) Lord Fitzalan [Lord-Lieutenant of Ireland] to Sir James Craig MP   5 July 1922

I have telegraphed today giving assent to four bills, but not to the Local Government Bill. This only reached me this morning, and it really is too short notice. There can be no reason why I should not have had a draft copy of this as introduced, and then a wire to say what alterations had or had not been made.

Moreover, I find the government here are hesitating about this bill and think it may be wise to make it a reserved bill, at any rate pending further consideration with you upon it. . . .

Another point I want to write about is that I have received from the [N.I.] Home Secretary a long list of recommendations for magistrates — there are eighteen for Belfast and some half a dozen for other counties.

There is not one Catholic. I can quite imagine this is all right, and that very likely no Catholic eligible for the appointment can be found who will consent to serve. But it seems to me to be a large order and likely to cause what may be considered a legitimate criticism if so many are now appointed without one of them being a Catholic.

I should be glad if you would wire to me, e.g. 'Please sign' and I shall then know it is your wish for the whole lot. Or if you wire 'Wait' I shall know you are writing on the subject. . . .*

PRONI, Cab. 9B/40/1

(b) Northern Ireland Cabinet minute   27 July 1922

The Prime Minister [of N.I.] indicated that Mr Churchill was withholding the Royal Assent to the Local Government Bill on the grounds that the change from proportional representation in county council elections was a matter affecting the whole of Ireland therefore one in which the Imperial Government were justified in withholding their Assent. It was agreed that this constituted a very grave step on the part of the Imperial Government and that to allow this precedent to be created would warrant the interference by the Imperial Government in almost every Act introduced in Northern Ireland. Although it was recognized that the resignation of the Government of Northern Ireland did not probably create the same crisis as would a resignation in similar circumstances of a Government in one of the Colonies, it was decided that this would prove the most effective course of action.

PRONI, Cab. 4/50/1

(c) Winston Churchill (Colonial Secretary) to W.T. Cosgrave

---

*Three days later Fitzalan wrote again, 'On receipt of your wire 'Please sign' I signed and returned the list of magistrates, so that is all right. . . .'

(Chairman of the Provisional Government of the Irish Free
State)   9 September 1922

I told General Collins in my last letter to him that after
exhaustive examination of the Constitutional issues I have come,
though most unwillingly, to the conclusion that the Local Government (Northern Ireland) Bill could not be vetoed. In view of your
further Memorandum on the subject I felt that the matter ought
to be discussed by the British signatories to the Treaty — a view
with which the Prime Minister agreed. After full discussion we
came to the unanimous conclusion that for us to veto a measure
clearly within the powers delegated to the Parliament of Northern
Ireland would form a dangerous precedent. I have never
concealed from Sir James Craig my opinion that the measure was
inopportune.

The same might, however, be said of other measures submitted
from time to time for the Royal Assent but such considerations, if
allowed to weigh, would tend to a dangerous enlargement of the
prerogative. Sir James Craig assures me that the measure is in no
way intended to prejudice the Boundary question. . . . It is
useless, as I repeatedly told the House of Commons, for you or me
or any one else to make predictions about what the Boundary
Commission will or will not take into account. . . .

PRONI, Cab. 9B/40/1

100 Political work in Fermanagh

The abolition of PR for local elections, though likely to favour the Unionists as
the largest party, could not entirely reverse the balance of forces in areas where
Catholics possessed a local majority. But political parties were able to obtain,
from the population census and from their own records, precise information
on the religious distribution — and thus the likely voting behaviour — of all
areas in Northern Ireland down to the level of the townland, the smallest unit
of rural measurement. The drawing of electoral boundaries, therefore,
frequently decided the outcome of future elections, or at least made clear how
many fabricated votes would be necessary to turn the tide. In disputed areas of
Tyrone, Fermanagh and elsewhere Unionist and Nationalist registration
agents, usually local solicitors, were very experienced at this kind of work.
James Cooper of Enniskillen (1882-1949), a member of the first Northern
parliaments, was one such practitioner. Interestingly, his initial advice to
Craig was to retain PR for a while, though this should probably be put down to

exasperation at having to overturn detailed arrangements which he had only recently made.

James Cooper MP to Sir James Craig MP   9 August 1922

A remark you dropped today that we must proceed by installments and get back the old county council and rural council areas first and then proceed to revise them at a later date rather fills me with alarm.

Any such procedure would result in a fearful hash so far as the county Fermanagh is concerned. At our last county council election we were only a few votes short of three quotas in two divisions and the Nationalists just had the two quotas. So 1600 Unionist votes were thrown away for nothing. The winning of either of the seats would have won our county council and we took steps last winter and went all through these divisions and manufactured votes wholesale, so that we would have the quota at the election. The peculiar part of the thing is that our strongest divisions in votes were our weakest under PR and that it was in our strongest divisions we needed to manufacture the votes. These manufactured votes of course are useless in a straight voting system, as they are largely in areas where we already have the majority.

. . .Fermanagh is absolutely Unionist all over except in two or three mountain areas. The fact is Fermanagh is about the most skilfully rigged county in favour of the Nationalists you could possibly conceive. In the rural councils as they stand 50 or 60 Nationalist voters often equal a Unionist division with 400 to 500 voters. Enniskillen and Lisnaskea councils are particularly bad. Under PR they could not run away with us (though even under it the district council areas were rigged) but if we are to go back to the old system we are swamped.

Personally I have gone to very considerable trouble just over the manufacture of the new votes and then in carving up the county vote into new divisions and arranging the different areas. This meant going carefully into the composition of every townland in the county and fitting them together. . . . In Fermanagh we have been fighting for the last ten or twelve years and every time we came close to victory we were knocked at in some way and I very much fear if this final blow falls it will knock the heart out of the people altogether. I may also say that I called a few days ago with Mr Miller [Unionist MP] at Newtownstewart on my way here and found him plodding away on the Tyrone maps. He has a very big job to tackle and the people all over are most enthusiastic about the whole thing. . . .

If areas are not revised the only result of the present bill so far as

Fermanagh is concerned will be to hand back to the Nationalists the
county council we would have won this time under PR and probably a
couple of district councils with it.

. . .Mr John McHugh [Nationalist] late chairman of Fermanagh
county council has already stated that of course the Unionists will
revise the areas and win the county council and he and the Nationalists
will be equally disappointed as they do not expect anything else. The
first act of the Free State government was to abolish the only Unionist
council in Donegal which had been set up by the Local Government
Board as a result of the dividing of a Union between Donegal and
Tyrone.

PS, I scarcely like to mention it at all owing to the difficulties which
arise over the boundary question but if any opportunity arises to
arrange the matter by agreement I could give you 36 townlands round
the borders of Fermanagh in which there is not a *single* Protestant
which or portion of which we would be quite willing to exchange for
the Pettigo area of Donegal and the Unionist townland of Clyhore [*sic*
for Cloghore] at Belleek just inside the Donegal border, in which
townland the floodgates of Lough Erne are situated.

PRONI, Cab. 9B/40/1

101   Electioneering in Omagh

Although the work of 1922 greatly strengthened the Unionist grip on local
government in west Ulster, these successes only served to intensify the eagerness
of less fortunate Unionist parties to emulate them. The situation in the town of
Omagh, Co. Tyrone, was outlined in a letter from Sir Charles Blackmore
(1880-1967) who, as Secretary to the N.I cabinet, was a public official, to the
Minister for Home Affairs on 17 July 1934. His unfashionable assertion of the
political rights of property against persons echoed Bates's (1876-1949) parliamentary declaration of 31 October 1928 that 'strong financial interests. . . are
entitled to preferential treatment' in the matter of voting qualifications.

Sir Charles Blackmore to Sir Dawson Bates   17 July 1934

Representations have been made to the Prime Minster in regard to
the Urban District Council of Omagh which has for the past fourteen
years been under Nationalist control, notwithstanding the fact that
the Unionists pay over three-quarters of the capital rates and are
owners of all the large residential and business premises in the town.
The Nationalists have consolidated their position by large building
schemes in the South Ward in which they had formerly only a trifling

majority, the present position being that the Unionists hold the North Ward whilst the Nationalists hold the South and West Wards.

As a result of the municipal building schemes carried on by the Nationalist Urban Council, in which it is stated over 95 per cent of all the houses were given to the Nationalist tenants, they have now increased the Local Government electorate in South Ward out of all proportion to the other two Wards. It is understood that in March last the Unionist Party in the town petitioned the Ministry of Home Affairs pointing out this anomaly and asking that there should be a redistribution of the Wards, and they prepared and submitted a scheme whereby the Unionists would have obtained control of the Council. . . . In view. . . of the present law the scheme will not be effective for the election next year, and even if the scheme may be adopted during the present year, the Nationalists will be left in control of the town for the next three years with ample opportunity of building and otherwise to upset the Unionist proposals.

It is pointed out that the Unionists of Omagh feel their present position very keenly and are prepared to make any sacrifices before admitting defeat, and the local Nationalists are boasting that they have already defeated the Unionists' proposals even before an Inquiry is held.

I shall be glad if you will let me have full particulars as early as possible.

PRONI, Cab. 9B/13/2

102   The saving of Derry

Bates's reply to the above came in the form of a direct communication to his Prime Minister. He explained the technical difficulties which impeded a rapid settlement of the Omagh situation, and went on to raise the question of keeping the Unionists in power in the much larger city of Derry. In the face of mounting demographic adversity this was accomplished effectively until the local government reorganization of the 1970s.

Sir Dawson Bates to Lord Craigavon   24 July 1934

You will recollect that the Omagh people got into touch with you direct with regard to the question of Home Office adopting a scheme for the alteration of Wards there, the effect of which would be to change the balance of power from the Nationalists to the Unionists in the Urban District.

The difficulty that arises in this case is that unfortunately the promoters of the scheme delayed coming to me until it was too late to hold the necessary enquiry, etc., giving the other side time to make representations in the meantime. . . .

If we had risked it and made the order, I have not the slightest doubt that the Nationalist Party would have applied to the Court for an Order restraining us from making the Order, and in my opinion, and in the opinion of our legal adviser, we would have been beaten. The result would have been held up to the charge of 'indecent gerry-mandering'.

It is, of course, impossible for me to explain all this in public, but I think it well to let you know the true facts of the case. It has occurred to me, however, that, as we are introducing a Local Government Bill in the Autumn, we might consider the possibility of postponing all Local Government Elections for a year, as we did in 1923. This is a matter which we can discuss at a later date, but I just mention it to you mean-time.

A similar situation, though not quite so acute, is cropping up in Derry. The Derry Unionists find increased difficulty, as is felt in other areas, in getting suitable people returned to the Corporation and therefore they are promoting a scheme for the alteration of the Wards and reducing the number of members. I have discussed this privately with the people concerned, and the scheme has not yet come up to me, but I have warned them that any publicity at the present time or speeches on the subject would only add to difficulties which I must always have in dealing with the alteration of Wards where the two parties are closely effective. I need hardly point out to you that in Derry, unless something is done now it is only a matter of time until Derry passes into the hands of the Nationalist and Sinn Fein parties for all time. On the other hand, if proper steps are taken now, I believe Derry can be saved for years to come.

PRONI Cab. 9B/13/2

103   Religious education: The 'humbug' of public control

Education was one area in which the Northern government attempted to deal more cautiously with the Catholic minority. Before partition, most schools had in practice been controlled by denominational managers, under the general supervision of the Commissioners of National Education, and all were funded on the same basis. There existed practically no public initiative for building the new schools which were desperately needed in Belfast and elsewhere, and no local authority control on the English model. A new structure for Northern

Ireland, headed by a Ministry of Education, was inevitable. But the Lynn Committee, appointed in 1921 to draft a scheme, was boycotted by Catholic clerical and political leaders, partly because they objected to public control, partly because they were not at that stage prepared to recognize the existence of the Northern state. The 1923 Education Act provided for the continued payment of salaries and some maintenance for those schools (almost all Catholic-managed) which opted to remain outside public control, but not for any capital costs. Schools coming under public control on the other hand (which the great majority of Protestant children attended) were fully financed, but were not permitted to provide bible instruction in school hours, nor impose a religious test for the appointment of teachers. Either of these might have been construed as *ultra vires* under the Government of Ireland Act, 1920. Protestant critics argued that in predominantly Catholic areas Nationalist councillors would control the schools of Protestants though not those of 'their own people'.

Following a vigorous clerical campaign by the United Education Committee of the Protestant churches however, this arrangement was eroded by amending acts in 1925 and 1930 so that the publicly-controlled or state schools became effectively Protestant schools in terms of staff and religious instruction as well as pupils. Protestant clergymen thus obtained the same degree of effective control as their Catholic counterparts without the financial sacrifice. The Catholic response, now that the Nationalist political leaders had ceased their abstention policy, was vociferous, along the lines of Joseph Devlin's (1871-1934) bitter speech on the second reading of the 1930 bill. Following this protest and threats by Catholic bishops to prod the British government into testing the legal validity of such proposals, the Northern Ireland government purchased acquiescence by conceding for the future fifty per cent capital grants to Catholic schools and any others which remained under private management (This was increased in 1947 to seventy-five per cent). State schools were able to consolidate their Protestantism while retaining one hundred per cent grants.

Does the right hon. gentlemen who is at the head of the government realize that on the rolls of the public elementary schools in Northern Ireland the children of this minority which he proposes to treat with contumely and contempt, form a larger percentage of those receiving instruction than the children of any other religious denomination? Here are the figures which supply, I think, a damning indictment of the policy of religious intolerance which the present bill proposes to intensify. The Catholic children on the rolls of the elementary schools number 36.1 per cent; the Presbyterians represent 32.3 per cent; the Episcopalians represent 25.9 per cent. . . .

. . .It is interesting to observe the way in which complete change in one respect in this Northern system, so loudly boomed as the greatest

in the British Empire, was first brought about. At first it was thought
that the Catholics had been dished, and that everybody else was satisfied. That was the mentality of the right hon. and hon. members
opposite and of those for whom they spoke; but the militant leaders of
some of the churches suddenly discovered that there was a flaw in the
ministerial masterpiece. There were Protestants who were not satisfied
with the provision for teaching religion that they conscientiously
desired for their children, and their leaders joined with the Orange
Lodges in organizing an agitation for religious instruction in the
schools. The Government, anxious to placate every aggrieved section
of the Protestant community. . . found a formula that met the wishes
and needs of every section of Protestants, and therefore what is known
as simple bible teaching is introduced to meet what they regard — and
I do not dissent — as the just claims of the Protestant body. . . .

By the Act of 1923 the Catholics had already been robbed of the
rights which they enjoyed under the British regime, namely, a grant of
two-thirds of the cost of the building of their schools. It might
reasonably have been expected that when you were introducing an
amending bill you would have at least restored that right to the
Catholic body. . . .

. . .Catholics do not in the least degree object to what you are doing
in the building, extension and lighting, and cleaning, of schools for
the Protestant children. . . and they do not desire directly or
indirectly in any shape or form to interfere with Protestant schools or
with the teaching of religion as they conceive it in their schools. But
they do claim, and claim emphatically and justly, a similar right for
themselves. . . .

This performance is bad enough, but the shabby pretence by which
it is sought to buttress it up is in many ways worse; it is even more
contemptible. That is the pretence that all this is caused by the fact
that we will not accept popular control. Under the Act of 1923 you
invented what is called four-and-two committees. . . . Under this
system of so-called popular control. . . four of the committee are
appointed by the manager and two are chosen by the elected
authority. This popular control is mere empty camouflage. . . .

And then the humbug of all this talk about 'we will not give public
money without public control.' Without public control you are paying
the teachers' salaries. I could see the consistency of your policy if you
came along and said, not one farthing of public money will be paid to
any school unless there is public control of that school. But they dare
not do it. What they do is pay the teacher, and they pay, I think, some

proportion of the equipment of the school, and of lighting and heating. But because there is no public control you are not going to give grants for building. . . .

> *NI HC Deb.* vol. xii, cols. 714-20 (9 April 1930)

104   The depression in Ulster

The development of the Northern Ireland state between the wars took place for the most part against a steadily worsening economic background. Although the impact of the depression on the province's economy was no more severe than in a number of the older industrial areas of Britain, the region was perhaps less well equipped to cope: the general standard of social provision was rather lower than in Britain; the financial arrangements of devolution were such that unemployment benefit, for instance, could only be maintained at the British level at the expense of other much needed reforms; while the rural economy, despite derating for farmers, was not strong enough to support the market towns which depended upon it. The political implications of the situation were alarming.

Cabinet memorandum by Sir Dawson Bates   8 July 1932

Distress is now very acute in most parts of the province and there is every indication that during the coming winter matters will become worse and that special measures will become necessary in very many localities. It is true that legally the responsibility for dealing with the situation belongs to the Board of Guardians, but in view of the abnormal character of the present situation and the widespread character of unemployment and acute poverty, the matter is getting beyond the control and the capacity of Boards of Guardians and local authorities, and I feel it my duty to bring it before my colleagues. . . because all my information goes to show that unless adequate measures are taken in good time and on some settled plan there is grave danger that the peace of the province will be endangered.

I do not desire to take an unduly alarmist view, but there can be no doubt that unless some ameliorative measures are adopted there will be a large body of the population driven to desperation by poverty and hunger, and the only alternative to relief measures is to keep order by force, and for this purpose, in the face of widespread discontent, the existing force is not adequate. The time has come, therefore, when the matter must be thoroughly considered by the cabinet.

> PRONI Cab. 4/304/21

105   Sir Basil Brooke: The employment of Catholics

Bates's memorandum was an accurate prediction. That October both Catholic and Protestant districts of west Belfast were disturbed by the looting of food shops and riots against the police. But the fears of Bates, and the hopes of those on the left who looked to the discontent to provide a new basis for nonsectarian working-class political organization, were quickly undermined.

Sir Basil Brooke (1888-1973), cr. Viscount Brookeborough, 1952, a former Indian Army and Special Constabulary officer, and large Fermanagh landowner, became Prime Minister of Northern Ireland in 1943. Ten years earlier, as a backbench Unionist MP, he made a series of speeches on religion and employment in Ulster which have come to occupy a prominent place in the litany of Catholic criticisms of the Northern state.

Continuing, Sir Basil said there was a great number of Protestants and Orangemen who employed Roman Catholics. He felt he could speak freely on this subject as he had not a Roman Catholic about his own place (Cheers). He appreciated the great difficulty experienced by some of them in procuring suitable Protestant labour, but he would point out that the Roman Catholics were endeavouring to get in everywhere and were out with all their force and might to destroy the power and constitution of Ulster. There was a definite plot to overpower the vote of Unionists in the North. He would appeal to loyalists therefore, wherever possible to employ good Protestant lads and lassies (Cheers).

. . .Mr Cahir Healy [Nationalist MP] complained that no appointments were given to Roman Catholics, but in that he was quite wrong as in his (Sir Basil's) opinion they had got too many appointments for men who were really out to cut their throats if opportunity arose (Hear, hear). It would be sheer madness to keep on giving such men appointments under existing conditions. . . .

Fermanagh Times, 13 July 1933

106   Lord Craigavon: I am an Orangeman

A few months after making the above speech Brooke joined the N.I. cabinet as Minister of Agriculture, and his extreme utterances quickly ceased. But they had been defended at Stormont by the Prime Minister, and when the Nationalist opposition sought to raise the question of job discrimination in debate, the outcome was not a reversal of policy but simply a modification of terminology. Unionists now objected to the employment not of 'Catholics' but of 'disloyalists' — to outsiders a position which could be logically defended in terms of liberal values. But to those who knew the political language of Ulster, the message was clear enough.

THE PRIME MINISTER (Lord Craigavon): I suppose I am about as high up in the Orange Institution as anybody else. I am very proud indeed to be Grand Master of the loyal County of Down. I have filled that office for many years, and I prize that far more than I do being Prime Minister. I have always said I am an Orangeman first and a politician and Member of this Parliament afterwards. Therefore, if hon. Members think for a moment that by taunts and jeers at the Orange Institution they will make me withdraw in the slightest degree anything I have done in my capacity as a loyal Orangeman, they make a very great mistake. . . . When my colleagues have passed the Resolution it will read like this:

> 'That in the opinion of this House the employment of disloyalists entering Northern Ireland is prejudicial, not only to the interests of law and order and the safety of the State, but also to the prior claims of loyal Ulster-born citizens seeking employment.'

All through this debate the charges made by hon. Members opposite have been grossly exaggerated. Since we took up office we have tried to be absolutely fair towards all the citizens of Northern Ireland. Actually, on an Orange platform, I, myself, laid down the principle, to which I still adhere, that I was Prime Minister not of one section of the community but of all, and that as far as I possibly could I was going to see that fair play was meted out to all classes and creeds without any favour whatever on my part.

MR LEEKE (Nationalist): What about your Protestant Parliament?

THE PRIME MINISTER: The hon. Member must remember that in the South they boasted of a Catholic State. They still boast of Southern Ireland being a Catholic State. All I boast of is that we are a Protestant Parliament and a Protestant State. It would be rather interesting for historians of the future to compare a Catholic State launched in the South with a Protestant State launched in the North and to see which gets on the better and prospers the more. It is most interesting for me at the moment to watch how they are progressing. I am doing my best always to top the bill and to be ahead of the South.

NI HC Deb. vol. xvi, cols, 1031-5 (24 April 1934)

107   Extremists and papists

Sectarian tensions remained at a high level throughout the mid-1930s, culminating in a very severe outbreak of inter-communal rioting in Belfast

during the summer of 1935 which resulted in 12 deaths and large-scale population movement in the city. Demands by Nationalists and by opposition MPs
in England for an official enquiry were overruled. A private investigation by
the English-based National Council for Civil Liberties in 1936 suggested that
Catholics and holders of nationalist views were unfairly discriminated against
by the Civil Authorities (Special Powers) Act of 1922, which gave strong
summary powers to police officers. But the N.I. government was also under
pressure, inevitably more persuasive, from what it regarded as its own side. A
body known as the Protestant League had surfaced during the early 1930s in
Scotland and Ulster, articulating very direct sectarian sentiments which
threatened for a while to find a considerable measure of support amongst
working-class Protestants.

(a) Anonymous communication, marked 'Seen by the PM 20 Sept.
1935'.

Some reasons for Protestant dissatisfaction with the Northern
Government
1   Prosecution of Protestant speakers including a well-known
clergyman who warned the Protestants to oppose the invasion
of the Dublin Catholic Truth society in 1934.
2   Placing papist officers in charge of York Street [police]
Barracks [Belfast] thus ensuring the success of the papist
attack on the twelfth demonstration.
3   Placing a papist school inspector [name given] in charge of
such a Protestant district as east Belfast and north Down, and
permitting him to abuse and maltreat Protestant teachers.
(This information has been supplied by Protestant teachers in
the area).
4   Appointment of a papist senior counsel [name given] to
prosecute Protestants, especially in the Recorder's court.
For these and other reasons a movement has been started to
oppose government candidates at next election.

PRONI, Cab. 9B/326/1

(b) R. Gransden (N.I. Cabinet Office) to W. Hungerford (Unionist
Party Secretary)   20 September 1935

I should be very much obliged if you could obtain, for the PM's
information, a full account of the position which arose in Glasgow
recently, when the corporation was handed over to the Socialists
and RCs owing to the splitting of the Protestant and Conservative
votes by the extreme Protestant party (i.e. the 'Leaguers'). If you

could get the information out, what the PM would like to see is the position which arose in the various wards, and the platform on which the extremists waged the election contest.

PRONI, Cab. 9B/236/1

108   Alex Donnelly: Nationalists are not hybrids

The morale of the Nationalists after 1921 was for the most part very low. Their one experienced political leader, Joseph Devlin, had engineered an end to parliamentary abstention by 1927, and some public financial support for Catholic school-building in 1930. But Nationalist political rhetoric in the north had, ever since 1912, been geared towards demonstrating the demographic injustice of partition. After the failure of the Boundary Commission such arguments were useless. Long before his death in 1934 Devlin appears to have given up hope politically, leaving the movement in the hands of various local spokesmen, without any real party structure or political programme other than an arid assertion of nationalist principles and a residual opposition to the border. Alex Donnelly (d. 1958) an Omagh solicitor and Nationalist MP for Co. Tyrone (later West Tyrone), 1925-49, was one such spokesman.

. . .The hon. and learned member was good enough recently to describe the Nationalist members as Hybrids. If the hon. and learned member had thought for a moment he would have realized that there is a contradiction in terms between the words Nationalist and hybrid. In every country in the world it is an honour to be known as a Nationalist because, obviously, the Nationalists are the party of the people from the people, and for the people. Our connection in this country extends back through the centuries. Most of the members opposite can trace their connection with the country only to the plantation, a mere three hundred years ago. Nationally they are neither fish, flesh nor even good herring, and this is the party that talks of hybrids. Hon. members opposite are not Irishmen. They would not wish to be known as English or Scotch. They are not even Ulstermen, because they betrayed their colleagues in Ulster and betrayed the province. With regard to the employment of hybrids in the six-county area the government, after they came into power, found it necessary to take steps to prevent Catholics from getting employment. . . .

NI HC Deb. vol. xvi, col. 1088 (24 April 1934)

109   Strategists and fighters

Antony Mulvey (1882-1957), a journalist and local newspaper proprietor, was elected to Westminster in 1935 as one of the two Nationalist MPs for Fermanagh and Tyrone. For ten years he abstained, but in the more optimistic political climate of 1945 his constituents authorized him to attend the new parliament with its large Labour majority. This decision, coupled with the formation of an Anti-Partition League in Ireland and Great Britain, implied a more serious attempt to put the northern Nationalists' case before a wider public than had been attempted for more than twenty years. Within the British Labour party a number of backbenchers, mainly left-wingers or, like Hugh Delargy, with Irish and/or Catholic connections, formed the anti-partitionist 'Friends of Ireland' lobby. Mulvey was in touch both with this group and also, through the journalist Gabriel Diskin, with Dublin politicians. He was also in receipt of advice from men more sceptical of parliamentary methods.

(a) Hugh Delargy MP to Antony Mulvey MP   6 November 1945

. . .The Catholic persecution angle is, as you say, peculiar to handle in England. It must by all means be mentioned, but it might be well to stress:
(a) it is a persecution of a minority—just as was the Jewish persecution in Germany.
(b) labour and progressive organizations have also been roughly handled. For propaganda purposes here it would be well to link the two. . . .

PRONI Mulvey Papers, D. 1862/5

(b) Gabriel Diskin to Antony Mulvey MP   6 September 1945

. . .Not only should there be support by you of Labour in Britain but in the *six counties* also. Remember we are one-third of the voters, and one-third and one-sixth makes one-half. In other words if a proportion of Protestants vote Labour we could see a Labour-Nationalist or Nationalist-Labour government in power in the six counties. This at least would mean fair play for Catholics, and the two parts of the Irish people, north and south, would then have some kind of hope for and of the future.

If you agree with this suggestion—your recent pre-election visitors who came to see me did not—would you let me know if there are any Labour groups on Tyrone-Fermanagh local bodies and would the Nationalists work in some kind of general cohesion with them on matters relating to people's welfare? I don't want you to canvass this suggestion around and if you do *make it your own.*

There could of course be no formal agreement as Unionist workers might say it was a trick. But Labour and us need not clash. Take North Tyrone for instance. Protestant voters might be for a Protestant Labour man (for Stormont) and if *all* Catholics did, a gerrymandered constituency will be won.

This in my belief is the *only* way to beat the Tories in Belfast. I am not imposing it upon you but I see it as the only course of early redress of our people's ills.

Ibid.

(c) Ciaran McAnally to Antony Mulvey MP   Good Friday, 1947

I quite agree with your policy, as outlined in a previous letter, of driving our propaganda into every influential circle in England, but as to the attitude and tone we should adapt towards Englishmen collectively and individually, and towards the British government, it should be one of unconditional hostility and spoken with the rigour of an ultimatum. . . .

The lesson of the Anglo-Irish conflict is that England bows to force and the threat of force. She despises the Irish politician when he starts trying to play the diplomatic game.

Another serious aspect of this is that you yourself speak with one voice to Westminster and another voice to the Anti-Partition League audiences. I saw a *Derry Journal* report recently where you stated that, efficient or inefficient, you wanted *no* Stormont Administration. But why was that attitude not adopted towards the Westminster audience? I can only conclude that an artificial enthusiasm is being fomented in the Six Counties which will pass off as did the other anti-partition leagues of the past.

The Anti-Partition League will organize mass meetings from America to England, will increase its membership to half a million, and will then be faced with the cold sober fact that the British Government laughs at such behaviour and is not impressed. What course that League will take at that juncture remains to be seen. I fancy that it will split into a moderate and clerical group and an extra-parliamentary group, but I cannot see either section achieving their aim. Partition will remain because the Anti-Partition League is not prepared to *fight* the British Government.

Ibid. D. 1862/16

110 Chuter Ede: No business of ours

After 1922 a convention had been quickly established whereby the Westminster parliament did not discuss affairs which came under the jurisdiction of Stormont. The practice continued until the late 1960s, notwithstanding attempts to raise discussion under the umbrella of apparently non-contentious, routine measures such as the Northern Ireland Bill of 1947. Chuter Ede (1882-1965), Home Secretary in Clement Attlee's Labour government, resisted these attempts strongly, even to the extent of wrongly attributing virtual sovereignty to the devolved legislature. In fact his reference here to the dominions was probably conditioned less by constitutional ignorance than by a desire to help out the N.I. Prime Minister, Sir Basil Brooke, in an intra-Unionist tussle with a group of right-wingers in Ulster who campaigned briefly for dominion status in order to escape the 'socialistic taxation' of the British welfare state.

MR EDE: Rightly or wrongly, this House has specifically delegated to the Northern Ireland Parliament the oversight of certain matters. I have no more right to inquire into how they discharge their functions in that matter than I have to inquire into the way in which the Dominions of South Africa, Canada, Australia, or New Zealand discharge the self-government which this Parliament has, in time passed, bestowed upon them. I have no such powers. . . .

> *HC Deb.* 5th series, Vol. 438, col. 1556 (13 June 1947)

111   Herbert Morrison: No business of the dominions

A new twist was given to relations between Westminster and Stormont by the announcement in September 1948 of the Dublin government's intention to withdraw formally from the Commonwealth and declare an Irish Republic. In view of the relatively favourable status of Irish citizens in Britain and the free movement between the two countries, the move threatened to cause serious complications in the lives of many thousands of Irish people. In Ulster the support of Protestants for the Unionist party, somewhat weakened by the inroads of Northern Ireland Labour in 1945, became solid once again. The British government, while declaring in its Ireland Act of 1949 that the new Republic was 'not a foreign country', was drawn into a more explicit *de facto* defence of partition. Herbert Morrison (1888-1965), as Leader of the House of Commons, was the government's chief spokesman.

MR MORRISON: It is, of course the case that Ireland, geographically. . . is very very near to our shores and we cannot be indifferent to the circumstances which obtain there. I think it is the case that if Ireland had been situated close to some other great Powers and countries in the world, the change would not have come about as smoothly as it has done, and that is very fortunate for Ireland. The country has taken this quietly. . . .

Quite frankly, This Government is not going to seek and take the initiative for the purpose of losing a part of the United Kingdom. . . . If Irishmen get together and make agreements among themselves that is a situation which we will consider, but it is no part of the business of this Government — and it is not going to do it — to take the initiative to diminish the territory of the United Kingdom. . . .

. . .without this Bill the Republic of Ireland would be a foreign State, with all the consequences that that involves, both there and to Irish folk in this country. That is another reason why we want to get the Bill through in order to remedy that state of affairs. It was, therefore, a Commonwealth issue, and it was right that the Dominions should be consulted. But with respect to Northern Ireland, I would impress upon my hon. Friend that that is essentially a United Kingdom matter. Northern Ireland is part of the United Kingdom. Therefore, that is the domestic business of the United Kingdom Government and the Government of Northern Ireland. I will be quite frank in saying that the Dominions were not consulted about that particular point: but I am sure that they would not expect to be consulted. . . .

. . .if it be the case that the British Parliament is going to declare that what was known as Eire becomes the Irish Republic and has ceased to be part of His Majesty's Dominions, surely it is logical and rational that we should in the same subsection declare what is the position regarding Northern Ireland. It is ungenerous — if I may say so, it is somewhat intolerant and unreasonable — that we should be criticized for declaring what is the position of Northern Ireland when we have been exceedingly generous in declaring the position of our country to the Republic of Ireland. Therefore, having declared the Republic of Ireland not to be part of His Majesty's Dominions, we declare that

> Northern Ireland remains part of His Majesty's dominions and of the United Kingdom and affirm that in no event will Northern Ireland or any part thereof cease to be part of His Majesty's dominions and of the United Kingdom without the consent of the Parliament of Northern Ireland.

That is not banging doors, but it is not unlocking doors either. It is leaving the situation fluid if the Parliament of Northern Ireland should wish to make a change, but if it does not wish to make a change, then we are affirming that the present position remains of Northern

Ireland being part of the United Kingdom and part of His Majesty's Dominions and part of the British Commonwealth. . . .

. . .It must be remembered that at the moment legally the Republic of Ireland is a foreign State, and Irish folk in this country are foreigners. Indeed, the Republic of Ireland does not want to be in the Commonwealth but it does not want to be foreign — it is as far as I know quite sincere on both points. (Laughter).

Ibid. Vol. 464, cols. 1957-65 (11 May 1949)

112   Geoffrey Bing: A positive duty

Although the declaration of the Republic and the Ireland Act were clear setbacks for anti-partitionists and those who sought fundamental reforms in Northern Ireland, the extended debates offered an unusual opportunity to discuss Ulster's affairs at Westminster.

Ever since 1921 anti-partitionist arguments from all quarters had tended to be couched in rather arid quasi-demographic terms — the distribution of Catholics/Nationalists in Ulster, the gerrymandering of constituencies, the overall gerrymander of the six-county state itself, and so on. During the years of the Attlee government a number of MPs began to direct attention to social injustices in Northern Ireland which conflicted not only with the aspirations of Irish nationalism but also with the fundamental principles of British social democracy. The most formidable of this group was Geoffrey Bing (1909-77), an English barrister with Ulster antecedents, who later played a prominent role in the Nkrumah government in Ghana. Although Bing's efforts, and those of the 'Friends of Ireland' group in general, petered out after 1949, his arguments in particular foreshadowed the more successful criticisms of the Northern Ireland state developed in the late 1960s.

MR BING: It can be put like this. It is impossible to divorce the struggle for the abolition of partition from the struggle for social justice for the whole of Ireland. The evils of this Clause are that it enables those on both sides of the Border who are opposed to the social reforms that must be the necessary prerequisite for the union of Ireland to carry on a barren dispute over nationalism. It will perpetuate that sort of nationalism which prevents the reunion of Ireland by preventing the very problem itself from ever being discussed. So far as political mistakes are made by the political parties of the Irish Republic, I do not think it is for us to go into them, for we have no direct responsibility. Where, however, Northern Ireland is concerned, this Parliament sitting here has a direct responsibility. . . .

We have a positive duty in Northern Ireland. Northern Ireland is not a dominion but a subordinate Parliament. Section 72 (of the Government of Ireland Act, 1920) deals with the powers of this Parliament. I will read it as amended by subsequent legislation.

> Notwithstanding the establishment of the Parliament of Northern Ireland or anything contained in this Act, the supreme authority of the Parliament of the United Kingdom shall remain unaffected and undiminished over all persons, matters and things in Northern Ireland and every part thereof.

In the face of that, we on this side simply cannot get rid of our responsibility for Northern Ireland, much as we should like to do so, or at least much as some of us would. It may well be, and I accept the argument, that Northern Ireland has a great strategical value. I have always held the view that it was wrong for the Irish Republic not to come into the war, and I should have defended, I think, the position of seizing bases in order to defend ourselves. But if we occupy an area for strategical reasons, then surely we have a duty to the inhabitants, not to the majority only, but all the inhabitants majority and minority.

A second point—we are paying for the Northern Ireland social services. I was glad to see, when the superior social services in Northern Ireland were being pointed out by my hon. Friend the Member for Wycombe, that the hon. Member for Armagh (Mr Harden) nodded his approval. Naturally so—they occupy the best part of his election address. What was not said, and what it is important should be said, is that these social services are paid for, not by the people of Northern Ireland but by the people of this country. That is quite proper. It is part of the United Kingdom, but we at least have a right to say how that money shall be spent.

In the event of any sort of trouble in Northern Ireland, as the hon. Member for Antrim said, the Northern Ireland Government would rely on British troops. That is quite proper, but the House ought to remember that these British troops will contain British conscripts and not any Northern Ireland conscripts, because there is no conscription in Northern Ireland. If the conscripts of this country are going out to defend another country which is subordinate to this Parliament, we have a duty to the people of this country to see that there is not a Government in that country of Northern Ireland which needlessly provokes an incident.

Ibid. Vol. 465, cols. 59-71 (16 May 1949)

113   The threat of a socialist economy

For the devolved government of Northern Ireland also, Dublin's declaration of a Republic offered opportunities to make political gains. The British government's Ireland Act of 1949 indeed gave a specific guarantee that partition would not be ended without the consent of the people *and parliament* of Northern Ireland. But some Ulster Unionist politicians, disenchanted with the apparent advance of socialism in Britain, hoped that the situation might offer wider opportunities for restructuring the relationship between Belfast and London. The following extracts are taken from a longer memorandum put before the Northern Ireland cabinet at the end of 1948 by the Minister for Commerce, Senator Roland Nugent.

I believe that we are in an exceptionally favourable position to get anything in reason for which we ask, but I think it is of the greatest importance that we should ask *now*, in time for our wishes to be included in the legislation now in preparation in England. . . . We are in a new phase of constitutional relationships, the old distinctions between dominion and other status have gone, and the Imperial Government is obviously ready to adopt improvised relationships of an almost experimental nature with individual units of the Commonwealth. . . .

EXTERNAL TRADE AND DUTIES OF CUSTOMS
    There are two principal reasons for independence in this respect:
(a)   The British Tariff, devised for the protection of the home market of a great industrial nation, tends to be too high for a semi-agricultural country such as Ulster, which in so far as it is industrial at all converts imported raw material and exports the product. Free import of a large range of commodities would best suit our economic interests. . . .
(b)   The other reason is inherent in the possible effects of nationalization in Great Britain. If nationalization raises the cost of British semi-manufactured materials, the export industries which use them as raw material will be very seriously handicapped if they cannot turn to an alternative source of supply. To take steel as an example, where the double effect of coal nationalization and its own will probably raise prices substantially. We might well be in a position in which we could only save our shipbuilding and textile machinery industries by importing foreign steel. Control of our own import duties might, therefore, be essential to our continued existence as an industrial country.
    Free trade with the rest of the United Kingdom is, of course,

essential, but control of our own tariff need not prevent this. . . .

TAXATION

As I see the position our two chief dangers are either being forced into an Irish Republic against our will through constitutional pressure, or a complete economic breakdown, which apart from the direct harm it did to the country might, through unemployment and general dissatisfaction, produce a government which was unwilling to employ the constitutional safeguards. . . . [with regard to the latter point] . . . *There is no safe course in present circumstances.* I must, however, emphasize in the strongest possible manner my own apprehensions as to the consequences of continued taxation even for a few years at the present levels and in the present forms on the economic well-being of the country. The main arguments for control of our own taxation follow. . . .

(i)   The present system of British taxation is. . . abnormally high (over thirty per cent of the total national income). Very high taxation, ill-adjusted, while harmful to Great Britain, must be even more harmful to a much poorer community.

(ii)   It is especially harmful to Ulster, because it prevents the accumulation of new capital. Ulster is, and always has been, very short of capital. The main cause, though of course not the only cause, of our chronic unemployment in past years, and of our present 'hard core' in spite of boom conditions, is lack of capital equipment with which to provide the employment.

(iii)   Ulster has few natural resources, fuels or minerals. Like all countries which depend on human brains and efforts rather than natural riches, she is very vulnerable to high taxation which not only prevents capital accumulation but reduces the incentive to work and enterprise. . . .

(v)   It is dangerous for a poor country to follow step by step the social expenditure of a much richer country, especially when that policy is being pushed to the edge of recklessness. Yet as long as taxation is reserved there is no incentive to undertake the difficult task of economy, the money is going to be taken from us in any case.

(vi)   British expenditure now covers a wide range of objects which do not interest or benefit Ulster, and as Socialist measures increase the proportion of such expenditure to the expenditure on matters which do benefit Ulster, such as defence, will probably increase. . . .

(vii)   There is a political aspect to this problem. No free enterprise economy can continue unless there is a constant renewal of capital in private hands. If taxation prevents this renewal, then the only alternative source of capital is the Government. We might have to choose between increasing unemployment or increasing Government participation in industry. The process has already started with the Industrial Development Act and Housing Subsidies. . . . A continuance of high taxation in its present form may well drive us in spite of ourselves and in spite of all constitutional safeguards [?] into a Socialist economy. . . .

PRONI Cab. 4/772/5

114   Economic expansion without political change?

The political tone of the 1950s was quieter. The IRA's 'border campaign' of 1956-62 provided the press with a number of colourful exploits and may, in retrospect, be said to have re-glamourized the IRA for a new generation of young republicans. But its impact on Northern Ireland was small, both in military terms (19 deaths from violence in six years) and in its failure to produce any hint of political crisis. The Northern Ireland Labour party (nonsectarian but, since 1949, committed to the maintenance of the British link) which had been annihilated at the polls immediately following the declaration of a Republic in the south, actually made its best showings ever in the Stormont elections of 1958 and 1962.

The Unionist party changed little during these years. The Orange Order continued to demonstrate the influence which it had held within the party since its formation, especially when it was suggested in 1959 that the party might begin to seek members among the Catholic community. Lord Brookeborough asserted in reply that there was 'no change in the fundamental character of the Unionist party'.

Under no circumstances will the suggestion that Roman Catholics could be admitted to membership of the Unionist party be countenance or accepted by the Orange Order, said Senator Sir George Clark in a speech at Scarva [Co. Down]. He made this declaration as master of the Grand Orange Lodge of Ireland.

Sir George was referring to the speeches made by Sir Clarence Graham and Mr Brian Maginess, the Attorney-General, at the Young Unionists' weekend school at Portstewart.

He said the reports and press comments 'were of such a nature that the implication of a change of policy in the Unionist party by the admission of Roman Catholics as members was, if not actually stated, suggested as a possible development in the future.

. . .I would draw your attention to the words 'civil and religious liberty'. This liberty, as we know it, is the liberty of the Protestant religion given to us by King William, who at the same time secured the Protestant succession to the throne, and gave us our watchword 'The Protestant religion and liberties of England I will maintain'.

. . . In view of this it is difficult to see how a Roman Catholic, with the vast differences in our religious outlook, could be either acceptable within the Unionist party as a member or, for that matter, bring himself unconditionally to support its ideals.

. . . Further to this, an Orangeman is pledged to resist by all lawful means the ascendancy of the Church of Rome; abstaining from uncharitable words, actions and sentiments towards his Roman Catholic brethren. . . .'

Sir George said that since 1922, the Northern Ireland government had always, and rightly so, been able to rely on the Orange Order, whose members played so large a part in its formation. . . . During those years there had been no discrimination, and Ulster prosperity had been shared by all. It was possible, therefore, that many Roman Catholics might wish to remain within the Commonwealth and continue to enjoy the expanding economy and resulting benefits.

'To those of them who wish to do so the way is quite clear and open, namely, by supporting through the ballot box the Unionist party. . . .'

Belfast Telegraph, 10 November 1959

115   Richard Crossman: A large, expensive secret

During the long period of Conservative government from 1951 to 1964, Northern Ireland affairs attracted scant attention in Britain, apart from the IRA sideshow. After 1964 a back-bench Labour pressure group, the Campaign for Democracy in Ulster, aroused a little interest among some members of the Labour cabinet. But the Ulster Unionist party, which always returned nine or more of the twelve Ulster MPs at Westminster, was until 1972 formally linked with the British Conservative party, and consequently ill-equipped to lobby a Labour government effectively for economic favours. On the very eve of the outbreak of serious trouble in Ulster the British cabinet's perception of the situation was alarmingly vague.

Diary, 12 September 1968

The third political item was Short's* of Belfast. Since we last

*Short Brothers and Harland, aircraft manufacturers

discussed it we had asked a commercial consultancy to advise us on the problem and they had come to the conclusion that for social and political reasons more subsidies had to be given. Thank God the PM said straightaway that we hadn't asked this firm of accountants to advise us on our social and political duties but on the strictly commercial side, where they admit that the firm has no future. Why should we pay vast sums to a firm in Belfast? What good do we get out of the twelve Ulster MPs? What social results do we achieve by pouring into Belfast money which we deny to Millom [Cumberland] or the North-East coast? Then (he was in great form) Harold [Wilson] evolved an ingenious scheme under which we would say to the Government of Northern Ireland, 'We're going to stop the subsidies to Short's and you can take the firm over.' At once it was pointed out that if we did this they would still get the subsidies from us because of the way Northern Irish finances relate to UK finances. At this point I said, 'I am an ignoramus; may I be told what is the exact financial arrangement?' Nobody could say. Neither Jack Diamond nor the Chancellor knew the formula according to which the Northern Ireland Government gets its money. In all these years it has never been revealed to the politicians and I am longing to see whether now we shall get to the bottom of this very large, expensive secret.

R.H.S. Crossman, *The Diaries of a Cabinet Minister* (Hamish Hamilton, London, 1977), iii, 187

IX Ulster since 1968: Troubles

116 Civil rights for Catholics?

Northern Ireland carried into the 1960s its traditional burden of high unemployment, low wage levels, and stagnant industries. When Brooke-borough retired in 1963 his successor Captain Terence O'Neill (b. 1914), though sharing a similar landed-elite background, associated himself more positively with growing pressures for economic and social change. Major efforts and concessions were made to attract multi-national corporations to the province, making Ulster a centre for the artificial fibre industry. The trade unions' representative body, the Northern Committee of the Irish Congress of Trade Unions, received official recognition on establishing its autonomy from the south. O'Neill visited Catholic schools in the north and discussed economic development with political leaders in the south, neither of which his predecessor had ever attempted. A new town, a new university and a new road system were planned for the province.

First indications for the government were encouraging. The industrial transformation was implemented smoothly, apparently undercutting opposition from the right wing of the Unionist party and from the NILP on the left. The Nationalist party, meanwhile, broke with tradition to accept the status of official parliamentary opposition. O'Neill seemed to have satisfied the mild interest which the new Labour government at Westminster was showing in Northern Ireland community relations.

But this was the lull before the storm. Both economic and political pressures encouraged the concentration of growth points in the less remote and predominantly Protestant areas of the province closest to Belfast. Political pressures alone caused the new city in north Armagh to be named 'Craigavon' and the new university to be sited in the Protestant market town of Coleraine rather than the much larger city of Derry, where a small university college already existed. The new economic promises raised false hopes of quick solutions to the problems of chronic unemployment and poor housing, while the changes of government at Stormont and Westminster rekindled old political aspirations and fears. By 1968 O'Neill was being squeezed between a growing body of Protestant working-class and traditional Unionist opinion on the one hand and an increasingly vociferous movement for Catholic civil rights on the other. The riot which followed the stern suppression of a banned civil-rights march in Derry on 5 October 1968 brought this conflict onto the television screens of the world — with shattering results. The commission of enquiry set up under Lord Cameron took a wide-ranging view, placing the emphasis in its recommendations on the reform of Catholic grievances.

. . . The immediate causes of the outbreaks of violence which began on 5 October 1968, and their continuance thereafter, arose from a wide variety of sources. Some and not the least powerful, as we have found, are deep-rooted in the continuing pressures, in particular among Catholic members of the community, of a sense of resentment and frustration at the failure of representations for the remedy of social, economic and political grievances. On the other hand, among Protestants, equally deep-rooted suspicions and fears of political and economic domination by a future Catholic majority in the population calculated to build up a dangerous, and politically explosive, sectarian tension. . . . What was considered by many Catholics and others who had been pressing for certain political reforms as the failure or delay of government to match promise and performance, introduced an element of disappointed expectation into the political atmosphere in the early summer months of 1968. In addition, we do not think it is wholly accidental that the events of last autumn occurred at a time when throughout Europe, as well as in America, a wave of reaction against constituted authority in all its aspects, and in particular in the world of universities and colleges, was making itself manifest in violent protests, marches and street demonstrations of all kinds. . . .

In large measure the general complaints made to us have traditional and historical roots, arising as they do from the permanent divisions in the community, and represent a protest against the tradition that Protestant and Catholic representatives ought primarily to look after 'their own' people. In the past for example it was considered natural that a Protestant Council would employ Protestants in all senior posts, and conversely that a Catholic-controlled Council would employ only Catholics. In the matter of local authority housing there has frequently been what is called a 'gentleman's agreement' amongst members of certain local authorities that houses in Catholic wards would be allocated to Catholics by Catholic councillors, and conversely in Protestant wards. . . .

Another matter of complaint which played a considerable part among the grievances felt particularly among the Catholic section of the community is the continued retention of the U[lster] S[pecial] C[onstabulary], commonly known as the 'B Specials'. This force. . . is of long standing and is designed to serve a dual purpose of providing something in the nature of a 'home guard' or defence force and a reserve supplementary to the civil police. The recruitment of this force, for traditional and historical reasons, is in practice limited to members of the Protestant faith. Though there is no legal bar to Catholic membership it is unlikely that Catholic applications would be favourably received even if they were made. Until very recent years, for drilling and training purposes, the Ulster Special Constabulary made large use of Orange Lodges and this, though it may have been necessary for reasons of economy and because of the lack of other suitable premises, tended to accentuate in the eyes of the Catholic minority the assumed partisan and sectarian character of the force. . . .

We now turn to the actions of the organizations directly involved in the disturbances, and the aims and actions of the participants. The Northern Ireland Civil Rights Association was founded at a meeting held in Belfast in February 1967. . . . Its constitution was modelled on that of the National Council for Civil Liberties in Great Britain with the consequence that the same breath of political and cultural outlook was sought in its membership. . . . The membership of the first Council was politically varied in range and undoubtedly included persons of known extreme Republican views and activities as well as members of the Northern Ireland Labour and Liberal Parties. In addition, the membership is predominantly Roman Catholic in religion. . . . It is and always has been a fundamental rule of the association to place no bar on membership because of particular political affiliations. . . . There is no doubt that the IRA has taken a close interest in the Civil Rights Association from its inception. . . .

. . .Following the march of 5 October 1968. . . a definite programme calling for specific reforms was adopted and publicized. These may be summarized thus — (1) Universal franchise in local government elections in line with the franchise in the rest of the United Kingdom. (2) The redrawing of electoral boundaries by an independent Commission to ensure fair representation. (3) Legislation against discrimination in employment at local government level and the provision of machinery to remedy local government grievances. (4) A compulsory points system for housing which would ensure fair allocation. (5) The Repeal of the Special Powers Act. (6) The disbanding of the USC; and later (7) The withdrawal of the Public Order (Amendment) Bill. It will be readily appreciated that support for these varied objects would be likely to come from a wide variety of quarters and be inspired by differing and frequently conflicting motives. . . .

Disturbances in Northern Ireland [Cmd. 532]
(Belfast, 1969), pp. 55-78

117   TV sets for Catholics?

The escalation of conflict proved too much for O'Neill to handle. Historical circumstances suggested that his chances of securing substantial Catholic support were negligible, while every Unionist politician who supported him risked rejection by his own grass-roots. Thus a general election called by O'Neill in February 1969 did nothing to improve his position. He failed to gain the decisive majority he needed in order to bring forward meaningful electoral reform, and resigned a few weeks later. A widely-quoted radio interview which he gave shortly afterwards indicates his rather stilted vision of the route to community harmony.

The basic fear of the Protestants in Northern Ireland is that they will be outbred by the Roman Catholics. It is as simple as that.

It is frightfully hard to explain to a Protestant that if you give Roman Catholics a good job and a good house they will live like Protestants, because they will see neighbours with cars and TV sets.

They will refuse to have eighteen children, but if the Roman Catholic is jobless and lives in a most ghastly hovel he will rear eighteen children on national assistance.

It is impossible to explain this to a militant Protestant, because he is so keen to deny civil rights to his Roman Catholic neighbours. He cannot understand, in fact, that if you treat Roman Catholics with due consideration and kindness they will live like Protestants in spite of the authoritarian nature of their church.

Transcription from the *Belfast Telegraph,* 5 May 1969

118   Ian Paisley: The intervention of almighty God

O'Neill was defeated from within the ranks of his own party. But behind the more inflexible Unionists, at the same time threatening them and stiffening their attitude, stood another group which was centred on Ian Paisley's (b. 1926) Protestant Unionist party (expanded and renamed in 1971 as the

Democratic Unionist party). Paisley had won some notoriety as a Catholic-baiter in the 1950s, operating through his own 'Free Presbyterian Church', and in 1962 travelled to Rome in a sack cloth to protest against ecumenical trends in the main Protestant churches. In 1964 he had intervened more directly in Ulster affairs by pressing the police to remove the flag of the Irish Republic which was being displayed on the Belfast Sinn Fein offices. The outcome was a major riot. By the end of the decade Paisley had become a more serious political figure however, using his mixture of social radicalism and religious fundamentalism to bring political coherence and direction to the old-established suspicions harboured by working-class and small-farm Protestants about the 'fur-coat brigade' leadership of the Unionist party. At the same time his crude but colourful sectarianism cut deeply into Labour's support in the Belfast Protestant community.

(a) The Rev. Ian Paisley stood at the fount of Orangeism this after-noon and said 'What Ulster needs now is the intervention of almighty God.'. . . .

Most of his address was a warning to the [N.I.] prime minister to toe the line with his strong brand of Protestantism. He said of the cabinet that they were almost all of the same conviction as O'Neill. Now they had lost their leader, but the same poison was still in their blood. 'We demand that these rebels, these attackers of Protestants, should go.'

When he wasn't attacking the villainy and anti-Christianity of the Catholic Church, he was hitting at the new creed, the spawn of the ecumenical movement. That movement had discovered that the Pope was not a bad fellow after all. He reminded members of the Church of Ireland, Presbyterian and Methodist Churches that they had 'ecumenical pansies' in their midst. . . .

He attacked Brian Faulkner for saying yesterday that he was not anti-Catholic and neither was the Orange Institution. 'I want to say that I am an anti-Roman Catholic as far as the system of Popery is concerned. . . but God being my judge I love the poor dupes who are ground down under that system.'

His concern particularly, he said, was for those Catholic mothers who had to go and prostitute themselves before old bachelor priests. It was the most shameful system on the face of the earth. . . .

Irish Times, 14 July 1969

(b) VOTE 'NO' TO THE COMMON MARKET!

1. *Because of its Religious Dimension*
RC [Roman Catholic] Shirley Williams, a member of Wilson's

Government, says 'We will be joined to Europe in which the Catholic religion will be the dominant faith and in which the application of the Catholic Social Doctrine will be a major factor in everyday political and economic life.' In the Six foundation countries of the Common Market there are 54 million RCs and only 21 million Protestants. Catholic Social Doctrine is completely repugnant to all freedom-loving people.

2.   *Because of its Constitutional Dimension.* . . .

3.   *Because of its Economic Dimension.* . . .

4.   *Because of its Irish Dimension.* . . .

Dr Fitzgerald the Foreign Sec. of the [Irish] Republic, writing in the *Catholic Herald,* sees the Common Market as the way to a United Ireland.

5   *Because of its Legal Dimension*

The Common Market is leading to the abolishing [sic] of 'Common Law' and the introducing of 'Roman Law'. Under Common Law a person is innocent until proved guilty. Under Roman Law the person is guilty until he proves himself innocent.

> Democratic   Unionist   Party   referendum handbill, May 1975

119   The intervention of Jack Lynch

O'Neill was succeeded by his cousin James Chichester-Clark (b. 1923), who was shortly able to promise 'one man, one vote' for future local government elections. But it soon became clear that the civil rights marchers and their occasional street encounters with the Paisleyites and the RUC had provided merely the overture for a more large-scale eruption of violence between Protestant and Catholic communities. During the summer of 1969 the sporadic clashes of the previous winter were emulated in many (though by no means all) towns throughout Ulster. On 8 August the RUC were barricaded out of the main Catholic areas of 'Free Derry', and the 'Battle of the Bogside' began. A section of the Fianna Fail cabinet in the Republic saw in the situation a chance to topple their own compromise leader, Jack Lynch (b. 1917), and implement a more active policy to secure Irish unity. Lynch's statement of 13 August 1969 is an indication equally of the seriousness of both the situation in the north and of his own political position.

. . . The Government have been very patient and have acted with great restraint over several months past. While we made our views known to the British Government on a number of occasions both by direct contact and through our diplomatic representative in London, we were careful to do nothing that would exacerbate the situation. But it is clear now that the present situation cannot be allowed to continue.

It is evident also that the Stormont Government is no longer in control of the situation. Indeed the present situation is the inevitable outcome of the policies pursued for decades by successive Stormont Governments. It is clear also, that the Irish Government can no longer stand by and see innocent people injured and perhaps worse.

It is obvious that the RUC is no longer accepted as an impartial police force. Neither would the employment of British troops be acceptable nor would they be likely to restore peaceful conditions—certainly not in the long term. The Irish Government have, therefore, requested the British Government to apply immediately to the United Nations for the urgent despatch of a Peace-keeping Force to the 6 Counties of Northern Ireland and have instructed the Irish Permanent Representative to the United Nations to inform the Secretary-General of this request. We have also asked the British Government to see to it that police attacks on the people of Derry should cease immediately.

Very many people have been injured and some of them seriously. We know that many of these do not wish to be treated in 6-County hospitals. We have, therefore, directed the Irish Army authorities to have field hospitals established in County Donegal adjacent to Derry and at other points along the border where they may be necessary.

Recognizing, however, that the reunification of the national territory can provide the only permanent solution for the problem, it is our intention to request the British Government to enter into early negotiations with the Irish Government to review the present constitutional position of the 6 Counties of Northern Ireland. . . .

> *Violence and Civil Disturbances in N.I. in
> 1969* [Cmd. 566] II, 43-44

120   The intervention of the British Army: Profound relief for Catholics?

Incensed by Catholic intransigence in Derry, and determined not to permit it in their own city, the main Protestant areas of west Belfast associated themselves with police efforts to clear Catholic barricades in a way that amounted to a major invasion of the Catholic Falls area. On the night of 14 August alone six died and 150 families were burned out. The heavy machine-guns deployed for the purpose of riot control by the RUC were no substitute for their lack of numbers on the ground, while events earlier in the year had shown that the

B-Special force, exclusively Protestant and not trained in riot control, could not be expected to have a pacifying effect. Thus on 14 August in Derry, and the following day in Belfast, the British Army was formally called onto the streets in aid of the civil power. In security terms a routine progression in face of escalating disorder, it was in Northern Ireland constitutional terms the most important development since 1921. Henceforward the British government had a measure of direct involvement in the day-to-day administration of law and order in the province. Ironically, in view of later developments, the move was widely welcomed on the Catholic side.

Some members of the British cabinet perceived the situation a little more clearly even at this stage, notwithstanding a degree of misplaced cynicism.

(a) Powdered with fine ash, exhausted by bloodshed, and brought under order by the arrival of more British troops, the grim city of Belfast settled down late tonight to what looked like being its first night's sleep since Wednesday.

The day had grown progressively tenser as the Northern Ireland Government delayed making the necessary request for troops to restore order in the Crumlin Road area, the large Catholic district not covered by yesterday's deployment of troops in the Falls Road.

The Army—two companies of the Third Light Infantry—arrived at 6.15 in the evening with fixed bayonets, loaded machine guns and armoured cars. It immediately set up wire barriers to divide the Protestant side of the road from the Catholic.

It was greeted with profound relief on the Catholic side, where community leaders had been attempting all day to communicate their plight after last night's widespread house-burning and shooting by Protestant extremists and police. But the troops were met with a cold and hostile reaction from many on the Protestant side. . . . .

The Observer, 17 August 1969

(b) Richard Crossman's Diary, 17 August 1969

Cabinet must now discuss the constitutional consequences of the involvement of British troops. I don't think we can get them out of Northern Ireland at all easily now they have gone into Belfast as well and I think we are bound to take over the responsibility for part of the government to try to see the reforms through. I fear that once the Catholics and Protestants get used to our presence they will hate us more than they hate each other. This is something we have all dreaded and looked away from but which has always been recognized as the inevitable consequence of letting the rioting get out of the control of the Ulster police. A year ago it was the Russian invasion of Czechoslovakia that dominated my life and now we have got this but, unlike Czechoslovakia, no sense of tragedy or principle is involved. It is so dirty, mucky, untidy; it really is street rioting, with boys and girls chucking beastly petrol bombs at each other and potting each other with old guns. It is the most messy kind of civil war one has ever seen and it doesn't give a sense of stirring, epic tragedy but is just awful and depressing. Nevertheless, from the point of view of the Government it has its advantages. It has deflected attention from our own deficiencies and the mess of the pound. We have now got into something which we can hardly mismanage. The Tories are with us on this.

> R.H.S. Crossman, *The Diaries of a Cabinet Minister* (Hamish Hamilton, London, 1977), iii, 620

121 Belfast: The lines are rigidly drawn

The 1969 riots produced a major upheaval in housing in west Belfast, and a two-mile long metal fence installed by the Army between the main Catholic and Protestant districts. The bitterness, especially on the Catholic side, produced an atmosphere in which the IRA could recruit and organize as 'defenders of the community' in a way that had not been possible since 1922. Efforts during 1970-1 by the British Army to prevent a build-up of IRA structures and weapons — with the inevitable cordoning-off of streets, dawn raids, broken doors and floorboards — were double-edged in their effect. When the Stormont government was finally allowed to implement large-scale internment without trial, in August 1971, over 300 IRA suspects were 'lifted' in one operation, and rioting once more broke out on a major scale. The refugee problem was intensified yet again.

About 8,000 people have moved house in Belfast in the past six weeks. Responding to a variety of pressures, they have trekked from one part of the city to another in a complex series of manoeuvres. . . .

One of the earliest, and certainly the biggest, movements of people came after the destruction by fire of about 250 terrace houses in three streets on the edge of the Ardoyne. It happened on the afternoon of August 9, the day of the Army's internment swoop. The Ardoyne is a Catholic enclave but the three streets, Farringdon Gardens, Velsheda Park and Cranbrook Gardens were occupied largely by Protestants.

As I watched the flames devour the houses that afternoon I was told by Protestants that they had been set alight by Catholics—one eye-witness even claimed to have seen petrol bombs being thrown by men wearing black IRA berets—and by Catholics that they had been fired by the Protestants. It appears to have been a combination of both an attack by the Catholics on the Protestants nearest to hand, and a scorched earth response by Protestants reluctant to see their homes occupied by Catholics.

Three further facts have to be considered. First, a militant Protestant leader admits to having been active in the area on the three nights before the fire. He says he was encouraging the Protestants to stay and fight and not be intimidated by the Catholics.

Secondly, nearly all the Protestants were rehoused that same night, most of them in Ballysillan, a new estate to the north, in homes previously vacated by Catholics who fled after their names had been painted on a wall. The rest went to new houses in Westland Road, the keys to which were quickly made available by a Protestant city councillor.

Thirdly, the Ardoyne triangle is now almost entirely cut off by waste ground on its north and east sides and by 10 ft corrugated iron barriers erected by the Army across most of the streets leading out of the south side. . . .

The. . . Belfast corporation housing manager, told me; 'Although before August, 1969, the different religions lived in separate areas, the lines of demarcation had become blurred, mainly through the movement of Catholics into Protestant districts. After that August the trend was reversed and we moved about 1,200 Catholic families out of Protestant areas. Then the lines were more sharply drawn than ever before.

'But now, after the explosion of movement this August, the polarization is pretty well complete. You can understand people living on the confrontation lines being frightened and wanting to move. You can also understand why they have a scorched earth policy: unless they do, by a process of leapfrogging, people are always going to end up living "cheek by jowl". . . .

The Times, 18 September 1971

122 Papist gangs

The riots thus generated spontaneous internal population transfer on a large scale. In Derry the balance of population, housing stock and topography facilitated a division along the lines of the river Foyle, bridged only at one point. But in Belfast the battle-lines, though clear at some 'historic' points, were elsewhere more blurred. The general inflow of Catholics into the large Falls district, for instance, produced inevitable pressure to expand the edges of that district. Such a situation, where public authorities had neither the machinery nor the information to act effectively, was tailor-made for the intervention of private armies, who came to win control of, and therefore allocate housing, in many areas. 'Paramilitary' gangsters were thus perceived to be performing valuable community services in both Catholic and Protestant areas, while the bitterness of their victims provided fertile ground for extremist politicians.

After several murderous attacks, the Presbyterian congregation at Henry Taggart Memorial Hall, New Barnsley, Belfast, faces extinction. A spokesman says that after several months of terrorism only about six families now remain. Petrol bombs, bottles and stones have been hurled at the building, and services and meetings have had to be abandoned because of the menacing mobs.

Already the Church of Ireland Lutheran Church has closed down due to attacks from Papist gangs in the same area.

There used to be 300 families connected with the Presbyterian Church until Roman Catholic mobs from Ballymurphy began to drive the Protestants out of the New Barnsley estate. . . .

Dr Ian Paisley MP tabled questions in Stormont to the Ministry of Home Affairs about these incidents, but the ministerial replies were evasive and unsatisfactory. The Papist mobs still control parts of this Province, and the Government is ashamed to admit it.

Protestant Telegraph, 21 November 1970

123   The bomb and the bullet

From 1956-62 the IRA had conducted a 'military' campaign against the border which totally failed to enlist the support of the Northern Catholic population. During the next few years the movement devoted itself instead to social and economic questions on both sides of the border. Its consequent lack of military preparedness in Belfast in 1969 (characterized in the ghettos as 'IRA — I Ran Away') provided the basis for what seems a permanent rift in the movement between the 'Officials', who retained a thoroughgoing left-wing revolutionary image, and the 'Provisional Army Council' which broke away at the end of that year, placing less emphasis on social revolution and anti-clericalism, and more on a straightforward military campaign for Irish unity. In the long run it was the 'Provisionals' who came to dominate, but until mid-1972 when they declared a 'cease-fire', the Officials too had a strong military role. The tone of this funeral oration by Chief-of-Staff Cathal Goulding, though self-consciously in the republican tradition of speechmaking and in part an attempt to counter 'Provisional' recruiting, was fully reflected in later 'Official' actions.

. . .It is our earnest wish. . . that the full emancipation of the Irish people could be achieved by peaceful means, but unfortunately it is not within our power to dictate what action the forces of imperialism and exploitation will engage in to repress, coerce, and deny ordinary people their god-given rights, and when their answer to the just demand of the people are the lockout, the strike breaking, evictions, coercion, the prison cell, intimidation or the gallows, then our duty is to reply as he replied, in the language that brings these vultures to their senses most effectively, the language of the bomb and the bullet. . . .

Transcription from the *Irish Times*, 9 July 1971

124   Edward Kennedy: Britain's Vietnam

The massive rioting, the developing IRA campaign, and the attempts of first the RUC and later the British Army to control the situation were all covered in meticulous detail by the world's press. In Irish-America interest was particularly strong and financial backing for revolutionary activity, channeled through bodies like Irish Northern Aid, was substantial. The response of Senator Edward Kennedy (b. 1932), while no doubt conditioned by electoral considerations, reflects the character of Irish-American feeling at this stage in the conflict.

In a fiery speech to the Senate, Senator Edward Kennedy called today for the dissolution of the Northern Ireland Parliament, the immediate withdrawal of British troops, and the reunification of Ireland.

Senator Kennedy, who has the support of a strong Irish Catholic element in Massachusetts, was co-sponsor of a resolution with Senator Ribicoff (Democrat, Connecticut). He said the conscience of America could not keep silent when Irish men and women are dying. Ulster was rapidly becoming Britain's Vietnam.

'Often alone, often without notice, brave men and women of Ireland given their lives for the principles they hold dear. Millions have been driven from their homes, forced to leave the land they love, obliged to seek a new life in nations where the yoke of oppression could not reach.'

Senator Kennedy accused the Ulster Government of ruling 'by

bayonet and bloodshed', and claimed the struggle in the ghettos of Londonderry and Belfast was the age-old story of oppressed minorities. 'The heart of the solution we offer today is the call for immediate withdrawal of British troops and the establishment of a United Ireland. Without a firm commitment to troop withdrawal and reunification, there can be no peace. . . .

The Guardian, 21 October 1971

125 Hitler and Ulster

By late 1971 the savage inter-communal rioting of previous years was brought to an end, only to be replaced by a sustained campaign of bombing shopping areas and sniping at soldiers by the IRA, by conflicts between the British Army and republican (and more occasionally loyalist) crowds, and later by some vicious spates of sectarian murders, many of them planned by Protestant paramilitary groups like the UDA and UVF. Some of the more notorious among the many major incidents were the deaths of 15 people from a bomb in a Catholic public house in December 1971, an explosion in a crowded cafe in March 1972 which injured 143, many seriously, and the halting of a works minibus and the execution by machine-gun of its 11 Protestant occupants in January 1976. During the course of 'Bloody Sunday', a riotous demonstration in Londonderry in January 1972, members of a British Army battalion shot dead 13 civilians, many of whom were guilty of nothing more than being present at a riot. In Dublin public feeling was assuaged only after the British Embassy had been burned down. A few weeks later a bomb attempt by the Official IRA to take revenge on the battalion responsible resulted instead in the deaths of six civilian women cleaners and a Catholic padre at a barracks in England. On 'Bloody Friday' in July of the same year, the Provisional IRA set off 22 bombs during one afternoon in Belfast, killing nine civilians and two soldiers. In all, between 1969 and 1979, 1,994 people died, including 573 members of the security forces. 1972 was by far the worst year, at 468 deaths, but the same intensity of terror re-emerged for shorter periods, like January 1976, when 47 died.

Events like the 'Bloody Sunday' episode on the one hand, and parked 'car bombs' and sectarian murders, ofter indiscriminate, on the other, encouraged the growth of large 'no-go' areas from which the Army and RUC were excluded, and where 'order' was imposed by local paramilitaries or vigilantes. For some months after Bloody Sunday more than half the population of Derry was included in such an area. Not until August 1972 did the Army's massive 'Operation Motorman' bring the no-go areas under control. It was against this background that an item such as the following could appear in a well-produced and widely read west Belfast community newspaper.

HITLER—HIS PART IN OUR DOWNFALL

The British are engaged in the final solution to the Irish question, and they do not intend to make the mistakes Hitler made. Their methods are more subtle but no less deadly. If you look at the situation in this light, the similarities are incredible. . . . In fact the British have done and are doing what Hitler did, but they have reversed the order and method with more deadly efficiency. Many of the Irish in the North were already in the ghettos, so they simply turned the ghettos into concentration camps, not surrounded by barbed wire but ringed by British troops and dotted with army forts. The process was simple. First use an Irish virtue to provoke them. The British attacked the Lower Falls in July 1970, and the Irish naturally resisted them. Thus the first steps were taken on the road to Motorman. The next step was internment in August 1971. One sided, indiscriminate, and brutal, it was designed to provoke and extend reaction. It was another step to Motorman. . . .

Hitler had the problem of rounding up the Jews. But the British had no such problem. They used the Planters to do their dirty work. Hence the intimidation and driving out of Catholics from mixed and Protestant areas with only token opposition from the British army. Hitler used Eichmann and the SS. England used the UDA. 50,000 Catholics were forced to flee to the ghettos in the largest population movement in western Europe since world war two. They fled to the concentration camps without the British lifting a finger, and largely unnoticed by the outside world. The British are now in the process of completing this project by withdrawing their protection from threatened Catholic communities—such as that in east Belfast. . . .

The final British solution is not physical genocide but psychological genocide. When this is achieved they can impose with the assistance of Irish quislings, lay and clerical, whatever political solution suits them.

Andersonstown News, 15 November 1973

126 A Protestant and the Republic

Stereotyped responses were not the prerogative of one side only. The following extract is from a statement made to an academic conference by a rising Unionist politician and leader of the Orange Order.

. . .What many of us in Ulster believe is that the imposition of a certain kind of authority on a whole population from childhood produces severe cases of psychological inadequacy and personality disorders.

Fear of committing supposed sins, educational thwarting of the capacity for exercising critical judgement and initiative, unhappy marriages arising from doctrinaire illusions about the relations between the sexes and the inferior position given to women, lack of opportunity arising from sectarian and Gaelic-oriented education unsuited to the demands of modern life, and many other social and personal handicaps, seem to make citizens of the Irish Republic unhappy and inadequate.

A major evidence of this is the extent to which citizens of the Republic seek to drown their sorrows in alcohol. To refer to this is not just the intrusion of a pussyfoot prejudice. The thing has reached the proportions of a national disaster. Last year £200 million was spent in the Republic on alcoholic drinks, the highest rate of all countries in the world keeping such statistics. . . .

Undoubtedly the various forms of Protestantism have their moral casualties; but in certain directions the casualties seem much more numerous and serious among our Roman Catholic neighbours. And this tragic state of affairs seems to be associated with communities in which the Roman Catholic Church takes its rather heavy-handed Irish form.

Many of us Ulster Protestants regard the Irish Republic as a very sick country; and we do not think this just because people drink too much. We see it as a place from which too many people emerge with an anti-social Mafia-type attitude. Indeed it has been a matter of speculation that it was only the chance violent deaths of certain Irish gang chiefs in Chicago in the early years of this century which caused what we now call the Mafia to be an Italian rather than an Irish phenomenon.

Even those who break away from the pattern of one kind of group uniformity tend compulsively to take up some other pattern of equally oppressive uniformity. For all its careful respectability, perhaps because of that quality of respectability, the Irish Republic is the place of origin of many extremists, people unable to settle down to any form of stable, public-spirited and responsible living. A culture tends to produce its own antithesis, and it has often been noticed that a dogmatic religion tends to produce the dogmatic Communist or Maoist or other active proponent of using physical violence as a political instrument. . . .

Rev. W. Martin Smyth, 'A Protestant looks at the Republic', in *Sectarianism—Roads to Reconciliation* (Proceedings of the 22nd Irish Social Study Conference, 1974), pp. 31-3

127   No Rent: Safety with moral commitment

The Protestant backlash against the civil rights campaign, the introduction of mass internment without trial, and the predictable growth of clashes between the Army and the Catholic community, inevitably provoked bitterness. In response to internment in particular, Catholic tenants of public housing were called upon by all shades of anti-partitionist political representation to withhold payment of rent and rates. At the end of December 1971, the peak of resistance, 25 per cent of all such tenants were involved—a measure of both the extent and the limits of the campaign. In all the campaign produced a cumulative debt of over £5 million, although by the time that this rather lame appeal was made support had begun to dwindle quite rapidly, to 12 per cent in early 1974 and to 4 per cent two years later.

The sheer size of the problem has prevented the authorities from isolating individuals to any extent. . . . It is a fact that very few people have been convicted, had goods seized or suffered seriously, because of going on strike. People have not been thrown out of their homes because they failed to pay rent and rates. The general experience has been that it is safe to strike! And it is even safer for people to strike if the numbers on strike are larger. . . . It is no trouble to join the strike. You simply *do nothing!* The way to join is to decide here and now not to pay rent or rates when the time is due. It will come as a pleasant surprise to discover that in the coming months, nothing will have happened to the new striker. . . .

As Christmas approaches, the Andersonstown Civil Resistance Committee will publicize means of remembering the internees. But we would remind you of the moral commitment to protest against the immorality of internment.

Andersonstown News, 29 November 1973

128   Urban blight: A Protestant perspective

The conflict continued at a significant though much-reduced level throughout the 1970s. By this time urban blight arising—at least in part—out of the troubles had become a major problem in its own right. The housing stock in Belfast, Derry and other towns, which in late Victorian times had compared favourably with that of British industrial cities, had not been sufficiently renewed during the depressed inter-war years. Thus the substantial, if segregated, public housing programmes of the post-1945 period merely alleviated rather than solved the basic problem. With the onset of serious trouble in 1969, coinciding unfortunately with plans—later abandoned—for a Belfast Urban Motorway, some areas were soon rendered uninhabitable, others were vacated *en masse* by all who could afford to move somewhere safer, and still others were drastically overcrowded by what was in effect an internal refugee problem. Large-scale vandalism was an additional by-product of the 'no-go' mentality.

Thus in Ulster the urban blight which characterizes so much of late urban-industrial society was compounded by the sectarian conflict. So too were the community responses to that blight.

The residents call Charles Street South the 'forgotten area of Sandy Row'. Only thirteen houses are occupied. . . . All the other houses in the hundred-yard long street are derelict. . . . The problems they complain of include. . . . Vermin. . . . Damp which invades their homes. Many of the derelict houses have leaking roofs and the rain soaks through to the tenanted houses next door. Lack of repairs. . . . Car parking by commuters. . . . Robberies. . . .

The above is even more sickening, with the news that £5 million is to be spent modernizing and renovating flats on the Falls Road. An average of £8,000 per flat is to be expended on part of the Divis Flats complex, a structure not of the Victorian era but the modern Elizabethan. If Republican areas can be graced with multi-million pound development why not in loyalist areas?

Protestant Telegraph, 16 June 1978

129 Employment: An official perspective

Northern Ireland is a relatively small and thinly populated area. As such its problems of urban blight are in the long run amenable to solution by a finite amount of British support. Differential levels of occupational status and unemployment between the two communities, as set out in this summary of a report by a recently-created government agency, may prove considerably less tractable, involving as they do the overall lack of dynamism in the local economy, the spatial distribution of the population, and the varied but deep-seated legacy of past as well as present discrimination.

The main points which have emerged from this examination of the 1971 Northern Ireland population census can be outlined as follows.

Unemployment is experienced at a much higher level by Roman Catholics than by Protestants. Overall, the level is two and half times greater. This higher level of unemployment is likely to be comprised of occupational, industrial and geographical components. The industrial profiling of Protestants and Roman Catholics demonstrated major areas of Roman Catholic under-representation, most notably engineering, the utilities and insurance, banking, finance and business services and the unhealthy over-dependence of Roman Catholic males on the construction industry. Extending the industrial profile to consider wages it was obvious that there was a tendency for those industries which had the highest weekly manual wage in 1971 to be predominantly Protestant, a tendency which was still more marked for women.

The occupational profile of Protestants and Roman Catholics revealed a distribution of Roman Catholics towards the unskilled occupations. The modal Protestant male is a skilled manual worker whereas the modal Roman Catholic male is unskilled. When occupations were matched with industry, which was only possible for construction and engineering, there was a tendency in construction for Roman Catholics to be employed in the lower status occupations while in engineering, a higher status industry, there was a general under-representation of Roman Catholics in most occupations, particularly marked at managerial level.

Overall, a Roman Catholic middle class exists. Its size, however, seems to be largely a product of meeting the demands of a segregated society rather than through performing a more general role as does the Protestant middle class.

> Fair Employment Agency for N.I. *An Industrial and Occupational Profile of the Two Sections of the Population in N.I.* (1978), p. 14.

X Ulster since 1968: Solutions?

130 The Downing Street Declaration, August 1969

The savage rioting in Derry and Belfast in the summer of 1969 had become a central focus of interest for the world's press, and stretched the RUC to breaking point. When the British Army was called onto the streets in aid of the civil power on 14-15 August it was clear that the *de facto* sovereignty which the Northern Ireland government had enjoyed in domestic matters since 1922 was about to be breached. On 19 August the British prime minister Harold Wilson (b. 1916) called Chichester-Clark and two senior colleagues to London. The subsequent press release, part of which appears below, spelt out the reforms which were the price of British intervention, but at the same time re-affirmed the constitutional status of the province.

Chichester-Clark also seems to have agreed in a vague way to the B-Special force coming under Westminster control. In October a commission under Lord Hunt recommended that this be achieved by the disbandment of the Specials and the recruitment from scratch of a part-time Ulster Defence Regiment, responsible directly to Westminster as a unit of the British Army. The new force, although always under-represented in the Catholic community, had at the outset a significant Catholic recruitment. Once the struggle moved into its later phase of direct conflict between the IRA and the British Army however, a Catholic UDR man living in a Catholic district was simply a sitting target, and Catholic membership inevitably shrank to almost nothing.

1   The United Kingdom Government reaffirm that nothing which has happened in recent weeks in Northern Ireland derogates from the clear pledges made by successive United Kingdom Governments that Northern Ireland should not cease to be a part of the United Kingdom without the consent of the people of Northern Ireland or from the provision in Section 1 of the Ireland Act, 1949, that in no event will Northern Ireland or any part thereof cease to be part of the United Kingdom without the consent of the Parliament of Northern Ireland. The border is not an issue.

2   The United Kingdom Government again reaffirm that responsi-

bility for affairs in Northern Ireland is entirely a matter of domestic
jurisdiction. . . .
3   The United Kingdom Government have ultimate responsibility for
the protection of those who live in Northern Ireland when, as in the
past week, a breakdown of law and order has occurred. In this spirit,
the United Kingdom Government responded to the requests of the
Northern Ireland Government for military assistance in Londonderry
and Belfast in order to restore law and order. They emphasize again
that troops will be withdrawn when law and order has been restored.
4   . . .In the context of the commitment of these troops, the
Northern Ireland Government have reaffirmed their intention to take
into the fullest account at all times the views of Her Majesty's Government in the United Kingdom. . . .
5   The United Kingdom Government have welcomed the decision of
the Northern Ireland Government relating to local government
franchise, the revision of local government areas, the allocation of
houses, the creation of a Parliamentary Commissioner for Administration in Northern Ireland [Ombudsman] and machinery to consider
citizens' grievances against other public authorities. . . .

> Transcription from *The Times,* 20 August
> 1969

131   The British and Irish dimensions, 1971

By the summer of 1970 good will between the British Army and the Catholic
community had eroded into chronic street conflict. The replacement of
Chichester-Clark by the more politically nimble Brian Faulkner (1921-1977) in
March 1971 was widely seen as Stormont's last chance. It was Faulkner who,
that August, persuaded the British cabinet to agree to internment. But as the
IRA campaign intensified, enlivened rather than crushed by the new measure,
so too did the search for new initiatives. In September 1971 the Northern
Ireland situation was the subject of talks between the British and Irish prime
ministers, Edward Heath (b. 1916) and Jack Lynch. The press release revealed
little, but the very fact of such talks, the first public admission by Britain since
1922 of Dublin's legitimate interest in the north, implied that Stormont itself
might be on the table.

'During the last two days we have discussed the situation in Northern
Ireland in all its aspects. We have done so, fully recognizing that each
of us remains committed to his publicly-stated position on the constitutional status of Northern Ireland; and we have been concerned to
see whether, without prejudice to those positions, we can find some

agreed means of enabling all the people of Northern Ireland to live in the conditions of peace and stability which any democracy should ensure to its citizens without regard to their religious or political conviction.

We are at one in condemning any form of violence as an instrument of political pressure; and it is our common purpose to seek to bring violence, and internment and all other emergency measures to an end without delay.

We also recognize that to bring violence quickly to an end, and to resume economic, social and cultural progress, means must be found to establish harmony and cooperation between the two communities in Northern Ireland. Our discussions in the last two days have helped to create an atmosphere of greater understanding between us, and it is our hope that the process of political reconciliation may go forward to a successful outcome.

We agree that our meeting has served a significant and useful purpose in present circumstances, and we believe that further such meetings may have a helpful part to play in the future.'

Mr Heath and Mr Lynch agreed to keep in close communication with each other, personally, through their Ministerial colleagues and at official level, as might be appropriate, on all subjects affecting the future of Anglo-Irish relations. In this respect, the meeting between the two Prime Ministers scheduled for the autumn, to discuss a range of subjects, including the Anglo-Irish Free Trade Area Agreement and the applications of both countries for membership of the European Community, will be held on dates to be announced later.

Transcription from the *Irish Times*, 29 September 1971

132   Harold Wilson: The dream must be there

As the violence continued to escalate, pressures grew for a major political initiative from Westminster. When the House of Commons debated the situation in November 1971 Harold Wilson, now leader of the opposition, came forward with a very radical proposal. In practice it came to nothing, although it may have served a purpose in holding the left-wing of the Labour party in line, at the expense of confirming the suspicions of many Ulster Unionists about British Labour.

. . .I have reiterated the Downing Street Declaration reaffirming the Attlee pledge, and insisted yet again that any settlement must be by agreement. But I believe that the situation has now gone so far that it is impossible to conceive of an effective long-term solution in which the agenda at least does not include consideration of, and which is not in some way directed to finding a means of achieving, the aspirations envisaged half a century ago, of progress towards a united Ireland. . . .

A substantial term of years will be required before any concept of unification could become a reality, but the dream must be there. If men of moderation have nothing to hope for, men of violence will have something to shoot for. . . .

Let us examine it — a constitution of a united Ireland, to be reached by agreement and requiring ratification by all three Parliaments and with enforceable safeguards for minorities, to come into effect 15 years from the date agreement is reached. Why do we not examine what would be involved — some may want to go into it with utter determination, others may wish to treat it as an exercise — in a constitution of a united Ireland to come into effect 15 years from the date agreement is reached, provided that violence, as a political weapon, comes to an end? It would be a subject for consideration — I am not sure whether this is right — that such a settlement should be deferred by, say, one month beyond the 15 years for every act of violence committed in the name of union after signature and ratification of this agreement.

Such a proviso might have the effect of minimizing support or tacit approval by non-violent members of the minority for those who seek a solution by violence. With such a provision, all acts of violence would be seen by all, whatever their views today, to be not advancing but actually retarding the cause of unity of Ireland.

. . . If progress were made in the freely constituted Constitutional Commission, with the last word held by the three Parliaments, the Irish Republic should undertake to seek as a Republic, membership of the Commonwealth, recognizing the Queen as head of that Commonwealth. It has long been my view that, had the Indian formula providing for a sovereign republic to be a member of the Commonwealth been devised in time to affect the Irish settlement, Ireland could well have remained within the Commonwealth. I recognize the great difficulty this would present to Irish leaders, having regard to history; but more than at any time in Irish history, we have to regard the struggle of the past as an inspiration for the future, not an impediment to securing a peaceful future so different from that past.

HC Deb. 5th series, Vol. 826, cols. 1586-90
(25 November 1971)

133 Anders Boserup: The windmills of British imperialism

Wilson's proposal remained very much a dream, scarcely mentioned again by him or by anyone else on the Labour front bench. But it remains the case that almost all socialist theoreticians follow Lenin and, more specifically James Connolly, in identifying 'British imperialism' as the problem in Northern Ireland and a 'united Ireland', delivered by socialist midwives, as the solution. Only a small propagandist group in Ulster, the 'British and Irish Communist Organization', and more recently the rump of the Northern Ireland Labour Party, have publicly advocated an alternative left-wing strategy. One statement of that general position was put forward in 1972 by the Danish political scientist, Anders Boserup, in an article entitled 'Contradictions and Struggles in Northern Ireland'.

As is nationalism elsewhere, Catholic Irish nationalism is a relatively recent phenomenon dating from the mid-nineteenth century and the period of the Gaelic revival. Like other nationalisms, it has sought to establish a continuity with a past which has been reinterpreted in romanticized terms. It thus incorporates an entire set of myths about the Irish struggle against English domination and the Protestant Ascendancy and about a pre-plantation Gaelic society of a communistic type — all of them myths, the foundations of which in historical fact are as tenuous as those of the corresponding Protestant ones.

British domination is thus seen as the root of all the problems of Ireland. In the socialist ideology British domination becomes British imperialism. In this way everything fits nicely into place in what appears to be a consistent socialist theory. The severing of the links with the British oppressor becomes the precondition for socialism in Ireland. The Orange oligarchy in the North (as well as the Green Tories in the South) become the middlemen, the neo-colonialist agents of British imperialism, and the Unionist workers, lured by petty privileges, its helpless tools. Most important: the existence of the common enemy, British imperialism, fuses Catholics and Protestants into one 'people' in so far as their *objective* interests are concerned. National differences conveniently recede into the background. . . .

Theories which ultimately reduce to notions like these are held with only minor variations by such diverse groups as the Communist Party, the IRA and People's Democracy. . . .

. . .Few nationalist ideologies could have provided a more fertile soil for socialist ideas than did the Irish since the socialist and anti-imperialist struggles were so easily shown to be two aspects of the same thing. In fact, of course, the Catholic left did not 'take over' a nationalist ideology; it was born of it and grew up in it. Its own ideology remained a variant of it, with somewhat different priorities, certainly, but with the main concepts and beliefs unchanged. This fusion of nationalism and socialism is particularly marked in the writings of James Connolly in the first decades of this century. Piety towards him has been such that all socialist groups today claim to be his heirs, and no-one even begins to ask whether his demand for an all-Irish Socialist Republic is as valid today as it was in his time. Instead, he has become part of the myths and the dogmas — a further 'proof', if any had been needed, that a Socialist Republic is a 32-county Republic as a matter of course. . . .

*   *   *

If it is to engage effectively in the struggle against the Orange system the left must necessarily dissociate itself from 32-county nationalism and accept the existence of the Northern State. As long as the left does not do this but, more or less wholeheartedly, plays the tune of Catholic nationalism it is in fact shoring up that system by providing it with a badly needed scarecrow to frighten Protestant workers.

The affirmation that Northern Irish Protestants constitute a separate national entity with a right to refuse incorporation in the Republic is usually considered to be divisive of the working class and therefore anti-socialist. On the contrary I think that it is the stubborn affirmation of unity and solidarity where none exists and the extravagant claim of Irish Catholics to the whole island which is divisive. The Catholic left demands a 32-county Republic and tries to sweeten the pill for Protestants by affirming that this will be a socialist, and *ipso facto* a secular Republic. Protestants would be fools if they believed it. Socialism in Ireland is not for tomorrow, and, even if it were, deeply entrenched ideologies do not disappear overnight. The Catholic left, by its espousal of the demand for a united Ireland, has demonstrated that even those who claim to constitute the socialist vanguard are trapped in nationalist ideologies.

Ultimately it is to put the cart before the horse to demand a 32-county Republic and hope that it can then develop towards socialism. . . .

The unity of Ireland will come after the feudal and colonial remnants in the North have been swept away and after the South has given up its demands. Then, to paraphrase Marx, after the separation there may come federation, but federation on the basis of equal rights for nations and international working-class solidarity. To start with an imposed unity is to betray the ideals of internationalism, socialism and democracy. . . .

To conclude I submit that there is a need for a reorientation of the struggle of the Catholic left, by which it would leave aside the windmills of British imperialism and the wholly counter-productive demands for Irish reunfication, and would concentrate on the real issue of today: crushing the Orange system; and doing this in a revolutionary, rather than a reformist way, exploiting the opportunities it gives for raising the revolutionary consciousness of the workers—which simply means their understanding of their own objective situation. Both among Protestants and among Catholics it is widely assumed that the Protestant ascendancy and the Union with Britain are two sides of the same coin: that the interests of 'colonialism' and those of imperialism, those of Orange rule and those of Westminster and British capital are coincident. I have tried to show that on the contrary it is here that the principal contradiction is to be found. To develop correct insight and hence revolutionary consciousness among Irish workers the best strategy seems to be to expose and to sharpen the contradiction. For in so doing both Protestant and Catholic workers will be forced to revise their received notions. As this contradiction is brought out into the open they will have to align with one side and against the other, but they cannot continue to align (or to believe they align) with both as do the Protestants, or against both as do the Catholics. Thus, whatever realignments occur they will facilitate common action by workers on both sides of the fence. The most pernicious aspect of the current struggle against 'British imperialism' is precisely that it perpetuates the false identification of Union with Unionist rule which lies at the very core of those ideologies which divide the working class. . . .

R. Miliband and J. Savile (eds.) *The Socialist Register 1972*, pp. 181-90

134   Neal Blaney: Time to change ends

In Dublin too, a range of possibilities was debated. Neal Blaney (b. 1922) had been dismissed from Lynch's cabinet in May 1970 following his implication in the importation of arms for use in the north, but his strong personal position in Co. Donegal enabled him to continue in politics as an independent Fianna Fail deputy. Although during the 1950s he had been a member of a cabinet which brought in internment in the south for IRA suspects, his position on the northern situation now came very close to that of the Provisional IRA.

. . .I do not attach blame to those who have perpetrated these deeds of discrimination because the very setting-up of this puppet state [Northern Ireland] 50 years ago, and the manner of its setting-up, could only bring in its train an effort by those in control to maintain that control at any cost. While Britain persists, as she is now persisting, in supporting that regime by money and by arms we will have an effort to continue that Government by those in control of the power and the influence and to retain the power and influence that it gives. So long as that situation continues, we will have the efforts of the minority, the oppressed, the discriminated-against minority, to break out of this position and to get for themselves the freedom which the Twenty-six Counties got the hard way 50 years ago. In talking of getting this freedom the hard way, is there not evidence for all of us to see that no freedom has been won by any people in any part of the globe without violence? There were many parts where Britain predominated, suppressed and colonized. In all the lands in which this was attempted Britain's yoke was only broken the hard way by violence meeting violence. It is true to say, in my estimation, that we are now nearing the end of the Six Counties and, perhaps, nearing the ultimate unity of our territory and ultimately the true unity of our people because of the hard way being taken by the minority there. . . .

. . .It is not right or helpful to say that this matter can be settled between Irishmen. It can, but there is the necessity for Britain to take her paws out of the nest, to take herself out of the Six Counties before there can be any rational or reasonable discussion with the people who are in control in the Six Counties today. You cannot expect, and you will not get, any reasonable or rational approach or even useful discussions with Mr Faulkner or his successor, if there is one, until Britain has taken away the guarantee that she repeatedly gives that she is going to maintain the Six Counties regime until the majority in the Six Counties are satisfied to come in with us.

. . .It is true to say that all of our people, the entire land, has suffered as a result of Partition, and regardless of any question as to who inside the Six Counties wants an end to Partition, we in the rest of the country have a right to bring about the end of Partition in any way we can.

It is not good enough, as I said at the outset, to start talking about a million reasons why you cannot end Partition unless that million agree. Are we to continue in the future, as we have done in the past 50 years, to look to the million and say that they do not want it, so we cannot have it? Is there no right on the side of the majority in this island of ours? Have we no right to say there must be a second half to be played, that 50 years is a long enough first half, that it is time the whistle was blown and that we should change ends?

> *Dail Debates*, Vol. 256, cols. 142-9 (21 October 1971)

135   Conor Cruise O'Brien: An aspiration or a claim?

Conor Cruise O'Brien (b. 1917), writer and journalist, and former academic and diplomat, was a Labour member of the Dail from 1969 to 1977. More than any other southern politician he has acknowledged the impracticability and in many cases insincerity of the call for Irish unity in the short-term. His frank treatment of the national myth was perhaps chief among the factors causing him to lose his Dail seat in 1977.

. . . The northern Catholic bishops ask the question: who in their sane senses think they can bomb 1,000,000 Protestants into a united Ireland? The answer seems to be: Deputy Blaney and his friends, if we regard them as being in their sane senses.

I have said that the claim that Northern Ireland is ours by right and that the Dail has a right of jurisdiction over it, asserted in Article 3, though then suspended is at the root of the trouble; but there is a vital distinction to be made here, a distinction which is blurred over in the Taoiseach's speeches and is the troubled source of their confusion and ambiguity. That distinction which should be made and is not is the distinction between a claim and an aspiration.

As regards the aspiration, the aspiration towards the unity of Ireland and all its people, I think we are all in agreement and those whom we represent are in agreement. . . . We in the Labour Party have as our objective the attainment of a 32-County socialist Republic of Ireland. That is our objective, to which we hold; but we are not claiming that that 32-County socialist Republic is already here as of right, is already here but is wrongly being withheld from us by the perversity of the Protestant workers of Northern Ireland.

We are not claiming that, and that is the distinction between an aspiration and a claim. We know that this is something which can only be achieved gradually— God alone knows how gradually— through a growing understanding between Catholics and Protestants. We know also that one of the great barriers to such an understanding is precisely the claim, the pretention of the Dublin Government that the Six Counties, including areas with massive Protestant and Unionist majorities in the eastern part of the area, rightfully belong to the Catholic majority of Ireland because that is the substance of the claim. . . .

Our claim to take over the Six Counties, a claim still formally sustained repeatedly, was a claim to impose our will on the Protestant population there. It was essentially that. We do not like to call it that, but that is what it was and that is what it still is. Is it altogether surprising then, in view of that, that the majority there feel justified, in imposing their will on the Catholic minority? We say, of course, that we would not behave as they do. We would be nice to the Protestant majority if we had them in. We would treat them decently. We would bring them cups of tea from time to time. If, of course, they ignored and cut themselves off from all their past political traditions we would be very nice to them indeed. But what would we do if they resisted incorporation, or if many of them resisted and some of them disliked it? What if they were felt not to be absolutely on our side as the Catholic minority in the North are felt to be absolutely on another side. I am not sure. . . .

Dail Debates, Vol. 256, cols. 236-9 (21 October 1971)

136   Noel Browne: Who wants a secular state?

O'Brien's Labour colleague Noel Browne (b. 1915) began his political career in 1948 as a member of the neo-republican Clann na Poblachta party. But his primary interest had always been in radical social reform, and in his later career he has endeavoured to find an association between his social goals and a rather different tone on the national question.

. . .I believe that if we are serious about attempting to create a climate in which we can seriously consider the eventual union of our people — geographical unity is unimportant; unity amongst our people — we must recognize the genuine fears of the Northern Protestant worker that in a united Ireland he would be a minority, a significant minority, and that in the situation of a united Ireland he would suffer in much the same way as the Catholic minority have suffered in the Six Counties since the State was created. He has a sense of guilt and a sense of simple reality that he might be exploited in a united Ireland.

We must make some gesture of sincerity if we are serious about our belief that in a united Ireland he would not find himself exploited in any way or subjected to a sectarian way of life of which he disapproved.

None of the parties who have held power over the years was prepared to make the sacrifices needed. Sacrifices are needed not to end Partition or to unite Ireland but to make it easier to begin the long debate which could be entered into so that eventually our people could accept unity in some form or other. There are the obvious constitutional guarantees. There is the position of the Catholic church as the most important church in the community. This is not simply an academic point in the Constitution. In fact it is used in the courts in relation to certain questions dealing with marriage settlements of one kind or another. There are the *Ne Temere* decree, the right to contraception and family planning, the right to divorce. There is the question of non-sectarian schools, mixed schools. In fact, who are prepared to say that they want to see a united community and want to see it so badly that they are prepared to consider the establishment of a secular constitution and a secular State?

. . .There is the question of the social services. We all know that they have better health services, better education services, better unemployment rates and old age rates. If we had been serious over 50 years surely we would have done something about these barriers; they are not the main obstacle but they are obvious impediments to some kind of rapprochement between the South and the North. Instead of reinforcing the two separate cultures which were established by the plantations at the beginning, we have, by law, in our Constitution, in our general attitude and behaviour, and in our educational system, created two separate communities a Catholic community and a Protestant community, inalienably hostile and opposed to one another.

I believe the Taoiseach simply cannot go across to Downing Street to Mr Faulkner and Mr Heath without being faced with these logical and legitimate criticisms of his tenure of office and of his predecessors. It is not a special Fianna Fail failing. We have all failed. . . .

> *Dail Debates*, Vol. 256, cols. 73-5 (20 October 1971)

137   Edward Heath: More radical measures

The IRA campaign in the north continued to escalate through the winter of 1971-2, aided by Catholic — and indeed world-wide — reaction to the events of 'Bloody Sunday'. Large sections of Derry city and west Belfast became ungovernable 'no go' areas for the security forces. In March 1972, as Heath explained to the House of Commons, the British government took the fateful step of transferring responsibility for law and order in Northern Ireland directly to Westminster, thereby precipitating at least an interim period of direct rule.

At a meeting. . . . on 22 March, we made it plain that in the British Government's view new and more radical measures were necessary, if there was to be any prospect of breaking out of this deadlock.

We made three main proposals. First, in the hope of taking the border out of the day-to-day political scene, and as a reassurance that there would be no change in the border without the consent of a majority of the people of Northern Ireland, we proposed periodic plebiscites on this issue.

Second, we proposed that a start be made on phasing out internment. Third, we were concerned about the present division of responsibility of law and order between Belfast and Westminster, whereby control remains largely with the Northern Ireland Government while the operational responsibility rests with the British Army, and therefore with the United Kingdom Government. . . .

. . .We therefore told the Prime Minister and Deputy Prime Minister of Northern Ireland that we had reached the conclusion that the responsibility of law and order in Northern Ireland should be transferred to Westminster.

The first two of our proposals were in principle acceptable to the Northern Ireland Government. But Mr Faulkner told us that his Government could not accept proposals for the transfer of responsibility for law and order from Stormont to Westminster. . . .

. . .The Northern Ireland Government's decision therefore leaves us with no alternative to assuming full and direct responsibility for the administration of Northern Ireland until a political solution to the problems of the province can be worked out in consultation with all those concerned.

. . .A new office of Secretary of State for Northern Ireland is, therefore, being created. . . .

> *HC Deb.* 5th series, Vol. 833, cols. 1859-61
> (24 March 1972)

138 'Binding the minority': Constitutional proposals, 1973

William Whitelaw (b. 1918), a senior minister, became the province's first Secretary of State, taking responsibility along with junior ministers for both security and constitutional reconstruction. During the autumn and winter of 1972-3 he held talks, formal or informal, with almost all political groupings in

Northern Ireland and in March brought forward a white paper outlining new constitutional proposals. At the insistence of the SDLP an 'Irish dimension' was included in the plan. But the central features were the creation of a new provincial assembly with as yet undefined powers, and the proposal for institutionalized 'power sharing' between representatives of the Catholic and Protestant communities at the executive or cabinet level.

51 . . .Hitherto, the executive dispositions in Northern Ireland have been made by the Governor under the Act of 1920 and in accordance with the current British constitutional conventions. But those conventions have been applied to Northern Ireland in a situation where: (a) the same party has been the majority party after each general election; and (b) that party has never returned to parliament in the course of half a century a member from the minority community which comprises more than a third of the population. It is from this situation that there flows the problem, as described in the Paper for Discussion, of 'binding the minority to the support of new political arrangements in Northern Ireland.'

52 There is no future for devolved institutions in Northern Ireland unless majority and minority alike can be so bound. This is not to say that any 'right of veto' can be conceded to violent, subversive or unconstructive elements determined, if they can, to undermine any new system from the outset. But the Government does not believe that this is the wish of the overwhelming majority in either community. What has to be found — through their representatives — is a system of exercising executive power in Northern Ireland which is broadly acceptable to them. One important means of ensuring this will be more effective participation by the Assembly as a whole, through its structure of committees, in the development of policy; but it is the view of the Government that the Executive itself can no longer be solely based upon any single party, if that party draws its support and its elected representation virtually entirely from only one section of a divided community. . . .

53 . . .When the Government is satisfied: (a) that the procedures of the Assembly and the proposed method of exercising executive powers will, taken together, be a reasonable basis for the establishment of government by consent (that is to say, with substantially wider support from the community as a whole than would necessarily be indicated by a simple majority in the Assembly); (b) in particular, that executive powers will not be concentrated in elected representatives from one community only; and (c) that any proposed arrangements will represent not just a theoretical framework for fair and acceptable

government, but a system which can and will be worked effectively by those concerned, it will seek the approval of Parliament for the devolution by subordinate instrument of extensive law-making powers to the Assembly, and for a broadly corresponding devolution of executive powers to a Northern Ireland Executive, which will be constituted in accordance with the arrangements that have been agreed.

PP 1972-3, cxxvi (Cmnd. 5259), *Northern Ireland Constitutional Proposals*, pp. 13-14.

139   Harold Wilson: Who do these people think they are?

Elections for a new 78-seat Assembly in May 1973, held under the proportional representation system for the first time since 1925, served as a test of public opinion on the white paper proposals and gave them a substantial majority. Only two minor parties on the Protestant side, running as a 'Loyalist coalition', opposed it entirely. But the Unionist party was badly split, almost a third of its votes and seats going to avowed opponents of the white paper. Faulkner's majority Unionists held the ring as the largest party, but it gradually transpired that many of his grass-roots supporters were not clear exactly what they had voted for and some of his Assembly followers were less than resolute. A power-sharing executive of Faulkner Unionists, Alliance and SDLP Assemblymen was formed, and in December 1973 met with British and Irish government leaders in conference at Sunningdale, near London, where plans for a two-tier Council of Ireland, with limited powers of decision-making by unanimous agreement in the economic and social sphere, were settled. For the Unionist side it was the price of SDLP participation.

The fury of the Loyalists quickly found an outlet when Heath's Conservative government called an unexpected UK election in February 1974. With the Faulkner Unionists in organizational disarray, the opponents of power-sharing won almost all the seats and a narrow overall majority of votes cast in Northern Ireland, under the straight-vote system. Focusing their opposition on the Sunningdale agreement, they now set out with renewed vigour to undermine the executive altogether. When the agreement received Assembly ratification, on 14 May 1974, a group of Protestant trade unionists, styling themselves the Ulster Workers' Council, called a general strike against its implementation. Widespread and often savage intimidation by loyalist street gangs stiffened the resolve of luke-warm Protestants, making the stoppage almost total in Belfast and many other areas of the province. Loyalist coalition members and anti-Faulkner Unionists joined the leadership of the movement as its strength grew.

Apart from taking control of 27 petrol stations on the fourteenth day of the strike, the British government made no significant intervention. The strikers' control of the electrical power supply, and the apparent inability of the army to operate the system, was the alleged explanation. The government adamantly refused either to intervene effectively to break the strike or to negotiate with the UWC. The SDLP members of the executive threatened to resign if the former was not done, but they were beaten to the point by their Unionist colleagues who had wanted negotiations. With the resignation of the Faulknerites on 28 May the executive collapsed, and full governmental responsibility reverted to Westminster. Harold Wilson's television address of 25 May, announced in advance and expected to initiate firm action, had offered only abuse, which served rather to strengthen the strikers' resolve.

. . .It is a deliberate and calculated attempted to use every undemocratic and unparliamentary means for the purpose of bringing down the whole constitution of Northern Ireland so as to set up there a sectarian and undemocratic state, from which one third of the people of Northern Ireland will be excluded. This is not — this has not been at any time over these past few difficult years — a party matter in the House of Commons or in this country at all. Where the political wildcats of Northern Ireland seek to divide and embitter, all the major parties in Britain have sought to heal and to unite. In the years before 1970 the then Conservative opposition supported the action the Labour Governemnt took when we put the troops in, in a security role, and issued the Downing Street Declaration which gave the most specific guarantees to the people of Northern Ireland about their right to determine their own future. When Labour was in opposition we supported Mr Heath, Mr Whitelaw and later Mr Francis Pym, first when they suspended the old one-sided Stormont parliamentary system which had broken down, then when they devised a new constitution aimed at reconciliation and shared power in Northern Ireland and again in the initiatives they took to secure better relations between Ulster and the Irish Republic. . . .

The people on this side of the water — British parents — have seen their sons vilified and spat upon and murdered. British taxpayers have seen the taxes they have poured out, almost without regard to cost — over £300 million a year this year with the cost of the Army operation on top of that — going into Northern Ireland. They see property destroyed by evil violence and are asked to pick up the bill for rebuilding it. Yet people who benefit from all this now viciously defy Westminster, purporting to act as though they were an elected government; people who spend their lives sponging on Westminster and British democracy and then systematically assault democratic methods. Who do these people think they are?

. . .Tonight I ask for the continued support of a long-suffering people in dealing with a situation in which the law is being set aside and essential services are being interrupted. It is our duty as the United Kingdom Parliament and the United Kingdom Government to ensure that minorities are protected, that those in greatest need are helped, that essential services are maintained, not by the condescension of a group of self-appointed persons operating outside the law, but by those who have been elected to ensure that these things shall be done.

The people of Northern Ireland and their democratically elected Assembly and executive have the joint duty of seeing this thing through on the only basis on which true unity can be achieved — democratic elections, constitutional government and the spirit of tolerance and reconciliation. And in doing that they will have the support of the British Government, with our responsibilities within the United Kingdom and our responsibilities in world affairs, for law and order in Northern Ireland. We intend to see it through with them.

Transcription from *The Times*, 27 May 1974

140 The search for wider agreement: Constitutional proposals, 1975-6

As direct rule continued under the Labour Secretary of State Merlyn Rees (b. 1920) and a growing team of ministers, elections were held in May 1975 for a 78-seat Constitutional Convention. During the latter part of the year it held regular sessions, but the 'United Ulster Unionist Coalition' of Loyalists and anti-power sharing Unionists had a clear overall majority, and their majority convention report, produced in November 1975, excluded the possibility of power sharing at executive level, and so failed to meet the British government's required condition of widespread support from both communities. Rees reported this predictable failure to the House of Commons, and called for a brief extension of the Convention in the vain hope that a compromise along the lines of a temporary power-sharing coalition for the duration of the present emergency might be forthcoming.

. . .Let me deal with one major matter at the start. The continuing and appalling violence in Northern Ireland has undoubtedly added to the groundswell of opinion in Great Britain that we should withdraw from Northern Ireland, cut Northern Ireland adrift and let the Northern Irish, whether Catholic or Protestant, fend for themselves. The Government are in no doubt that this would be a grave mistake. . . . Equally, a united Ireland is not in the gift of this Parliament. . . . It would be a mistake also to think that we could impose or enforce a constititional system and expect it to work.

. . .This Government took the decision, which was supported by the

House and by many people in Northern Ireland, that the people of Northern Ireland should be given an opportunity, through elected representatives called together for the purpose, to put forward recommendations as to how they thought Northern Ireland should be governed — that is, that they should have a chance to contribute to the solution of their own problems. The Convention which was elected on 1 May last year was devised by this Government to give the people of Northern Ireland that chance. But it is for this House to reach final decisions. That is what being part of the United Kingdom is all about.

. . .Northern Ireland is a divided community. Experience in recent years has made plain that no system of government within Northern Ireland will be stable or effective unless both parts of the community acquiesce in that system and are willing to work to support it. I must tell the House that, in spite of those matters on which the Convention has agreed, support from both sides of the community is not at present forthcoming for the total system proposed in the Report. The Government share with the Convention the strong desire that direct rule may be brought to an end and that a new system of government may be established within Northern Ireland. But the Report does not, in the view of the Government, command sufficiently widespread acceptance throughout the community to provide stable and effective government.

. . .Those who argue in favour of independence ignore the economic weakness of Northern Ireland and its lack of natural resources. The forecast of public expenditure there in 1975-6 is about £1,300 million. The plain fact is that Northern Ireland could not sustain anything like its present living standards if it were not part of the United Kingdom. . . .

. . .Northern Ireland will continue to be governed by, and from, this Parliament. It is in accordance with this principle that the Northern Ireland Act 1974 provided for the functions of government to be exercised by me. As I have made clear to this House, under the terms of that Act, the Convention is not, and cannot be, an advisory body to me, nor can it play a wider role in the government of Northern Ireland. The Convention will soon come to an end. I have no power to prolong its existence or to preserve the position of its members except for the constitutional purposes laid down in the Act of 1974.

. . .As for direct rule, we govern Northern Ireland. That is the way it will be, but I do not see direct rule as a method for governing Northern Ireland. . . .

The overriding need now is for a wider measure of agreement in the

Convention. It is because of the very fact that the society of Northern Ireland is divided and that the political parties within Northern Ireland reflect these divisions that violence on both sides can operate under a political guise. The gangsters can masquerade as politicians with guns instead of what they are—criminals. . . .

HC Deb. 5th series, vol. 903, cols. 51-65 (12 January 1976)

141   Betty Williams: Peace, peace, peace

The Convention came to an end in March 1976 and all its members except for the three who were also Westminster MPs faced political unemployment. A number of them had been virtually full-time politicians for many years. The Convention's failure marked a tacit end to the search for a political settlement and an emphasis instead on tackling terrorism as ordinary crime. The trend towards *de facto* integration of Northern Ireland into the Westminster govern-mental structure intensified, and it was agreed to increase the number of Northern Ireland MPs so as to reflect this. The ensuing vacuum in the headlines was filled, alongside continuing IRA activity, by a women's peace movement begun in Belfast in August 1976. It differed from the earlier Alliance party in that it was directed explicitly at the predominantly working-class areas of Belfast where terrorism flourished, and in its prudent avoidance of political party status or commitment. The movement later widened to include men as well as women, and in 1977 its leaders were awarded the Nobel Peace Prize. But later developments did not suggest that the movement had gained the overwhelming support which would be necessary to remove terrorism's slender but apparently firm base in the community.

The Belfast peace movement doubled in strength yesterday when at least 20,000 people flocked in warm sunshine to another rally at a park in east Belfast. The marchers, led by a group of women from the Catholic Andersonstown area of Belfast, defied threats from the provisional IRA by parading with a 'Peace with Justice' banner through Protestant and mixed areas. Earlier Dr Ian Paisley's extremist Protestant newspaper the *Protestant Telegraph* added its voice to Provisional IRA attacks on the women's peace movement, describing it as 'spurious' and 'priest-inspired'. . . .

Mrs Betty Williams, the 33-year old organizer of the movement, said simply 'Peace, peace, peace' when asked about the attacks. She said she was 'overwhelmed' by yesterday's response. She and Miss Mairead Corrigan, an aunt of the three Maguire children who were killed 11 days ago when an IRA man's car crashed into them, led the

march from the BBC's offices in central Belfast to the Ormeau Park.
In a symbolic gesture of reconciliation at the entrance to the park, Mrs
Williams hugged and kissed Mrs Winnie Jordan, leader of the
Protestant women from east Belfast. . . .

Protestant and Catholic ghettos of Belfast, including the Ardoyne,
Turf Lodge, Shankill and Springfield, were represented by banners in
the crowd. Shops closed early to enable workers to attend the
rally. . . .

As Protestants streamed back to east Belfast and Catholics to the
west, Mrs Williams and Miss Corrigan said that next Saturday they
plan to hold the biggest peace rally yet seen. Instead of being in a
Catholic or mixed area it will march through the Loyalist heartland of
the Shankill Road. . . .

It is partly a symptom of the journalistic silly season and partly
instinctive well-wishing from the British media that the activities of
two ordinary Belfast women have received so much publicity. But
there is also their patent sincerity, and their conviction that, this time,
they are really going to do something to end the violence. . . .

The Observer, 22 August 1976

142   Edward Kennedy: America's opportunity

In August 1977 the new American president Jimmy Carter published an 'initiative' on the Northern Ireland crisis. It was but a small part of his administration's efforts to demonstrate a liberal and humane interest in world
problems, and appeared to have little direct impact in Ulster. But when
endorsed by politicians with a more direct involvement in Irish-American
affairs, such as Edward Kennedy, the   gesture developed a potentially
important new dimension so far as Irish-American support for the IRA, both
emotional and financial, was concerned.

While properly avoiding any specific US involvement in the details of a
settlement, the President has unequivocally endorsed a solution
involving a form of government in Northern Ireland broadly acceptable to both the Protestant and Catholic communities. By endorsing
this concept of partnership between the two communities the
President has given strong and much-needed support to moderate
political leaders on both sides in their continuing negotiations to
achieve a peaceful settlement. . . . My hope is that once a peaceful
settlement is reached, the United States would undertake a Marshall-
type programme of assistance to heal the wounds of the present

conflict and to benefit all the people of Northern Ireland, Protestants and Catholics alike. I believe there would be broad support in Congress for such a programme of jobs and other assistance, linked to a peaceful settlement.

Finally, by strongly denouncing the violence of both sides and by calling for vigorous Federal law-enforcement efforts against those who violate US laws, the President has taken the strongest possible step to ensure that American guns and dollars will not be used to support those engaged in violence. . . .

> Transcription from the *Irish Times*, 31 August 1977

143   Ian Paisley: 'Blood on his hands'

A frequently-expressed hope of the early 1970s was the view that British and Irish membership of the European Economic Community would create the conditions for an improvement in community relations in Ulster, gradually rendering petty localisms irrelevant in face of a new supra-national consciousness. It is too soon to judge whether this is likely to be the case. At present all that can safely be said is that electoral activity in Northern Ireland during the 1970s has consistently increased political polarization while at the same time providing the occasion for upsurges in terrorist activity. The 1979 campaign for seats in the first directly elected European Parliament was no exception in this respect. While EEC pressures may eventually work towards greater harmony in Ireland, the first evidence from Strasbourg was not encouraging.

A major row blew up in the European Parliament in Strasbourg today with the Rev. Ian Paisley accusing Irish Prime Minister Jack Lynch of supporting the IRA and having 'blood on this hands'. . . .

The trouble started when Mr Lynch, as acting President of the EEC Council, started to make a ceremonial speech — but his first few words were in Irish.

Mr Paisley, obviously enraged, started shouting out from the back of the Chamber. The words 'blood' and 'terrorism' were heard.

Outside the chamber — after Mr Paisley had been refused permission to continue his protest — he said that the Irish Government was the only nation in the Council of Europe to have refused to sign the European Convention on the Suppression of Terrorism. . . .

Mr Lynch's opening remarks in the Irish language were drowned as Mr Paisley leapt to his feet and began shouting protests 'in the name of Ulster's dead'. . . .

Asked if this was the right occasion for such an outburst he replied:

'This is the first time an Ulster representative has had the opportunity to face Mr Lynch and make this point.'

'I am not here to play a Parliamentary game — I came here just to fight for the people.'

He described Mr Lynch as 'a hypocrite, a man who had blood on his hands.'

Mr Paisley was involved in a bitter exchange with Irish Euro-MP Mr Noel Davern as he left the chamber.

Clutching a Bible he shouted at Mr Davern, a member of Mr Lynch's Fianna Fail Party: 'You are a papist lout and your leader is one too.'

'You are a bigot,' replied Mr Davern. . . .

Belfast Telegraph, 18 July 1979

144 The intervention of Pope John Paul II: Call murder by no other name?

At the end of the 1970s the political future of Northern Ireland appeared little clearer than it had been at the fall of the Stormont Parliament in 1972. Response to the visit of the Pope, whose speech on the Ulster troubles was delivered to an estimated audience of a quarter of a million Catholics, said to have been predominantly Northerners, at Drogheda on 29 September 1979, indicated that even amongst pragmatic politicians and journalists perceptions of the situation differed widely. Many, perhaps the majority of observers, in Britain and Ireland welcomed the speech and noted its clear denunciation of violence — 'call murder by no other name'. Others, however, expressed concern at His Holiness's use of terms like 'political vacuum' and his apparent implication that IRA terrorism, though its methods were morally unaccept-able ought to be, and was capable of being, defused by political concil-iation — that direct rule of Northern Ireland by successive, democratically elected UK governments, did not constitute political justice.

. . . Now I wish to speak to all men and women engaged in violence. I appeal to you, in language of passionate pleading. On my knees I beg you to turn away from the paths of violence and to return to the ways of peace. You may claim to seek justice. I, too, believe in justice, and seek justice. But violence only delays the day of justice. Violence destroys the work of justice. Further violence in Ireland will only drag down to ruin the land you claim to love and the values you claim to cherish. . . .

I appeal to young people who may have become caught up in organizations engaged in violence, I say to you, with all the love I have for you, with all the trust I have in young people: do not listen to voices which speak the language of hatred, revenge, retaliation. Do not follow any leaders who train you in the ways of inflicting death. . . .

To all who bear political responsibility for the affairs of Ireland, I want to speak with the same urgency and intensity with which I have spoken to the men of violence. Do not cause, or condone, or tolerate, conditions which give excuse, or pretext, to men of violence.

For those who resort to violence always claim that only violence brings about change. They claim that political action cannot achieve justice. You, politicians, must prove them to be wrong. You must show that there is a peaceful, political way to justice. You must show that peace achieves the work of justice, and violence does not. . . . If politicians do not decide to and act for just change, then the field is left open to the men of violence. Violence thrives best when there is a political vacuum and a refusal of political movement. . . .

Transcription from the *Irish Times*, 1 October 1979

SHORT LIST OF BOOKS FOR FURTHER READING

The Making of Modern Ireland (1966)
Beckett, J.C.

An Economic History of Ireland since 1660 (1972)
Cullen, L.M.

Internal Colonialism: The Celtic Fringe in British National Development
(1975)
Hechter, M.

Minorities in History (1978) chs.4-6
Hepburn, A.C. (ed.)

The Green Flag: A History of Irish Nationalism (1972)
Kee, R.

The Modernisation of Irish Society, 1848-1918 (1973)
Lee, J.J.

Ireland since the Famine (1973 ed.)
Lyons, F.S.L.

Ireland in the Twentieth Century (1975)
Murphy, J.A.

Ireland before the Famine, 1798-1848 (1972)
O Tuathaigh, G.

John Foster: The Politics of the Anglo-Irish Ascendancy (1978)
Malcomson, A.P.W.

The Fenian Movement (1968)
Moody, T.W. (ed.)

The Liberator: Daniel O'Connell and the Irish Party (1965)
MacIntyre, A.

The Politics of Repeal (1965)
Nowlan, K.B.

The Year of Liberty (1969)
Pakenham, T.

The Origins of Ulster Unionism (1975)
Gibbon, P.

Queen's Rebels
Miller, D.W.

Approach to Crisis: A Study of Belfast Politics, 1613-1970 (1973)
O' Leary, C. and Budge, I.

The Narrow Ground: Aspects of Ulster, 1609-1969 (1977)
Stewart, A.T.Q.

Land and the National Question in Ireland, 1858-82 (1978)
Bew, P.

Irish-American Nationalism, 1870-90 (1966)
Brown, T.N.

Coercion and Conciliation in Ireland: A Study in Conservative Unionism (1963)
Curtis, L.P.

Anglo-Saxons and Celts: Anti-Irish Prejudice in Victorian England (1968)
Curtis, L.P.

The Roman Catholic Church and the Creation of the Modern Irish State, 1878-1886 (1975)
Larkin, E.

John Dillon (1968)
Lyons, F.S.L.

Charles Stewart Parnell (1977)
Lyons, F.S.L.

Irish Unionism I: The Anglo-Irish and the Making of the New Ireland, 1885-1922 (1972)
Buckland, P.J.

Irish Unionism II: Ulster Unionism and the Origins of Northern Ireland, 1886-1922 (1973)
Buckland, P.J.

Politics and Irish Life, 1913-21 (1977)
Fitzpatrick, D.

Culture and Anarchy in Ireland, 1890-1930 (1979)
Lyons, F.S.L.

Church, State and Nation in Ireland, 1898-1921 (1963)
Miller, D.W.

Labour in Irish Politics, 1880-1930 (1974)
Mitchell, A.

The Secret Army: A History of the IRA, 1916-70 (1970)
Bell, J.B.

Patrick Pearse: The Triumph of Failure (1977)
Edwards, Ruth D.

Michael Collins: The Lost Leader (1971)
Forester, M.

The Government and Politics of Ireland (1970)
Chubb, F.B.

The Restless Dominion (1969)
Harkness, D.W.

Representative Government in Ireland, 1919-48 (1958)
McCracken, J.L.

Nationalism and Socialism in Twentieth-century Ireland (1977)
Rumpf, E and Hepburn, A.C.

Church and State in Modern Ireland, 1923-70 (1971)
Whyte, J.H.

A Mirror to Kathleen's Face: Education in Independent Ireland, 1922-60
(1975)
Akenson, D.H.

Education and Enmity: The Control of Schooling in Northern Ireland,
1920-50 (1973)
Akenson, D.H.

The Northern Ireland Problem (1972 ed.)
Barritt, D.P. and Carter, C.F.

The State in Northern Ireland, 1921-72 (1979)
Bew, P. Gibbon, P. and Patterson, H.

The Factory of Grievances: Devolved Government in Northern Ireland,
1921-39 (1979)
Buckland, P.J.

Conflict in Northern Ireland (1976)
Darby, J.P.

Northern Ireland: The Orange State (1976)
Farrell, M.

Ulster (1972)
Sunday Times Insight Team